the Buddhist experience
sources and interpretations

Stephan Beyer

University of Wisconsin

Wadsworth Publishing Company
Belmont, California
A Division of Wadsworth, Inc.

BQ
4012
.B49

The Religious Life of Man Series
FREDERICK J. STRENG, *Series Editor*

Understanding Religious Life, Third Edition
Frederick J. Streng

African Cosmos: An Introduction to Religion in Africa
Noel Q. King

The Buddhist Religion, Third Edition
Richard H. Robinson and Willard L. Johnson

The Buddhist Experience: Sources and Interpretations
Stephan Beyer

The House of Islam, Third Edition
Kenneth Cragg and R. Marston Speight

Islam from Within: Anthology of a Religion
Kenneth Cragg and R. Marston Speight

Japanese Religion: Unity and Diversity, Third Edition
H. Byron Earhart

Religion in the Japanese Experience: Sources and Interpretations
H. Byron Earhart

Native American Religions: An Introduction
Sam Gill

Native American Traditions: Sources and Interpretations
Sam Gill

The Hindu Religious Tradition
Thomas J. Hopkins

The Life of Torah: Readings in the Jewish Religious Experience
Jacob Neusner

The Way of Torah: An Introduction to Judaism, Fourth Edition
Jacob Neusner

The Christian Religious Tradition
Stephen Reynolds

Chinese Religion: An Introduction, Third Edition
Laurence G. Thompson

The Chinese Way in Religion
Laurence G. Thompson

ISBN-0-8221-0127-0

Library of Congress Catalog Card Number: 73-93289

Printed in the United States of America

Printing (last digit): 10 9 8 7 6 — 91 90 89 88 87

Translations by Stephan Beyer.   Drawings by Marianne Bodine.

contents

iii

PART THREE: WISDOM

fORewORd

The power of religious life is often self-evident to the participant, but very difficult to communicate to the uncommitted observer. Therefore, in an attempt to allow students to understand the thoughts, feelings, and attitudes of participants in the major religious traditions, we present companion volumes of readings in the Religious Life of Man Series.

The aim of this series of readings is to introduce the literature of a tradition, and provide sympathetic interpretations and descriptions of important activities which expose the dynamics and some of the concrete variety in a religious tradition. Every book of readings is selective in the material it includes, and the focus here is on religious life, in the past and present, that defines the religious options available today. The selections seek to reveal the goals, experiences, activities, symbolic imagery, and community life of a religious tradition. Hopefully the reader can thereby imaginatively participate in some of the feelings and experiences which are exposed.

Each of the volumes is edited by a university or college teacher who is also a specialist in the major languages and cultures of a religion. Several volumes have new translations of material made especially for them, and each reading is introduced with a brief comment about its place in the tradition and its general religious significance. Further background is found in the companion textbook in the Religious Life of Man Series; at the same time, these books of readings might well be used in combination with other books and media.

Frederick J. Streng
Series Editor

PREFACE

Critic: What conceivable reason could there be to produce yet another anthology of Buddhist writings?

Author: No reason at all, actually.

Critic: Then why did you do it?

Author: I enjoyed it. Translation is a challenge, and it is the only chance a scholar has to carry on his love affair with language.

Critic: But are your translations accurate?

Author: No translation is accurate. Every translation flirts with the original text; no translation is married to it.

Critic: But look at the word you have translated as "wisdom." Professor X has conclusively proved that it should be translated as "intuitive-discriminative-noetic-apprehension."

Author: You cannot whistle "intuitive-discriminative-noetic-apprehension," but you can say "wisdom" while you are brushing your teeth.

Critic: What about the texts you have selected? I see very few of the standard Buddhist works.

Author: You see very few of the usual Buddhist works.

Critic: Then you have distorted the tradition.

Author: Of course I have. Any anthology is a tomb filled with dry bones, and I have packaged the Buddhist tradition in paperback.

Critic: But do you feel the texts you have selected are representative of the tradition?

Author: I think they are representative of the way the tradition is perceived by those within it; they are certainly representative of my own vision of what the Buddhist tradition is.

Critic: And what is this vision?

Author: Buddhism is a religion. Buddhism is a performing art.

Critic: That's it?

Author: That's enough.

Critic: Then the texts are just a personal selection.

Author: Can anyone make an impersonal selection? I tried to stand face-to-face with the tradition, to let the Buddhists speak for themselves, through what they themselves had written. But this stance is personal, subjective, and dialectical, for here the Buddhists are speaking *to*, and in this case they are speaking to me. I am just passing it on.

Critic: But they speak in Sanskrit and Tibetan, in Chinese and Japanese. Are you not a bit presumptuous to translate from all these languages by yourself?

Author: No more presumptuous than to put my name on the cover of a book filled with the work of other people.

Critic: And so some of your translations look a bit peculiar.

Author: I tried to let each language speak in its own form, to translate complex syntax into complex space, and to leave simplicity alone; to translate the concrete concretely, and to turn it all into the poetic vision of the original.

Critic: And the arrangement?

Author: Again, a traditional Buddhist arrangement, for virtue is the basis of meditation, and meditation is the source of wisdom. Within each category I chose the texts I most enjoyed translating, the texts that would throw the most light on the living Buddhist experience: these are the basic texts, not those enshrined by Western scholars before me. And I have dug a tomb for my texts as deep as they for theirs.

Critic: Then why should anyone buy your book?

Author: So they can share it with me.

Critic: Is that the only reason?

Author: A monk once asked Jōshū: If a poor man comes, what should I give him? And Jōshū replied: We do not lack anything.

Critic: Are there any people whose help you would like to acknowledge in this work?

Author: My daughter was born the other day.

Critic: Are you putting me on?

Stephan Beyer
University of Wisconsin

part one
VIRtue

1
the model

1. IN PRAISE OF THE BUDDHA

Virtue underlies the entire Buddhist path, for virtue is the post to which one ties the refractory elephant of the mind; and the Buddha himself is traditionally taken as the exemplar of virtue in all its forms. Even in the earliest texts, the Buddha is more than a mere human teacher; his arduous quest for wisdom had led him through eons of self-sacrifice, and these eons are the model, the ideal path of perfect virtue.

Buddhist literature is filled with hymns of praise to the virtues of the Buddha, but few works have achieved the fame of a simple devotional poem written by Mātṛceṭa in the second century A.D. The reason is not hard to find. The poet prized simplicity over rhetoric, and humanity over abstract principle. He speaks without affectation of the Buddha's courage and patience, of his skill and compassion, of his kindness and his love. His is a reflective poem, but a moving one, for its directness and humanity lend to it a sort of joy, a kind of wonder at the miracle of Buddhahood.

Mātṛceṭa, Śatapañcāśatka, [The 150 verses], ed. D. R. Shackleton Bailey (Cambridge: At the University Press, 1951), pp. 28-150.

              no flaw is : in any way
  where)   (there
               virtue is : in every way

              it is fit for the wise
              to go for refuge
                 praise
                 serve
         abide in his teachings

1

HOMAGE

to you   selfsprung
to your works   diverse & wonderful
to your virtues   uncircumscribed
                        so many are they, & glorious

how many are your virtues?   infinite
how glorious are they?   no words
                            and yet

they grant merit
so I pour them forth in song

you shook off doubt (is it possible? is it impossible?)
& freely came to the help of a helpless world

unbought you were kind   :   a friend to the stranger
uncaused you were tender   :   a kinsman to the lonely

you gave your own flesh
        (no words for all you gave)
            kind one
with your life's breath you paid heed to the suppliant:
             a hundred times
        your own body purchased the bodies
        your own flesh the flesh
            of beings about to die

not from fear of suffering, not from hope of happiness
but from purity of heart alone you made virtue your habit

much tormented, your noble heart
        unleashed its bright violence upon impurity
        but loved the impure

from the mixture you took the essence   the stainless speech
        & drank it all
but you shunned the evil speech like poison

you did not envy the distinguished
        despise the lowly
           strive with equals
but simply became the best in the world

you have so increased yourself with good actions
        that even the dust of your feet
          is an abode of merit

every worldly thing is limited by time & space
      subject to destruction
          obstruction
             & easy to attain
then what metaphor have I for your virtues?
      unrivalled
      unapproachable
      unchanging
      irreversible
      supreme

when I see the profundity of your wisdom
      the depth of the great salt sea
         becomes a mud puddle:
            Sage
the light of your knowledge (destroying the darkness of ignorance)
      makes the sun
         less than a firefly

though they rise against you in great rage
         to assail you
it is not too much for your patience to bear
         in such a worthy vessel

three things are conquered by three things
      the lustful by one free of lust
      the wrathful by one who has conquered wrath
      the deluded by one without delusion

that you might free a world bound by defilement
      you placed yourself in bondage
         to compassion:
            shall I first praise you? or the great compassion
              which long held you in the world
               knowing its flaws

you were used to the joys of solitude
      but gave free rein to compassion
         & she carried you among the crowds
            (she is ever kind to others
            & cruel to her own household)
    Lord: to you alone was compassion pitiless

for resolute compassion would cut you into a hundred pieces
& scatter you to the quarters like some scattered sacrifice
         to serve the aim of others

your speech has threefold beauty
                not false, for it has seen the truth
                not confused, for it has no passion
                but convincing, for it is reasoned

your words first steal the hearts of those who hear them
& then (thought upon) they steal their gloomy ignorance

seen a hundred times
                                    :your form delights the eye
beheld for the first time   equally

the ordinance of death
                unhindered
                without obstacle
                            over all the triple world
            is transcended by your teaching
for he who knows your teaching could remain for an eon
                if he wished
            but freely he goes
                beyond the realm of death

                        to praise you removes all sin
                        to think of you brings joy
                        to seek you is understanding
                        to know you is purity

you are the island of those swept by the flood
            the armor of those wounded in spirit
            the refuge of those who fear existence
            the resort of those who seek for freedom

you are a rampart for those who stand at the edge of the precipice
                        careless of their own interest
                        their own worst enemies

        you have eaten sorry food   sometimes dwelt in hunger
        you have trod rough paths   slept where oxen trample
                    though you are mighty
            you have taken a service filled with abuse
                    changed your dress & speech
                        Lord
            out of love for your followers

men are not so kind to those who love them
as are you to those who do you harm
            to an enemy bent on evil
                you are a friend bent on good

to him who ever seeks out faults
   you respond by seeking out his virtue
to him whose invitation is with poison & fire
   you come bearing compassion
      & immortality

with patience you conquer those who revile you
   with blessings those who harm you
   with truth those who slander you
   with love those who injure you

      sometimes you are asked, & say nothing
      sometimes you approach, & speak
   sometimes you awaken thirst, & speak later
            for you know time & mind

I do not know how we can repay you:
   even those who have reached nirvana
   are not free of debt to you
         they stand in your Law
            but work for their own aim
         you labor for their sake
            how can we repay that?

you look upon the hearts of the sleeping
   & awaken them
         heedful kinsman of heedless beings

you have pounded your bones to pieces
   with the diamond of meditation
& even at the end have not escaped
   doing what is hard to do

firmness   conduct   form   virtue
there is no quality of Buddhahood which is not wondrous

tranquil   beautiful   calm in speech & action
but even to you men are hostile
         see how savage are the deluded

         to those who honor you
            (ocean of merit
            treasure of jewels
      heap of qualities
fountain of virtue)
            it is well to pay homage

Lord, your virtues are inexhaustible
but my power fails me
I stop (unsatisfied)
for fear I stammer

not a fraction of your virtue have I praised
& yet my heart is filled with joy
a mighty lake will cool the thirst of men
without diminishing

2. THE TALE OF THE HAWK AND THE DOVE

When the Buddha was enlightened, he looked about the world, and he found few people indeed who were ready to receive his teachings. He seriously considered simply passing away into nirvana and leaving the world to its own devices. But King Brahma descended from his high heaven to plead with the Buddha to preach the holy Law, and he recounted stories of the Buddha's own past lives to persuade him to persevere in self-sacrifice this one last time.

At least that is the way the Chinese storytellers told it, and that is the way it was translated into a Tibetan collection of edifying tales called *The Wise Man and the Fool,* from which we have taken our "Tale of the Hawk and the Dove."

The Buddhists had borrowed many popular Indian forms to express their vision of exemplary virtue: animal fables and ancient tales of righteous kings became stories of the prior births of the Buddha and models for moral action. Many of these stories retained their charm, and praised cleverness and wit as often as righteousness. But their occasional didactic hyperbole can have a rather dizzying effect upon the modern reader: a rabbit will commit suicide simply to feed a hungry wanderer; a man will give his body to a starving tigress; or a king may either sacrifice himself for his people or impoverish them with his extravagant charity—and all in the name of perfect virtue.

The simple folktale style of our story cannot hide its deep concern with the nature of moral responsibility, even as it is set within the framework of the Buddha's own responsibility to teach the Law he had discovered. King Shibi (the Buddha himself in a former life) provides the model: he will not impose his own standards upon the hungry hawk, but he is willing to shoulder the full burden of his nonviolence, to back up his moral choice with his own body, and accept the consequences of his moral decision.

But to the modern reader his commitment seems to go beyond reasonable necessity. The king would give up his life to feed a hawk who harbors not the least gratitude for it: he would cast aside all considerations of state and family to save a single dove, and would forget his conflicting responsibilities in the face of a single and admittedly subtle moral distinction.

In effect, however, this hyperbole is a literary convention; it expresses the world-transcendence of true moral purity. The charity and nonviolence of the Buddha are indeed perfect, for his virtue is totally selfless and completely impartial. Given the convention, the model is clear: virtue knows no degrees; true morality makes no exceptions.

'Dzangs-blun zhes bya-ba'i mdo [Damamūko-nāma-sūtra] [*The wise man and the fool*], in the Peking Bka'-'gyur *HU 137b–140a (Tokyo: Suzuki Research Foundation, 1958) 39, no. 1008.*

Blessed One: in eons past (numberless and beyond counting) you were born in the world as a king named Shibi; and the palace where the king dwelt was called Land-of-the-Gods, endowed with the countless pleasures of wealth and joy and bountiful harvest.

And the king ruled over the world: he had five million vassals, and eight hundred thousand cities, and twenty thousand queens, and twenty thousand courtiers, and five hundred princes, and ten thousand great ministers; and he ruled them all with compassion and with love.

Now King-of-the-Gods (to whom are due a hundred sacrifices) was drawing near to death; his body had lost its five heavenly virtues, and his heart grew sad. And Divine-Artisan saw his sadness and said to him, "Why are you so grieved and sorrowful?"

"Now the time of death draws near," King-of-the-Gods replied. "I have seen the signs that my life is over, and the Law of the Buddha has waned in the world. I grieve that there is no bodhisattva in the world, and I can find no place of refuge."

"A great king named Shibi yet abides in the world," said Divine-Artisan, "who practices the conduct of a bodhisattva: firm is he in his vows, and he has set forth in striving. Go to him for refuge; surely he will become a perfect Buddha; surely he will be your protector and free you from evil destiny."

"Let us then go and test him," said King-of-the-Gods, "to see if he is truly a bodhisattva. Change yourself into a dove. I shall become a hawk and pursue you swiftly, that you may go to the dwelling of the king to seek his refuge. And by this test we shall learn what is illusion and what is truth."

But Divine-Artisan objected and said, "It is wrong to injure a bodhisattva, a great person who is worthy of our worship. Do not be so harsh, nor impose so difficult a task."

And King-of-the-Gods (to whom are due a hundred sacrifices) replied, "I wish him no harm, but true gold is revealed only in the fire. If we want to find the truth of this, then let us test this bodhisattva."

So Divine-Artisan transformed himself into a dove, and King-of-the-Gods became a hawk. Swift was the pursuit, and the kill was near, when the dove settled upon the lap of the king and, panting with terror, begged for refuge of her life.

But instantly the hawk arrived and alighted by the palace. And he said to the king, "This dove is my food. Now she has settled upon you, so give her quickly to me, for I am much oppressed by hunger."

"I shall not give her to you," replied the king, "for I have vowed that I will never turn away any who come to me for refuge."

"By your own words, you are the refuge of every creature," said the hawk. "Then why am I not included among them? I cannot live without my food."

"Will you eat some other food that I give to you?"

"I will eat it," said the hawk. "But it must be meat, and raw and freshly killed."

But the king thought, "If I give him raw and fresh-killed meat, then I must murder one creature to save another: this would be both purposeless and wrong. I must preserve the life of everything that lives, and my body alone is not included."

So he lifted his sharp sword and sliced off the flesh of his own thigh, and he gave it to the hawk to ransom the life of the dove.

"Truly, my king," the hawk said to him, "you are a most charitable person. But do one small thing for me, if you would be fair—make sure the weight is equal."

So the king ordered that a scale be fetched. He put the dove in one pan of the scale and piled the flesh of his thigh in the other: yet even when his thigh was cut to pieces, still it was lighter than the dove.

So he hacked off the flesh of his shoulders, and of his sides, and of his body; and still it did not equal the weight of the dove. Then the king himself climbed upon the scale, but he was overcome by weakness and tumbled to the ground, unconscious.

And in his faint he remembered the far distant past, and he reproached himself in his heart, saying, "From beginningless time you have been incapable of true forebearance, and so you have wandered in the triple world; you have tasted cruel sufferings and have gained no mass of merit. Now is the time to set forth in striving; now is not the time for laziness."

And thus he reproached himself in many ways; he gathered his strength and climbed upon the scale. "That is good," he thought, and happiness awoke within his heart.

And the earth and the sky shook in six different ways, and the mansions of the gods also quaked and trembled. All the gods gathered together and stood in space to witness the austerities of the bodhisattva—how he denied his body and paid no heed to his life, all for the sake of the Law. And they made offerings to him, so that a rain of heavenly flowers fell down and gathered like the dew.

And King-of-the-Gods (to whom are due a hundred sacrifices) changed back into his own body and said to the king, "What is it that you desire, my king, that you suffer such hardship? Do you wish to rule the world, or be king of the gods, or be lord of death? What is it that you wish?"

"I care not for the pleasures of power," replied the bodhisattva, "but let the merit of this deed help me gain supreme enlightenment."

"You have denied your own body," said King-of-the-Gods, "and you have tasted the suffering of bones and ashes. Have you no regrets?"

"I have no regrets."

"You say you have no regrets," said King-of-the-Gods, "but your body shivers and trembles, and so hot is your breath that you can scarcely speak. I see these things, and how can I believe what you say?"

And the king replied, "From beginning to end I do not regret the loss of a single hair of my body: surely I have done what I set out to do. And if these words I speak be true, then by the power of this truth may my body be as it was and whole again."

And no sooner had the king spoken than his body became even more beautiful than before, and in the worlds of gods and men all creatures rejoiced together, rejoiced and marveled at the wonder they had seen.

In that life you were King Shibi, and now you are the Buddha. Blessed One: in eons past you have devoted your body and your life to the welfare of many beings; and now the time has come to fill the ocean of the Law, to hoist the banner of the Law, to sound the drum of the Law, and to light the lamp of the Law, that you may serve our aim of benefit and joy. Why do you not teach the Law? Why would you cast aside all beings and think to enter nirvana?

And Brahma bowed down before He Who Has Come and praised him, saying: In all his former lives, the Blessed One has sought the Law, and has sacrificed his head a thousand times for the sake of beings.

And so the Blessed One consented to the prayer of Brahma, and he came to the land of Benares, to the place where deer have no terror, and there he turned the wheel of the Law.

And because he thus turned the wheel of the Law, the Three Jewels have appeared in the world.

2
personal morality

1. A LETTER TO A FRIEND

The retribution for sin is as swift as the rewards of virtue, and the ultimate responsibility for any act rests upon the individual, even as it rested upon King Shibi. This theme is sounded again and again in Buddhist works and is reiterated throughout the following selections. Commit no sin for god or family, they say, for you will have no partner to share the result with you in hell.

Lust is the root of all sin; it is desire that binds us to the world. Virtue thus has a soteriological end, for virtue is a discipline for the extirpation of desire. Yet the rewards of personal morality ripen even within the world: true pleasure in this life comes from the peace of inner purity, undisturbed by lust even for the rewards of virtue.

The following letter is attributed to the great philosopher Nāgārjuna and is said to have been written to King Kaniska I, perhaps around 128 A.D. There have been many imitators of this epistolary style, but few writers have matched Nāgārjuna's power and concision: almost the entire Buddhist path is laid out before us, brought to life by a sincere moral fervor and a rather wry appreciation for human frailty.

Nāgārjuna, Bshes-pa'i spring-yig [Suhṛllekha] [*A letter to a friend*], in the Peking Bstan-'gyur Mdo-'grel GI 74a–81b (Tokyo: Suzuki Research Foundation, 1958) 103, no. 5409.

Accomplished and virtuous one:
I have compiled a few verses, that you may gain the merit which comes of hearing the Buddha's words. It is proper that you listen to them.
A wise man will worship any image of the Buddha, even of wood, however poorly made: then do not despise my poor poem, for it is based on the teachings of the holy Law.
You have already heard and comprehended many of the Sage's words, but even chalk looks whiter by moonlight: do not disregard my letter.
The Conqueror has taught us six things to bear in mind: the Buddha and the Law and the Community, charity and virtue and the gods. Bear them in mind, with all their qualities.
Ever practice the ten paths of good conduct, with your body and speech and mind. Avoid strong drink, and delight in a virtuous livelihood.

10

Know that pleasure is transient and worthless: then give properly to recluses and brahmans, to friends and to the poor, for your next life has no better kinsman than charity.

Practice virtue fully, bountifully, freely, ungrudgingly, for it is said that virtue is the foundation for all qualities, as is the earth for the living and the unliving.

Increase the vast perfection of your charity, virtue, forebearance, striving, meditation and wisdom: be the sovereign who reaches the other shore of the ocean of this world.

He who honors his father and mother is of the family of the gods and masters; in honoring them he gains fame, and heaven in the life to come.

Renounce killing and stealing, adultery and falsehood; renounce strong drink and untimely food; renounce your delight in your high throne; renounce song and dance, and adorning yourself with garlands.

If you have these eight qualities, then follow the virtue of a Worthy One and observe also the day of confession, which grants to men and women the beautiful body of a god of desire.

Behold your enemies: greed and cunning, covetousness and sloth, pride and lust and hatred, arrogance in your family, your looks, your learning, your youth, your power.

The Sage has said that concern is the abode of immortality, indifference the abode of death: then be ever and devotedly concerned to increase your virtue.

For whoever goes from indifference to concern shines like the moon moving from behind a cloud.

There is no austerity like forebearance, so give yourself no opportunity for anger: the Buddha has taught us that he who renounces anger will surely gain the goal.

"He abused me, he beat me, he robbed me": this resentment brings nothing but contention, but he who casts his resentment aside sleeps happily.

Understand that your thoughts can be like a drawing made on water, on earth or on stone: the first is best for the passionate, the last for the righteous.

The Conqueror has taught us that a man's words may be cogent or true or false, like honey or flowers or dirt: give up the last.

There are four types of people: those who move from the light to the light, those who move from the darkness to the darkness, those who move from the light to the darkness, and those who move from the darkness to the light: be the first of these.

Understand that people are like mangoes: the rotten who appear ripe, the ripe who appear rotten, the rotten who seem rotten, and the ripe who seem ripe.

Look not upon another man's wife: if you see her, think of her as your mother or daughter or sister, according to her age; if you lust for her, think well upon her impurity.

Guard your unsteady mind as your son, your treasure, your very life: turn your mind from lust as from poison, from weapons, from enemies, from fire.

For lust leads only to ruin; the Lord of Conquerors has said that it is like a poison fruit. Give it up, for it binds us with iron chains in the prison of the world.

One man conquers the objects of sense, ever unsteady and fickle; another conquers his enemies in battle. A wise man knows that the first is the greater hero.

Look at the body of a young girl without her ornaments: evil-smelling, foul at its nine apertures, an unfilled filthy vessel covered with skin.

Know that your desire for pleasure is like a leper, tormented with lice, burning himself with fire to find relief, but gaining no peace at all.

Become practiced in looking at things rightly, to see the truth; there is nothing else that has the quality of this.

A man of family and looks and learning is not respected if he lack wisdom and virtue, but he who has those two qualities is honored even if he lack the others.

A man wise in the world is indifferent to the eight worldly things: gain and loss, happiness and sorrow, flattery and slander, praise and blame. He says: I do not think upon these things.

Commit no sin for brahman or monk or god, for guest or parent, for wife or son: you will have no partner to share the result with you in hell.

A sinful deed does not cut you like a sword when you commit it, but its faults will be waiting for you when you come to die.

The Sage has said that faith, virtue, charity, learning, humility, modesty, and wisdom are the seven treasures: understand that other treasures are common and worthless.

Give up gambling and loitering at festivals, laziness and the company of sinful friends, strong drink and wandering in the night, for they lead to evil destiny and the loss of fame.

The teacher of gods and men has said: of all treasures, contentment is the best. Therefore be ever content with what you have, and you will be rich though you have nothing.

Brave king: Your sorrows are as many as your possessions and as few as your desires: the more heads a serpent-king has, the greater is his suffering.

Give up three sorts of wife: the "hangman" who loves your enemies, the "great lady" who despises her lord, and the "thief" who steals small things.

But honor as your family goddess a wife who is as helpful as a sister, as loving as a friend, as devoted as a mother, and as submissive as a slave.

Use food without desire or dislike, knowing it to be but medicine; use it not for sleekness, nor for pride, nor for pleasure, but only to sustain your body.

Lord of Good Family: In wakefulness pass the day and two watches of the night; only in the middle watch should you sleep, and then mindfully, that even your sleep will not be without use.

Ever meditate upon friendliness, upon compassion, upon sympathetic joy, and upon equanimity: though you reach not the most high, you will gain bliss in the world of the gods.

The four trances cast away lust and enjoyment, pain and pleasure, and thereby you gain your rightful share in the highest heavens.

Strive in virtue in five ways: continually, intentionally, freely, well, and ever as the foremost. These five great things are the foundation from which deeds spring, and it is they that determine the virtue of your deeds.

A few ounces of salt will change the taste of a little water, but not of the whole stream of the Ganges: so understand that a little sin cannot harm a vast store of merit.

Know that these five hindrances are thieves to steal the treasure of your merit: worry and regret, malice, sloth and torpor, lust and attachment, and doubt.

These are the five highest qualities: faith and striving and mindfulness and meditation and wisdom. Ever strive in these, for they are called strength and power, and are the very summit.

Think always how you have not passed beyond disease and old age and death, nor beyond separation from what is dear to you, nor beyond your narrow self, and be not proud.

If you yearn for heaven or for freedom, then become practiced in right views; for a man of wrong views may practice well, yet will never escape the full ripening of his deeds.

Understand that mankind is unhappy, impermanent, selfless, impure: those who bear this not in mind sink and are destroyed in the four perverted views.

For we are told that form is not the self, nor does the self possess form; the self does not dwell in form, nor form in the self; and the four other aggregates also are empty.

These aggregates do not appear by accident, nor from time, nor from an essence, nor from their own nature, nor from a creator, nor without a cause: know that they appear from ignorance, from deeds, from craving.

Know that there are three things that block the gate to the city of freedom and that you must cast aside: sole reliance on rites and penance, perverted views, and doubt.

Freedom depends upon you alone, for no one else can help you: then strive in the four noble truths, with study and virtue and meditation.

Ever train yourself in higher virtue, higher wisdom, higher meditation, for within these three are gathered more than a hundred and fifty trainings.

My Lord: The Well-Gone One has taught us that the only path to tread is mindfulness upon the body. Meditate thereon and guard it well; for when mindfulness is lost, all virtues are destroyed.

Life is full of danger; it is as impermanent as a bubble blown by the wind: just to breathe out again after you breathe in, just to awaken from sleep is a miracle.

So know that at last your body will be dust; it will shrivel and rot, impure and insubstantial; it will wither and decay, for it is a compounded thing; and it will pass away.

. The earth will blaze, and the mountains and the oceans, and seven suns will consume all living creatures, and not even ashes shall remain. And what will happen to frail mankind?

Best of Men: Withdraw your heart from the world, for it is a hollow reed; all is impermanent and selfless, without a refuge, without a lord, without a home.

Lord of Men: Practice the holy Law, and make it fruitful; it is harder for an animal to become a man than for a blind turtle to find the hole of a wooden yoke floating in the ocean.

A man who wastes his life in sin is a greater fool than one who uses a jeweled and golden vessel to vomit in.

You are a lord of four great dominions: you dwell in a suitable land, you rely on holy persons, you have made your earnest wish in former lives, and you have gathered merit.

The Sage has said that to serve a virtuous friend is to make perfect the practice of purity: therefore serve holy persons, for many are they who have gained peace by heeding the words of the Conqueror.

These are the eight adverse conditions: to be born a heretic, or an animal, or a hungry ghost, or in hell; to be born where the Conqueror has not appeared, or in a barbarian border land where his teachings have not spread; to be born a fool, or a long-lived god.

And now you have gained the benefit of freedom from these, so strive to put an end to birth hereafter.

Hear the faults of this world, know them, and be weary of the world, for it is where you lose what you most desire; it is the source of many sufferings, of death, of disease, and of decay.

The father becomes the son, the mother becomes the wife, the enemy becomes the friend: truly there are no certainties in this world.

Every one of us has drunk more milk than the four oceans could hold, and you will drink more than that before you are done with birth in the world.

Every one of us has piled up bones higher than Mt. Meru: if all the mothers you have had were small as seeds, they would still be beyond counting.

You might become the king of the gods, worshipped by the world, but still your deeds will cast you down to earth again. You might become a universal emperor, but still you can become a slave in this round of births.

Long may you taste the joys of caressing the full breasts of heavenly maidens: but still you will suffer the unbearable caress of the crushing engines of hell.

Long may you dwell on the summit of Mt. Meru, tasting the joys of pliant ground beneath your feet: but still you will touch the unbearable pain of walking upon hot coals and rotting corpses.

You may frolic in beautiful groves, and take your pleasure with heavenly maidens: but still you will abide in the forests of hell, where the leaves of the trees are sharp swords, to cut your feet and hands, your ears and nose.

With the fair-faced daughters of the gods you may enter a gently flowing river of lotus flowers: but still you will enter the hot and crashing river of hell.

You may attain great pleasures in heaven, or the unpassioned happiness of Brahma himself: but still you will become firewood for hell, and suffer without ceasing.

You may become the sun and the moon, to brighten the world with the light of your own body: but still you will come to the black darkness, where you cannot see your own hand stretched out before you.

For you must die. So seize the brightness of the threefold lamp of merit: in the end it is you alone who will enter the darkness, which neither sun nor moon can pierce . . .

And the evildoer is cut down between his very breaths; he has heard of the infinite sufferings of hell, but his heart is hard as diamond, else it would crack with fear into a thousand pieces.

He has seen pictures and sculptures of hell; he has heard of it, and thought of it, and read of it: if this is enough to make him fear, then need we speak of the actual taste of unbearable retribution?

Among all pleasures, the end of craving is lord of all happiness; and among all pains, the most unbearable is the suffering of hell.

Picture the pain you would feel here on earth, were you fiercely struck with three hundred spears in a single day: but this does not equal even the smallest part of the least pain of hell.

And there you will taste unbearable suffering for a hundred million years, and you will not die again until you have exhausted your evil deeds.

And sin is the seed of this evil fruit, sin with body or speech or mind: then strive with all your might and all your skill that you plant not even an atom thereof.

Those who cast aside peaceful virtue are born in the wombs of animals, to be slain and bound and beaten, and suffer all manner of pain, devouring each other.

They are slaughtered for pearls and wool, bones and blood, flesh and hide; powerless, they are used as slaves, driven by kicks and blows and whips, and jabbed with iron hooks.

And those born as hungry ghosts lose all that is most dear to them, and suffer pain unceasingly; they endure the unbearable pain of hunger and thirst, cold and heat, weariness and terror.

Some have a mouth as small as the eye of a needle, and a stomach as large as a mountain; and they suffer hunger, for they have not the power to eat even a piece of filthy garbage.

Their bodies are naked, skin and bones, like a withered tree; fires blaze in their mouths at night, and their food is drifting sand.

And the meanest of them cannot find even filth to eat, pus or excrement or blood; they hack at each other's faces, to eat the rotten pus exuding from goitres on their throats.

Even the moon is hot in summer for them, and the sun cold in winter; trees lose their fruit when hungry ghosts but look upon them, and rivers run dry.

They bear pain without stopping, their bodies bound with the hard noose of their evil deeds; nor will they die again for five thousand years, or ten thousand.

And the Buddha has told us that all their many pains have but a single taste, for the cause thereof was greed and avarice and corruption.

Even those born in heaven suffer far more by their death and their loss of pleasure: those who are truly noble think upon this, and yearn not for transient heavens.

Their complexion grows coarse, and their cushions give them no ease; their garlands wither, their garments grow soiled, and their bodies stream with strange sweat.

These are the five signs that appear to the gods in heaven to foretell their coming death, as signs of death appear for dying men on earth.

And if they have no merit left when they fall from the world of the gods, then powerless they are born as animals, or as hungry ghosts, or in hell, whatever is appropriate for them.

Those born as demigods suffer great anguish, for theirs is fierce unthinking envy for the glory of the gods; even those among them who are wise cannot see the truth because of the darkness of their destiny.

So understand that this is the way the world is: it is not good to be born as a demigod, or in hell, or as an animal, or as a hungry ghost, for birth is the vessel of many ills.

If your head or your clothes suddenly caught fire, you would try to put it out, and thus too should you strive to put an end to birth, for nothing else is more important than this.

With virtue and meditation and wisdom, gain nirvana; for it alone is the state of peace, calm and stainless, without decay or death or disease; for it is neither earth nor water, fire nor air, sun nor moon.

Mindfulness, investigation of events, striving, enthusiasm, serenity, meditation, equanimity: these are the seven factors of enlightenment, the accumulation of merit that leads to the attainment of nirvana.

Without wisdom there is no meditation; without meditation there is no wisdom; but when you have both of these, you make the vast ocean of this world into a mud puddle.

The Kinsman of the Sun has said that there are fourteen questions that cannot be answered in this world; so do not speculate upon them, for they lead not to calmness of mind.

The Sage has taught us that from ignorance comes the predisposition to existence; from the predisposition to existence comes awareness; from awareness comes name-and-form; from name-and-form come the six senses and their objects; and from the six senses and their objects comes contact.

And from contact come feelings; from feelings comes craving; from craving comes clinging; from clinging comes the ripening of deeds; and from the ripening of deeds comes birth.

And when there is birth there is sorrow and disease; there is old age and dissatisfaction, and death and terror: there appears the whole mass of suffering; and it ends only when birth is ended.

This chain of causation is the most profound and precious of the treasures bequeathed us by the Conqueror: whoever sees dependent co-arising has the highest vision, for he knows reality as the Buddha does.

Then contemplate these eight limbs of the path that you may gain peace: right view, right aspiration, right speech, right conduct, right livelihood, right effort, right mindfulness, and right meditation.

For birth is suffering, and craving is called the greatest cause thereof; to end it is freedom, and it is the noble eightfold path that leads us there.

Then ever strive to see the four noble truths, for even householders who live in luxury can cross over the river of passion, when they know them.

Those who have realized the true nature of things did not fall from the sky nor spring from the earth like grain, for in the past they also were ordinary people, under the sway of passion.

Then be not afraid. Need I say more? This is a teaching of benefit and of profit: subdue your mind, for the Blessed One has said that the mind is the root of all things.

Hard it is even for a monk to do what I have taught you, but just hold to the essential quality of whatever you practice and make your life fruitful.

Rejoice at all and every virtue and dedicate your every practice to the attainment of Buddhahood.

For it is by this heap of merit that you will gain countless births among gods and men, and gain glorious sovereignty.

You will practice like the noble bodhisattvas, to take in hand many tormented beings; you will be born to clear away their disease and old age, their lust and hatred.

You will create your own magical Buddha heaven, as did the Blessed Buddha of Infinite Light, and with everlasting life will you be the protector of the world.

The great and spotless fame of your wisdom and virtue will spread upon the earth and reach to the land of the gods in the sky; and surely you will calm the lust for pleasure of men on earth and gods in heaven, who delight in heavenly maidens.

You will be a Lord of Conquerors to calm the terror, the birth and death of hosts of beings, defiled and tormented; you will attain the deathless state, but fear not that you will be unmoving, for it is but words to say that you have passed beyond the world.

2. APHORISMS

The Indian literary tradition often seems committed to ornate and florid metaphor and a massive accumulation of adjectives, as we shall see in some of our selections; but it could equally strive for elegance, for the most perfect and concise statement of profound truths. The genre of aphorism begins early in Buddhist writings, and the *Dhammapada* is traditionally considered one of the earliest anthologies of these religious epigrams, attributed to the Buddha himself and worked by some skilled hand into a coherent statement of the most basic Buddhist beliefs.

The influence of this collection has been enormous, not only in content but in style as well. Versions exist in every major Buddhist language, and it is quoted constantly by later writers, including Nāgārjuna in the previous selection. Easily remembered and easily applied, the verses became the common inheritance of all Buddhists, and proverbs throughout Asia are indebted to them.

Dhammapada [*Verses on the Law*], *in* Khuddakanikāya [*Collection of little texts*] *gen. ed. Bhikkhu J. Kashyap (Bihar: Pali Publication Board, 1959), 1:17–57.*

All events are preceded by thought
        led by thought
        made by thought
speak or act with a wicked thought:
        sorrow follows
        as a wheel follows the foot of an ox

He abused me:
he beat me: who harbor such thoughts
he overcame me: their hatred does not cease
he robbed me:

Concern is the abode of immortality : the concerned do not die
indifference is the abode of death   : the indifferent are as if dead

A wise man should build an island
        by vigilance
        by concern
        by restraint
        by control
which the flood will not overwhelm

Who controls his thought
        far-reaching
        solitary
        immaterial
        dwelling in the heart
will be free from the bonds of death

Soon, truly, this body will lie upon the earth
        despised
        unconscious
        useless
        a stick of wood

He knows this body is like foam
he knows this body is a mirage
he breaks the flowery arrows of Evil
        he would go where the Lord of Death
        can't see him

These sons are mine:
                        the fool torments himself
this wealth is mine:
                his self is not his own
                how sons?
                how wealth?

As a deep lake is serene
            undisturbed
wise men are serene
    when they have heard the Law

Whose mind is rightly cultivated
    in the limbs of enlightenment
who delights in the rejection of desire
who has destroyed his passions
who is full of splendor:
            he has attained nirvana in this world

Who has destroyed his passions
who is indifferent to food
whose realm is empty
            signless
            liberation
    his path is hard to fathom
        like a bird in the sky

If a man conquer in battle a thousand thousand men
and another conquer himself:
        truly the latter
            is the greatest of conquerors

Do not think lightly of sin
            "it will not come near me"
even a water pot fills with falling drops of water
a fool fills with sin
            a little
            at
            a
            time

As a cowherd with a stick
drives his cattle to pasture
old age & death drive us
            from life to life

A town is made of bones,
plastered with flesh & blood:
in it dwell pride & self-deception
            old age
            death

House-builder! I see you:
        you won't build this house again
your rafters are broken
your roof is dismantled
my mind has gained
        destruction of craving
        freedom

The self is lord of self
                    who else could be the lord?
        with self well-tamed
you gain a lord
                    hard to find

Come, look at this world
            like a many-colored royal chariot
            where fools sink
the wise have no love for it

Who is not led anywhere
            by ensnaring poisonous craving
by what path will you lead him
            the awakened
            the infinite
            the trackless?

Who takes refuge in the Buddha
                    in the Law
                    in the Community
perceives the four noble truths
            with right wisdom

        Health   :   the greatest gain
        contentment   :   the greatest wealth
        trust   :   the greatest relation
        nirvana   :   the greatest happiness

When a man long absent from home
            returns safely
            from afar
his kinsmen and friends
            welcome him
When a man who has done good
            goes from this world
            to the next
his good deeds
            receive him
            as kinsmen a friend who has returned

This is an old saying, O Atula
this is not a modern saying:
            they blame the silent
            they blame the talkative
            they blame the moderate
there is no one in the world who is not blamed

As a smith refines silver
a wise man removes his impurities
   one by one
   little by little
   from time
      to
       time

You're not an honored elder
   just because your hair is grey
your age is ripe
you are called
   grown old in vain

You must strive : the Buddhas are only preachers
   enter the path
   meditate
     be freed from the bonds of death

The disciples of Gautama are well-awakened
     always
their minds delight in meditation
    day & night

The speaker of falsehood goes to hell
and he who says "I didn't do it"
   and did it.
After death they are the same
    men of evil deeds
    in the next world

This mind of mine used to wander
   where it liked
   where it wanted
   where it pleased
but today I shall rightly control it
   as an elephant driver controls
   a mad elephant

I tell you good counsel
all you who gather here:
   dig out the root of craving
     as you would dig up *birana*-grass
       to get at its fragrant root
    that death may not break you
    as the flood breaks reeds
      again
        and
         again

He treats as his own
    no name nor form
ungrieved at what is not: a monk

A monk who dwells in friendship
calm in the Buddha's teachings
attains a state
        calm
        happy
        where the thrust into existence
                is at rest

Monk: bale out the boat
    it goes lightly
    empty
cut off lust and hatred
    then you reach
    nirvana

A monk with tranquil mind
has entered an empty house
      he sees things rightly
      his delight is miraculous

    Meditative   work done
    pure   no passion
    settled   goal attained
         him I call
         a brahman

He has cast away sin   :   he is called a brahman
he lives in tranquility   :   he is called a monk
he has driven off impurity :   he is called a wanderer

3. PRACTICAL VIRTUE

Virtue, in the broadest sense, means knowing how to behave properly, and it is thus inextricably linked to the concept of cleverness. The ability to maneuver skillfully (without necessarily compromising principle) is an ideal enshrined in the literature of all of Asia. The Buddhists recognize the necessity for dealing with the world as it is; the truly virtuous man is the one whose virtue is effective, and virtue is defined operationally as that which is proved right by events. King Shibi turned out to be right after all; he gained his merit, and by his Act of Truth his body became even more beautiful than before.

This tradition of statecraft, of skillful and politic morality, was early and happily wedded to the aphoristic style; even Nāgārjuna was not above including a few pieces of sage and practical advice in his letter to the king. But the Tibetan monk who wrote the following epigrams actually lived his precepts

amid the Byzantine complexities of international politics, for Kun-dga' rgyal-
mtshan (1182–1251 A.D.) was both a religious scholar and a most extraordi-
nary diplomat, and is credited by tradition with almost single-handedly converting the entire Mongol nation to Buddhism. He illuminates his practicality
with a remarkable sense of humor as well as simple examples from daily life;
he teaches Buddhist virtue with one eye upon the world, and he maneuvers
through the world with one foot on the threshold of heaven.

*Sa-skya Paṇḍita, Legs-par bshad-pa rin-po-che'i gter [The treasury of
precious sayings], ed. James E. Bosson (Bloomington: Indiana University Press, 1969), Chapter VIII (Bya-ba brtag-pa), pp. 99–115.*

> People's desires are different
>> so it is hard to please everyone
> but if you are possessed of virtue
>> you're getting close

> Rely upon those of perfect virtue
>> or else make friends with the common people
> it is easy to carry a pitcher
>> when it is full
>> or when it is empty
> but who can serve a man of a few virtues?
> who can carry a half-filled pitcher on his head?

> Even those of little strength succeed
>> relying on the great
> a water drop is weak
>> but mixed with a lake
>> it cannot dry up

> If you lack wisdom yourself
>> then question well the wise
> if you cannot kill an enemy with your hands
>> don't you take a weapon?

> Take food & wealth properly obtained
> but renounce the thoughts which glory in the unworthy
>> you can pick fruit from the very top of a tree
>> but when you climb beyond that
>>> you fall down

> Until your strength is perfect
>> respect your enemies
> when your power is perfect
>> you can do anything you want
>> they say

Though an enemy speak sweetly
    the wise do not trust him
the crane & the cat
    kill their prey
        courteously

Though the lord of the land be angry
    stay & serve him with love
when your foot slips on the ground
    you steady yourself
        with the ground

Whoever longs with many desires
    will be destroyed
it is the fish who lusts for bait
    the fish-hook catches

Lords should gather taxes
    prudently
    without harm
when you take too much sap from the tree
        it dries up

Lords should be gentle
    & not be angered with little cause
a snake may have a gem
        but who would sit down with him?

Be not too friendly with kinsmen : loans to relatives cause grudges
be not too fierce with enemies   : it is easy to pay back harm

Gentleness conquers the gentle
gentleness conquers the fierce
gentleness accomplishes everything
    gentleness is sharpness
        the wise men say

Do not leave a place
    without examining the place you are going
make sure your lifted foot is down
    before you raise the other:
        when you lift both feet at once
            you fall

Strive to conceal your activities
    they are spoiled by display
if a monkey did not dance
    why would anyone tie a rope around its neck?

Do not speak words which touch the quick
    even to an enemy
        for their consequences rebound
           like an
      echo   :   echo

If you wish to harm an enemy
    possess yourself of virtue
for it will burn in your enemy's thoughts
        (& increase your merit)

When you do even a little harm
    clear it away quickly
    make friends again
have you never seen a flood
    enter a little ditch?

A wise man never does wrong
    even when he knows how
look: the elephant slays the enemy
      so the king keeps him
        tied up

Though your friends be angry
      do not leave them
though your enemies be friendly
      do not join them
a crow may harm a crow
    but when they trust an owl
    they are destroyed

The wise are always disciplined
    when doing a deed
      great or small
whether he kills a rabbit or an elephant
      a lion
        never relaxes

Who would stay in a place
    where they do not honor the virtuous?
who would sell crystal in a place
    where they use crystal as a flint?

A wise man either teaches
or dwells alone in the forest
      a gem is either made a crest ornament
      or stays in the ocean isles

You will not attain greatness
   if you rely on the great
      who are jealous
look: when it nears the light of the sun
   the moon grows dim

The wise man rejects
   both friendship & discord
      with the unruly
you neither hate nor befriend
   a tiger

When place & time are right
   speak a few words
      with restraint
too many words may be well-spoken
   but they are like excess merchandise:
      no demand

Give up an unruly friend
   however long you have known him
a loose tooth may be healthy
   but it's better to pull it out
      the ancients said

An ever-annoying retainer:
   give him a little something
      & turn him out
when a snake grabs your finger
   you slice it off
      or die

Serve a deserving sage with devotion
   but if you find he is cunning
      beware
protect a deserving fool with friendliness
   but if you find he is cunning
      get rid of him

Order someone to work he knows
   not to what he is incapable of doing
you don't get through the water with a wagon:
   can you go on the plains with a boat?

"I have no bad thoughts"
   well, don't trust anyone anyway
the deer have pleasant minds
   the fanged beasts think of them
      as food

If a fool takes a wrong path
    you can say he's just a fool
if a wise man takes a wrong path
    find out why

Though you know something well yourself
    do all deeds with counsel
when you do not enjoy advice
    you are buying repentance
        dearly

When you act after well investigating
    how can a deed go wrong?
if one has eyes to see
    and investigates
        would he step off a cliff?

If you want status
    by any means available
        then do benefit for others
those who would clean their face:
    don't they first wipe off the mirror?

The upright must examine
    the falsehood in the words of the cunning
what good is it to praise yourself
    "I am upright"
        after you have been swindled?

It is good for a wise man
    ever to act with friendship & courtesy
        even to an enemy
though he gain nothing from reconciliation
    it is a medicine
        to purge his evil thoughts

You do not get what you want in the world
    by speaking evil words
accomplish your aims in your own mind
    when you speak
        agree with everyone

When you rely on evil people
    you harm yourself
        with their evil
look: the fish who swim in ditch water
    wind up scattered on the field

If you praise the vulgar excessively
     later you will be despised
if you fling filth into the sky
       it falls
         on your head
If you dishonor the wise
     you are touched by harm
if you turn a lamp upside down
       it burns
         your hand

Keep everything in its place:
       a crest-gem is not bound to the foot
       a foot-ornament is not tied on the head

If you increase your wealth too much
     you are near a fall
if a dam holds too much water
       it must be drained
       or break

When doing a great deed
      diligently rely on a good friend
a fire may burn a mighty forest
      but it needs its friend
        the wind

It is easy to speak words
      drenched with friendliness
        & it is the best way
          to make others happy
who can content others with money?
you could give up your life
       & half of them
        still aren't satisfied

4. A VISION OF HELL

No rationalist bias can argue away the fact that hell is real for the Buddhists, an unquestioned possibility dwelt upon with Dantean relish. But hell is not eternal damnation: it comes to an end, though its sufferings may last for an almost incalculable length of time.

Hell is a choice that is made here and now, and the possibility of choice is symbolized by the five messengers of the gods: birth, old age, disease, punishment, and death—ever-present reminders of destiny and mortality. And it is simple indifference that postpones the choice of virtue: the Buddhists see no grand and tragic glory in even the greatest evil, for the motive of sin is seen as nothing more than the petulance of a rather foolish immaturity.

Devadūtasutta [*The messengers of the gods*], in Majjhima-nikāya [*Collection of medium discourses*], gen. ed. Bhikkhu J. Kashyap (Bihar: Pali Publication Board, 1958), 3:250–59, Sutta XXX.

The Blessed One said:

Suppose there were two houses with doors: a man with eyes to see, standing between them, could see the people entering a house, & leaving it, & going between the houses, & walking back and forth.

Thus do I (with my pure divine eye, surpassing that of men) see beings pass away & be reborn: I see beings that are lowly or exalted, ill-born or well-born, in good destinies or in evil destinies, according to the deeds they have done.

Truly, these beings (endowed with good conduct in body & speech & mind) speak no ill of the Noble Ones: possessed of right views, they collect the karma of their right views; and after their bodies break up & after they die, they are reborn in a good destiny, in the world of heaven, or among men.

But these beings (endowed with evil conduct in body & speech & mind) speak ill of the Noble Ones: possessed of wrong views, they collect the karma of their wrong views; and after their bodies break up & after they die, they are reborn in an evil destiny, in the realm of hungry ghosts, in the womb of an animal, in hell (the state of woe & pain & suffering).

And the guards of hell grab that person by both arms and show him to Yama, the King of the Dead. "This person, your majesty, did not honor his father or his mother, did not honor recluses or brahmans, did not respect his elders in the family. Your majesty, decree his punishment."

Then King Yama questions him carefully & closely, and asks him about the first messenger of the gods: "Silly person, didn't you see the first messenger of the gods who appeared among men?"

And he says: "No, sir, I didn't see him."

King Yama says: "Silly person, did you never see among men a baby boy, ignorant, lying on his back, wallowing in his own urine & excrement?"

And he says: "Yes, sir, I saw that."

King Yama says: "Silly person, you were a mature & intelligent adult. Didn't you think, 'I too am subject to birth, I have not passed beyond birth; then let me do what is good in body & speech & mind'?"

And he says: "Sir, I was not able: I was lazy & negligent."

King Yama says: "Silly person, it was because you were lazy & negligent that you did not do what is good in body & speech & mind; and surely, silly person, they will deal with you according to your negligence. For the evil you have done is yours: it was not done by your mother or father, your brother or sister; it was not done by your friends or relations, by recluses or brahmans, or by the gods. The evil deeds were done by you, and it is you who will taste their ripening."

Then King Yama questions him carefully & closely, and asks him about the second messenger of the gods: "Silly person, didn't you see the second messenger of the gods who appeared among men?"

And he says: "No, sir, I didn't see him."

King Yama says: "Silly person, did you never see among men an old man or woman, decrepit & bent, crooked as a rafter, leaning on a stick & trembling as he went, miserable, his youth gone, his teeth broken, his white hair falling out, his skin wrinkled, his body spotted?"

And he says: "Yes, sir, I saw that."

King Yama says: "Silly person, you were a mature & intelligent adult. Didn't you think, 'I too am subject to old age, I have not passed beyond old age; then let me do what is good in body & speech & mind'?"

And he says: "No, sir, I was not able: I was lazy & negligent."

King Yama says: "Silly person, it was because you were lazy & negligent that you did not do what is good in body & speech & mind; and surely, silly person, they will deal with you according to your negligence . . . The evil deeds were done by you, and it is you who will taste their ripening."

Then King Yama questions him carefully & closely, and asks him about the third messenger of the gods: "Silly person, didn't you see the third messenger of the gods who appeared among men?"

And he says: "No, sir, I didn't see him."

King Yama says: "Silly person, did you never see among men a sick man or woman, suffering & in pain, grievously ill, wallowing in his own urine & excrement, getting up with the help of others, & by others being put to bed?"

And he says: "Yes, sir, I saw that."

King Yama says: "Silly person, you were a mature & intelligent adult. Didn't you think, 'I too am subject to illness, I have not passed beyond illness; then let me do what is good in body & speech & mind'?"

And he says: "No, sir, I was not able: I was lazy & negligent."

King Yama says: "Silly person, it was because you were lazy & negligent that you did not do what is good in body & speech & mind; and surely, silly person, they will deal with you according to your negligence . . . The evil deeds were done by you, and it is you who will taste their ripening."

Then King Yama questions him carefully & closely, and asks him about the fourth messenger of the gods: "Silly person, didn't you see the fourth messenger of the gods who appeared among men?"

And he says: "No, sir, I didn't see him."

King Yama says: "Silly person, did you never see among men a king who would seize a thief or evildoer, and subject him to torture: lashing him with whips & sticks, cutting off his hands or feet or ears or nose, sticking his hands into blazing torches, setting him on fire, slicing off pieces of flesh with a razor, driving spikes through his limbs, breaking his bones with clubs until he was like a pile of straw; and then covering him with oil and casting him to the dogs to eat, or impaling him alive, or cutting off his head with a sword?"

And he says: "Yes, sir, I saw that."

King Yama says: "Silly person, you were a mature & intelligent adult. Didn't you think, 'Truly those who do evil deeds are thus tortured in this very life: and what about the next life? Then let me do what is good in body & speech & mind'?"

And he says: "No, sir, I was not able: I was lazy & negligent."

King Yama says: "Silly person, it was because you were lazy & negligent that you did not do what is good in body & speech & mind; and surely, silly person, they will deal with you according to your negligence . . . The evil deeds were done by you, and it is you who will taste their ripening."

Then King Yama questions him carefully & closely, and asks him about the fifth messenger of the gods: "Silly person, didn't you see the fifth messenger of the gods who appeared among men?"

And he says: "No, sir, I didn't see him."

King Yama says: "Silly person, did you never see among men a man or woman dead for one day, or two, or three, swollen & bloated & purple & festering?"

And he says: "Yes, sir, I saw that."

King Yama says: "Silly person, you were a mature & intelligent adult. Didn't you think, 'I too am subject to death, I have not passed beyond death; then let me do what is good in body & speech & mind'?"

And he says: "No, sir, I was not able: I was lazy & negligent."

King Yama says: "Silly person, it was because you were lazy & negligent that you did not do what is good in body & speech & mind; and surely, silly person, they will deal with you according to your negligence. For the evil you have done is yours; it was not done by your mother or father, your brother or sister; it was not done by your friends or relations, by recluses or brahmans, or by the gods. The evil deeds were done by you, and it is you who will taste their ripening."

And then King Yama falls silent.

And the guards of hell subject him to the torture of the fivefold pinion: they drive fiery blazing iron spikes through his hands & feet & the middle of his chest, and he feels pain that is sharp & bitter & severe. But he has not finished his time until he has exhausted his evil deeds.

And the guards of hell lay him down & chop him with axes, and turn him upside down & slice him with razors, and bind him to a chariot & drag him over the fiery blazing earth, and drive him up and down a great mountain of fiery blazing coals, and turn him upside down & hurl him into a fiery blazing iron cauldron; and there he boils, throwing up scum to the surface, rising & sinking & going across; and he feels pain that is sharp & bitter & severe. But he has not finished his time until he has exhausted his evil deeds.

And then the guards of hell hurl him into the Great Hell,

> square & four-gated, divided into equal parts
> with an iron wall about it & an iron roof above
> its iron ground flaming & blazing
> standing a hundred leagues in all directions

And the flames that leap up at one wall smash against the wall opposite, and he feels pain that is sharp & bitter & severe. But he has not finished his time until he has exhausted his evil deeds.

Every once in a great long while one of the gates of the Great Hell opens wide: quickly & hurriedly he runs to it, his skin & flesh & sinews burning, his bones smoking; but when he gets there, the gate is closed, and he feels pain that is sharp & bitter & severe. But he has not finished his time until he has exhausted his evil deeds.

And every once in a great long while one of the gates of the Great Hell opens wide: quickly & hurriedly he runs to it, his skin & flesh & sinews burning, his bones smoking; and he rushes through the gate, and falls into the Hell of Excrement.

And in that Hell of Excrement needle-mouthed creatures cut away his skin & flesh & sinews; they cut his bones, & they eat his marrow; and he feels pain that is sharp & bitter & severe. But he has not finished his time until he has exhausted his evil deeds.

Then he falls into the next hell, the Hell of Hot Coals, and he feels pain that is sharp & bitter & severe. But he has not finished his time until he has exhausted his evil deeds.

And next to that hell is the Forest of the Thorn Trees, which stand a league high, with fiery blazing thorns sixteen fingers long; and they drive him up and down the trees, and he feels pain that is sharp & bitter & severe. But he has not finished his time until he has exhausted his evil deeds.

Then he enters the next forest, the Sword-leaf Forest; and the wind stirs the leaves, and they slice off his hands & feet, his ears & nose, and he feels pain that is sharp & bitter & severe. But he has not finished his time until he has exhausted his evil deeds.

Then he falls into the next hell, the River of Acid, and he is carried with the current & against the current, and up & down the stream, and he feels pain that is sharp & bitter & severe. But he has not finished his time until he has exhausted his evil deeds.

Then the guards of hell haul him out with a fish-hook, set him on dry land, and say to him: "Silly person, what do you want?" And he says: "Sirs, I am hungry."

So they pry open his mouth with a fiery blazing iron spike and push a fiery blazing iron ball into his mouth; and it burns his lips & mouth & throat & chest and comes out below, taking his intestines with it, and he feels pain that is sharp & bitter & severe. But he has not finished his time until he has exhausted his evil deeds.

Then the guards of hell say to him: "Silly person, what do you want?" And he says: "Sirs, I am thirsty."

So they pry open his mouth with a fiery blazing iron spike and pour fiery blazing molten iron into his mouth; and it burns his lips & mouth & throat & chest, and comes out below taking his intestines with it, and he feels pain that is sharp & bitter & severe. But he has not finished his time until he has exhausted his evil deeds.

And then the guards of hell hurl him back into the Great Hell again.

. . . What I am telling you, monks, I did not hear from any other recluse or brahman; I am telling you what I know myself, what I have seen myself, what I have understood myself.

Thus spoke the Blessed One.

5. GHOST STORIES

The entire universe is a vast interconnected web of life, bound together by karma: heaven and hell are the moral poles of this world, and between them lie not only the realms of men and animals, but the more shadowy kingdom of the hungry ghosts. This is the stage upon which we act out the drama of moral responsibility, where virtue is rewarded by bliss, and the punishment is made to fit the crime.

For just as physical torment is the ripening of sinful deeds, the pleasures of the senses can be a reward for virtue: the mansions of heaven are as real as the pits of hell, and the choice is before us at every instant.

The following tales were once part of an extensive oral tradition of Indian ghost stories; even where these particular tales have disappeared, Buddhist lands have filled the gap with stories of their own. Throughout all of Asia, to the present day, the departed return to earth to tell of the consequences of their deeds, to report on the joys of heaven and the despair of hell, and the lonely terrors of the shades who flit and gibber in the night.

Two points in these stories deserve mention. If the texts are indeed as old as I believe them to be, they indicate that important elements of later Buddhism were in fact present in the tradition from the very start; for in some of these tales we find that the merit of virtue can actually be transferred from one person to another and that the act of worship is of the greatest moral consequence. We shall meet with both these themes again.

Vimānavatthu [*Tales of the heavenly mansions*], and Petavatthu [*Tales of the hungry ghosts*], in Khuddaka-nikāya [*Collection of little texts*], gen. ed. Bhikkhu J. Kashyap (Bihar: Pali Publication Board, 1959), Sect. 1 and 2, 2:3–229.

Herons and peacocks, and heavenly wild geese, and sweetvoiced cuckoos fly about: this delightful mansion is gaily painted, and strewn with flowers; it is filled with men and women.

There you dwell, goddess of great glory, exercising all your magic powers: heavenly maidens are all about you, and dance and sing to give you pleasure.

You have gained the magic powers of a goddess: what virtue did you do when you were human? Why have you such blazing glory, your beauty shining forth all around you?

When I was among men, when I was human, then was I a devoted wife, with thoughts for no other save my lord; I protected him as a mother her child; even when he angered me I spoke no harsh words.

I dwelt in truth and cast aside falsehood; I delighted in charity and was kind to all; with faithful heart I gave food and drink; respectfully I gave abundant alms.

This is how I gained such beauty; this is why I prosper here, where pleasures spring forth for me, whatever is pleasing to me.

I tell you the virtue that I did when I was human, that thus I have such blazing glory, my beauty shining forth all around me.

*
* *

Naked and ugly are you, lady: you are thin, with your veins showing; skinny one, with your ribs sticking out, who are you, standing there before me?

I am a hungry ghost, in evil destiny, a dweller in the world of death; for I have done evil deeds, and have gone to the land of hungry ghosts.

What evil did you do, with your body or speech or mind? Of what deed is this the ripening, that you have gone to the land of hungry ghosts?

I had no father or mother, no kinsman to take pity upon me and urge me to give charity, with faithful heart, to recluses and brahmans.

For five hundred years have I wandered, naked, consumed by hunger and by thirst; for this is the fruit of my evil deeds.

I bow down before you with faithful heart: have pity upon me; bestow some charity for me, and free me from this evil destiny.

And so he promised, for he took pity upon her; and he gave a bit of food to the monks, and a piece of cloth, and a bowl of water; and he dedicated the merit to her.

And immediately that virtue ripened, and food and clothes and drink were the fruit of his dedication.

And she approached him once more, clad in pure clean garments of Benares silk, wearing divers raiment.

You are of surpassing beauty, goddess, standing there before me: you shine in all directions like a healing star.

How did you gain such beauty? Why do you prosper here, where pleasures spring forth for you, whatever is pleasing to you?

Goddess of great glory, I ask you: what virtue did you do when you were human? Why have you such blazing glory, your beauty shining forth all around you?

You saw me pale and thin, hungry and naked, my skin wrinkled, in evil destiny; and you took pity upon me.

You gave a bit of food to the monks, and a piece of cloth, and a bowl of water; and you dedicated the merit to me.

See the fruit of that bit of food: for a thousand years I who love pleasure eat food of many flavors.

See the ripening of that piece of cloth: as many garments as are in the realm of a king of joy.

More raiment than that have I, silk and wool, linen and cotton.

Abundant and precious are they, hanging in the sky; and I clothe myself in whatever is pleasing to me.

See the ripening of that bowl of water: lotus ponds, deep and regular, well laid out.

Clear is their water and beautiful their banks; cool and fragrant are they, covered with blue and white lotuses; and the water is filled with flowers.

And here I delight, and play, and rejoice without fear; and I have come to bow down before you, for truly you have compassion.

*

* *

Naked and ugly are you, lady; your breath is foul and putrid; you are covered with flies. Who are you, standing there before me?

I am a hungry ghost, in evil destiny, a dweller in the world of death; for I have done evil deeds and have gone to the land of hungry ghosts.

In the morning I give birth to seven children, and in the evening to seven more; and I devour them all, nor am I satisfied.

My heart burns and smokes with hunger, nor is it quenched, for I scorch as though burned with fire.

What evil did you do, with your body or speech or mind? Of what deed is this the ripening, that you eat the flesh of your own children?

I had two sons, and both had grown to manhood; and I despised my husband, for I saw the strength of my sons.

And my husband was angered and took another wife, and when she was with child, I plotted evil against her.

With wicked mind I made her lose her unborn child; in the third month it came forth, foul and bloody.

Her angry mother led her kinsmen against me: she accused me and made me swear an oath.

And falsely I spoke this fearful oath: May I eat the flesh of my children if I have done this thing.

And this is the ripening of my deed, and of my falsehood: I eat the flesh of my children, foul and bloody.

*
* *

You are adorned with garlands; you wear bracelets; your limbs are rubbed with sandalwood perfume; your face is serene, and you shine like the sun.

You have a retinue of servants to serve you: ten thousand maidens are your servants; they wear bracelets and bangles, adorned with golden garlands.

Handsome are you, and of great glory; yet you hack the flesh from your own back, and devour it.

What evil did you do, with your body or speech or mind? Of what deed is this the ripening, that you hack and eat the flesh of your back?

To my own harm I acted in the world of the living, with slander and falsehood, with deception and fraud.

There I went into the assembly when the time for truth had come; but I despised the good and the true, and I turned to unrighteousness.

Thus must he devour himself, who is a backbiter, even as today I eat the flesh of my own back.

You yourself can see this thing: it is compassionate to speak the good; do not slander, nor speak falsely of others, lest you be a backbiter indeed.

*
* *

You stand there before me in the sky: your breath is foul and putrid; worms eat your rotting face. What deeds did you do in your former life?

They take up swords and hack you again and again: they sprinkle you with lye and hack you again and again.

What evil did you do, with your body or speech or mind? Of what deed is this the ripening, that you suffer such pain?

In the lovely city of the king, upon the delightful mountain peaks was I a lord of abundant wealth and property.

My wife, and my daughter, and my daughter-in-law went to the shrine to offer garlands and lotuses and new perfumes; but I stopped them, and that was the evil that I did.

There are 86,000 of us here in this hell of separate sufferings; and here I am boiled alive, for I despised the worship at the shrine.

Hold back those who thus do evil when others worship at a shrine, at the festival of the Worthy Ones.

See these ladies coming, adorned, wearing garlands: they enjoy the ripening of the garlands they have offered; rich are they, and beautiful.

The wise look upon this wonder, this thrilling miracle, and they pay homage; they bow down before the great seer.

When I have passed away from here and have become a man once more, surely I shall ever worship at the shrine, with faithful heart.

6. THE VOWS OF COMPASSION

The philosopher Josiah Royce once considered the moral issues raised by the Book of Job, and he wrote:

" . . . You are damned for your own sins, while all that I can do is to look out for my own salvation." This, I say, is the logically inevitable result of asserting that every ill, physical or moral, that can happen to any agent, is solely the result of that agent's own free will acting under the government of the divine justice. The only possible consequence would indeed be that we live, every soul of us, in separate, as it were absolutely fire-proof, free-will compartments, so that real cooperation as to good and ill is excluded.*

The mean and the selfish, then, are the dark side of individual moral responsibility. The Buddhists have been aware from the first how easily virtue can degenerate into narrow priggishness when it is not given life by compassion and sympathy. Meditations upon love and benevolence have always been part of the Buddhist tradition, but it was the religious movement called the Great Vehicle that placed compassion at the center of the moral stage and made it the most fundamental of all the virtues.

The Great Vehicle was a complex religious and social phenomenon; it was simultaneously a religious revitalization and a reworking of metaphysics, a revival of archaic and ecstatic modes of vision, and a progressive reordering of moral priorities. It was in essence a moral and philosophical revaluation of the world, an affirmation of virtue as mutual responsibility; and it drew on ancient sources of compassion and selflessness within the tradition to extend the concept of personal morality to include all living creatures.

Much of the movement was not really new, and we can see its ideals of self-sacrifice in the earliest strata of the Buddhist tradition, even to the giving away of one's own merit to those who need it more. But what was new was the

*Josiah Royce, "The Problem of Job" in *Studies of Good and Evil* (1898), reprinted in George Brantl, ed., *The Religious Experience* (N. Y.: Geroge Braziller, 1964), 124-142.

moral excitement of the vision, the quickening of the pulse at the thought that the perfect virtues of Buddhahood were indeed within the grasp of all. The movement was endowed with what we can only call enthusiasm, in its original and religious sense: an inspired and poetic fervor in the call to universal salvation.

Śāntideva became the foremost voice of this poetic fervor, despite the fact that he lived in the seventh century A.D., long after the movement had begun: he was a climax of the tradition, rather than a founder. A monk at a great monastic university, he seemed to be a loafer and a glutton. The other monks planned to humiliate him by exposing his ignorance, and they asked him to recite the scriptures. He responded by chanting a poem of his own, which was to become one of the most moving and important hymns in all of Buddhist literature.

Tradition thus tells us that Śantideva was a great bodhisattva, one skilled in wisdom and faith, who hid his virtues under humble ways and strange behavior. He was the secret saint who wanders through the whole of Buddhist folklore, and whom we shall meet again.

The following selection is drawn from two cantos of his lengthy work. The first canto is a hymn of praise to the awakening of the thought of enlightenment, a joyous expression of his sense of wonder at the possibility of salvation, not only for himself but through him for all living creatures. The second canto is the dedication of his merit for the benefit of others, so that whatever good he has done may be used by the entire world. The whole poem is a monument to the excitement of the ultimate moral challenge, the presence of Buddhahood in all things.

Śāntideva, Bodhicaryāvatāra [*Setting forth in the practice of enlightenment*], ed. *Vidhushekhara Bhattacharya (Calcutta: The Asiatic Society, 1960), chaps. 3 and 10.*

I am medicine for the sick & weary

may I be their physician & their nurse
until disease appears no more
may I strike down the anguish of thirst & hunger
with rains of food & drink
may I be food & drink to them
in famine & disaster
may I be an inexhaustible treasure
for those in need
may I be their servant
to give them all they desire

my body : my pleasure : my merit
   now & forever
   everywhere
       I care nothing about them
       I cast them aside
          to accomplish the aims of beings

nirvana is the giving up of all
& my heart yearns for nirvana
   if I am to give up all
       let it be given to beings
       let me give my body to them
          to do with as they wish
          to slay & abuse & cover with filth
       let them play with it
          laugh at it : frolic with it
I have given them my body
why should I care about it
       let them do what brings them pleasure
       let them suffer no misfortune
       because of me

   let them hate me : let them love me
      but let their feeling
        bring about all their aims
let them accuse me : let them wrong me : let them mock me
   but let them share in enlightenment

        may I be a protector for the unprotected
          a guide for wanderers
        a boat : a bridge : a causeway
      for those who desire the other shore
       a lamp for those who need a lamp
       a bed for those who need a bed
       a slave for those who need a slave
          for all beings

        & may I be a wishing gem
         an inexhaustible vase
         a magic spell
         a great medicine
         a wishing tree
         a cow of plenty
         for all beings

as the elements of earth & water & fire & air
  are for the use of all the beings
    who dwell in all of space
      in many ways

may I be the means of sustenance
        for the realm of beings
                in all of space
                        in many ways
                                until all have passed into nirvana

as the Well-gone Ones seized the thought of enlightenment
        & resolved upon the practice of bodhisattvas
                in ages past
so do I awaken this thought of enlightenment
        for the welfare of the world
                        & I shall follow their practice

and when the wise man joyfully seizes the thought of enlightenment
                        let him rejoice
                                (that it may grow
                                that it may thrive)
                                        & say

today my birth is worthwhile
        & my humanity is fruitful
today I am born again
                                in the family of the Buddhas
                                as a son of the Buddhas

(& I deeply care to act according to my birth,
let there be no stain upon that stainless family)

as a blind man might find a jewel in a pile of garbage
                by some miracle
this thought of enlightenment has appeared in me
                & there is born

an elixir of life to destroy death
        an endless treasure to conquer poverty
        a supreme medicine to cure disease

        a tree of rest for the weariness of wandering
                on the journey of existence

        an open bridge for travelers to cross
                beyond all evil destiny

        a rising moon to cool the heat of passion
        a great sun to dispel the darkness of ignorance
        fresh butter churned from the milk of the true Law

it is a banquet of happiness laid out
        to refresh all who come
                the caravan of beings
                        wandering on the journey of existence
                        hungry to taste some happiness

today I invite the world to Buddhahood
with happiness on the way
(let gods & demigods rejoice
in the presence of the protectors)

& by my merit:

may all beings be ornaments to the practice of enlightenment
& all those tortured in body or spirit
gain oceans of happiness & joy
nor lose their gladness
as long as the world shall last
& the world attain forever
the happiness of bodhisattvas

and may all the beings in the hells
throughout the worldly realms
taste the joys of paradise
those tormented by cold find warmth
& those tormented by heat
be cooled by oceans of water
pouring from great bodhisattva clouds

may all the regions of hell grow charming
& filled with lakes
fragrant with stretching lotuses
delightful with the pleasing cries
of cranes : of ducks : of ruddy geese
heaps of fiery coals be piles of jewels
& the blazing ground a crystal pavement
clashing mountains be temples filled with Buddhas
& the rain of coals & flaming stones & swords
a rain of flowers

(& may the combat of swords be a playful battle of flowers)

the yellowed skeletons (their flesh fallen off
sunk in the rivers of hell
sunk in the blazing waters)
be bodies of the gods
dwelling by celestial streams
with the daughters of heaven

and by the strength of my merit

the minions of death : the dreadful scavenging birds
will tremble as they see the darkness disappear
(suddenly : completely)
& wonder at the moonlight
which awakens happiness & joy

and silently behold the blazing bodhisattva
                    coming through the sky
        see the flood of joy which conquers pain
                as the suffering go to meet him
            (& a lotus rain falls down : mixed with perfumed waters)
they see the flames of hell put out
                    the beings of hell refreshed with joy
        & wonder as they see the sudden vision
                of the bodhisattva

come: come quickly, my brothers (who once were alive)
                    banish your fear
        he has come for us
                    (this necklaced prince : this blazing comforter)
        by his might all evil vanishes
                & a flood of joy bursts forth

look look : his lotus feet
        are worshipped by the crowns of gods
                    (& his eyes are wet with compassion)
            a flooding rain of flowers falls about him
        as the beings of hell let forth a roar . . .

                                        & by my merit:

            may the blind see & the deaf hear
            the fearful cease to tremble
            the afflicted be consoled
            & the weary be made content

        may the sick be made whole again : those in bondage freed
                may the weak be strong
                        (& loving to each other)

                may the gods protect the helpless
            from the dangers of disease and dark forests
                (the young & the old
                        the sleeping & the heedless)
                & send the rain in season

        may the harvest be abundant : may the world flourish
            may kings be righteous & medicines be potent
                may no creature ever suffer
                        be sinful or sick
                (be wretched : or despised : or forsaken)

                                        & by my merit:

            may we ever hear the sound of the Law
        (in the song of birds : in the whispering of trees)
                in dancing sunbeams

may the monasteries prosper : filled with recitation
    the Community be complete
        and achieving all its aims
    monks attain to wisdom : be anxious for training
    and meditate industriously
        without distraction

    may scholars be honored
        (received : supported)
    may they keep the lineage of teachings
        & their fame pervade the world

and every creature be a Buddha in the world
        (to taste neither sorrow nor hardship)
    attain the body of a god
& worship all the Buddhas (in many ways)
    be exceedingly glad
        with Buddhist gladness

    and as long as the earth and sky shall last
    may I remain here
        to heal the sorrows of the world

I take upon myself the sorrows of the world

    & may the world be happy . . .

3
worship

1. THE FRUITS OF WORSHIP

Devotion to the person of the Buddha has been a striking part of the Buddhist tradition from the very beginning. The texts describe him as approached with the greatest reverence by all his followers, who would walk about him three times in respect and kneel to one side, while the monks would bare their right shoulders before him. After his death, the same respect was paid to his relics and the shrines that enclosed them, to the holy places where he had walked, and to the memorial mounds that commemorated his teachings and his deeds. Here the faithful—both monk and lay—would place the traditional offerings of flowers and incense, of perfume and food, as they do to this very day.

As artistic traditions grew and developed, the same worship was offered to the image of the Buddha, and often the image became the central focus of the memorial shrine. To build these shrines, restore them, and adorn them with fine carvings and fluttering banners had always been of the greatest merit, and the virtue was extended to include the making of Buddha images, and the offering of worship before them.

This devotion is expressed even in the fundamental formula of the three refuges, the Buddha, the Law, and the Community: to take refuge in the Buddha is to enter into an existential relation with a living and potent spiritual force that is more than an abstract idea: the model of feudal loyalty on which the formula was based never became an empty metaphor. Thus the worship of the Buddha was the expression of an entire mode of being, a turning of the whole person toward the active good that governed the world. The intentionality of this relationship with Buddhahood could bring the worshiper the same merit as the intentionality of virtue itself.

The following text speaks of this merit in terms of building images of the Buddha, but it could just as well be speaking of any act of reverence and devotion. There is some stylistic reason to believe that it was composed in China or central Asia in the seventh century A.D., most likely using an older Indian text as a model. The first half gives the traditional account of how King Udayana built the first image of the Buddha ever made (although the text is rather free with its legendary materials) and of how the king became concerned that his innovation was a sin, for he had failed to capture the shining beauty of the Blessed One. The second half of the text, given here, is an assurance that a reverent intention is never wasted, and that it washes away even the most heinous and perverse of crimes.

Ta-ch'eng tsao-hsiang kung-te ching [*The meritorious virtue of making images*], *in* Taishō Shinshū Daizōkyō, *gen. eds.* Takakusu Junjirō *and* Watanabe Kaigyoku *(Tokyo: Taishō Issaikyō Kankōkai, 1924–29) 16, no. 694.*

And the Blessed One sat upon his lotus throne, upon the terrace of enlightenment; and each person in the four assemblies thought to himself:

Truly we wish to hear the Blessed One teach us the meritorious virtue of making images of the Buddha: for what blessings could we gain if we made an image in the form of the Buddha, yet with our meager talent failed to capture his likeness?

And the bodhisattva Maitreya knew their thoughts: he arose from his seat, placed his robe over his right shoulder, and knelt upon the ground: he joined his palms together, and said to the Blessed One:

King Udayana has made an image of the Buddha. Whether the Buddha is in the world or has passed away into nirvana, how much merit does one gain who follows the dictates of a faithful heart and builds an image such as his? My one wish is that the Blessed One explain this thing to me.

And the Buddha said to the bodhisattva Maitreya:

Listen attentively: listen attentively, and ever bear in mind what I shall explain to you.

Let a son of good family or a daughter of good family but be pure and faithful, and fix his mind solely upon the virtues of the Buddha, and meditate unceasingly upon his awe-inspiring virtue and majesty.

Let him think upon the ten powers of the Buddha, and upon his four-fold fearlessness; upon his eighteen special qualities, and upon his great love and compassion; upon his omniscience, and upon all his signs of greatness.

Let him see how every single pore of the Buddha's body glows with measureless multicolored brilliant light, with immensities of surpassing blessings and adornments and accomplishments, with measureless insight and perfect enlightenment, with measureless meditation and forebearance, with measureless magic and spiritual power.

Let him meditate upon the infinitude of all the virtues of the Buddha, upon his far removal from all the hosts of error, and upon his splendor unequaled in all the world.

And let him fix his mind in this manner, and awaken deep faith and joy, and make an image of the Buddha with all its signs: and then he gains merit which is vast, and great, and measureless, and limitless, and which can be neither weighed nor counted.

Maitreya, should a man draw and adorn an image with a host of varied colors; or cast an image of silver, or bronze, or iron, or lead, or tin; or carve an image of fragrant sandalwood; or cover an image with pearls, or shell, or well-woven and embroidered silk; or cover a wooden image with red earth and white lime plaster; or build an image to the best of his ability, even if it be so small as the size of a finger, as long as those who see it can see that it is in the form of the Blessed One—I shall now tell you what his blessed reward will be, and how he will fare in his next life.

For a man who does these things may be born again into this world, but he will not be born into a poor family, nor will he be born in a barbarian border kingdom, nor into a lowly clan, nor as an orphan; he will not be born stupid or fierce, nor as a merchant or pedlar or butcher; truly he will not be born into any low mean craft or impure caste, into any heretical practices or heretical views.

For by the power of his intention he has cast aside the cause for such rebirth, and he will not be born into such states; but rather he will always be born into the household of a universal emperor, having powerful clansmen, or perhaps into the household of a brahman of pure practices, rich and honorable, lordly and without error.

And the place where he is born will always be where Buddhas are served and worshipped; and perhaps there he shall be a king, able to maintain and establish the Law, teaching the Law which converts those of evil practices; and perhaps he shall be a universal emperor, having the seven jewels, bringing forth a thousand sons, and mounting into the sky to convert the four corners of the world.

And when his length of days has been exhausted, the lord will be abundantly joyful, perhaps to rule as the king of the gods, or as lord of the Heaven of Delights, or of the Heaven of Power; for there will be no joy either of gods or of men which he will not taste. And thus his blessed reward will continue in heaven and will not be cut off when he dies.

And he will always be born as a man: he will not take on the body of a woman, or of a eunuch, or of a hermaphrodite. And the body which he takes will be without defect or deformity: neither one-eyed nor blind; his ears not deaf; his nose not bent or twisted; his mouth not large or crooked; his lips not hanging down or wrinkled or rough; his teeth not broken or missing, not black or yellow; his tongue not slow; the back of his neck without tumor or boil; his form not hunched; his color not splotched; his arms not weak; his feet not large; and he will be neither too thin nor too tall, neither too fat nor too short.

And in this wise he will lack all unpleasant characteristics; and his body will be upright; his face round and full; his hair dark in color, soft and rich, bright and clean; his lips like red fruits; his eyes like blue lotus petals; his tongue broad and long, and his teeth even and close that he may skillfully form words which rid his listeners of sorrow; his arms strong and long; his palms flat and solid; his waist and thighs full and substantial; his chest broad; and his hands and feet as soft as silk: and he will be without any deficiency at all, and he will be as strong as a god.

Maitreya, it is like a man who has fallen into a latrine and who finally gets out of there: he scrapes off the excrement and dirt and washes himself with pure water; he splashes himself with perfume and puts on fresh clean clothes. Now how much difference is there for this man between being in that latrine and having gotten out, between being clean and being filthy, between being perfumed and stinking? These two states of affairs are separated by an incalculable amount.

Maitreya, if there is a man who, in the midst of this world, can awaken his faith and build an image of the Buddha, then between his having done so and his not having done so the difference is just as great: for anywhere this man is born, he is purified and free of all his past sins, and by all his skill may gain liberation even without a teacher.

If his destiny be birth among men, then he yet gains the faculties of a god; if it be birth among the gods, then he surpasses all the hosts of heaven.

And wherever he is born, he never suffers from disease; he is without itch or mange, ulcers or cancers, or any of those diseases which are spread among the demons and the hungry ghosts; he has no diseases of convulsion, or of madness, or of excessive thirst, no jaundice, fevers, constipation, asthma, malignant boils, syphilis, vomiting, diarrhea; never does he lack satisfaction from his eating and drinking; never is his whole body afflicted with pain, or half his body lame and paralyzed: in brief, never does he suffer from any of the four hundred and four diseases.

Nor does he suffer any of the hurts which come of harmful external conditions: never does he suffer from poison, or weapons, or fierce lions, or water, or fire, or enemies, or thieves; but rather he is always fearless, and commits no sins.

Maitreya, anyone who in the past has accumulated evil karma will taste all manner of grievous suffering and woe: he will carry a yoke and wear a lock; he will be fettered with handcuffs; he will be beaten and burned and flayed alive, have his hair pulled and his body hung upside down in the air, and be dismembered at all his joints; but if he can awaken his faith and build an image of the Buddha, then he will taste none of this bitter retribution for his sins.

He will not be born in a town which will be invaded and looted and destroyed by robbers, nor where evil stars bring forth strange famines and pestilences. And he lies who says he is born there.

And then the bodhisattva Maitreya said to the Buddha:

Blessed One, you have always said that good or evil deeds are never lost. Any being who has done such grievous sins should be born in a mean, low class and household, be poor and sick and die a speedy death. But if he can awaken his faith and build an image of the Buddha, then will he still experience the retribution for his host of sins?

And the Buddha said to the bodhisattva Maitreya:

Maitreya, listen attentively, and I shall explain it to you. Should this being, who has done all those sins, put forth his heart to build a Buddha image, seek to wail and repent, take himself strongly in hand and vow to transgress no more, then everything that he has done before is all annulled. Let me illustrate this case for you.

Maitreya, there was once a man who had been very stingy in a past life, and thus he now experienced poverty and suffered from his lack of wealth, for all his former possessions and pleasures were now exhausted. But one day it happened that a monk, who had entered into meditation, arose from his trance; and this man honored the monk and gave him alms of food and drink. And no sooner had he given alms than he was freed from poverty forever, and all that he wanted was just as he wished. Maitreya, that poor man had accumulated evil karma in a former life: but now what had happened to the retribution for what he had done?

And the bodhisattva Maitreya said:

Blessed One, it was because he gave food to the monk that the evil karma of his past life was annulled and exhausted, and thereby he could be free of poverty forever, and endowed with a sufficiency of great wealth.

And the Buddha said to Maitreya:

It is just as you have said. And you should know that a man who builds a Buddha image is the same: because he builds an image his evil karma is exhausted forever, without any reminder; and he experiences none of the retribution which he should experience.

Maitreya, there are three kinds of karma: (1) the kind whose results are experienced immediately, (2) the kind whose results are experienced in the next life, and (3) the kind whose results are experienced even after that: and each of these three kinds of karma may be either certain or uncertain. If a man has a faithful heart and builds a Buddha image, only a small part of his immediate and certain karma is experienced; and he experiences none of the others.

And then the bodhisattva Maitreya said to the Buddha:

Blessed One, you have always said that there are five kinds of grievous sin by which a man is sure to fall to the deepest hell: (1) killing his father, (2) harming his mother, (3) killing a Worthy One, (4) with malice aforethought causing blood to flow from the body of a Buddha, and (5) causing a schism in the Community. But if a man has done these things, yet later goes to the birthplace of a Buddha, awakens his faith, and builds a Buddha image, then will he still fall into hell?

And the Buddha said to the bodhisattva Maitreya:

Maitreya, I will now fully explain this to you with a parable. Suppose there is a man standing in a grove of trees, grasping a strong bow in his hands: he faces upward and shoots at a leaf; his arrow will penetrate that leaf and go on without hindrance. If there is a man who has done any of these perverse sins, yet later makes a Buddha image and repents with a sincere heart, then he gains faith by the grace of the Buddha: he himself realizes his own meanness, and at the same moment that he falls into hell he has passed through and beyond it, just as the arrow did not stop. He is like a monk who has gained magic powers, who can fly from shore to shore of the sea and circle the four continents, with nothing to hinder him: he may fall briefly into hell because of his previous transgressions, but his past deeds are unable to keep him there . . .

And then the bodhisattva Maitreya said to the Buddha:

Blessed One, suppose there is a man who steals things from a shrine, who steals things from the Community, and thinks he can treat the things of the Community as if they were his own. Blessed One, you have always said that it is a grievous sin to use things belonging to a shrine or to the Community. But if a man has done this thing, yet later upbraids himself and repents, awakens his faith and builds a Buddha image, then will his sin be annulled?

And the Buddha said to the bodhisattva Maitreya:

Maitreya, if there is a man who has appropriated these things, yet later examines himself, is deeply ashamed and repentant, pays back double the amount, and vows to transgress no more, then he is like the man in the parable which I shall now tell you. Suppose there is a poor man, carrying a heavy burden of debt, who suddenly happens on a hidden treasure and finds countless jewels; then even after he has paid off his debts he still has treasure left over. You should know that the thief, too, has treasure left over, even after he has paid back double the amount he stole; and by further building a Buddha image he remits all suffering, and gains peaceful joy forever . . .

But there were those in the crowd who had not yet awakened their faith, and they had doubting thoughts: Did the Blessed One himself make Buddha images in the past? For if he did, then how is it that his lifetime is limited, he has diseases and suffering, and the land wherein he dwells is unclean and corrupt rather than stainless and pure?

And King Prasenajit was blessed by the power of the Buddha: he arose from his seat and knelt upon the ground; he joined his palms together and said to the Buddha:

Blessed One, I see that your signs and faculties are foremost in the world, and your mind is without impediment. Yet once you cut and injured your foot on a piece of wood; once the wicked Devadatta pushed over the rocks scattered on a mountain and drew blood from your foot; once you cried that you were ill and sent for a physician to mix beneficial medicines; once you suffered from a malady of the back and had a monk recite the scriptures to ease your pain; once you were ailing and sent a monk to beg milk for you; once you spent the rainy season retreat eating nothing but foul food; and once you begged for food and got nothing at all, and returned with an empty bowl.

And yet the Blessed One has said that if a man makes an image of the Buddha, then all his past evil is annulled: he is freed from all his pain and suffering, and he is without disease. Now did the Blessed One himself make Buddha images in the past? For if he did, then how could such things as these have happened?

And the Buddha said to King Prasenajit:

Listen attentively; listen attentively and ever bear in mind what I shall explain to you.

In past lives I searched for enlightenment: with a host of precious things, sandalwood and rich colors, I made Buddha images exceeding the number of men and gods in this assembly. And by the merit thereof, although I was yet in the world, I exhausted all my passions, and the body which I took was firm as diamond and could not be injured or hurt.

I think of all those who have made Buddha images for numberless eons in the past: and some still had all the passions of lust and hatred, and thought that these passions were proper; yet even they have never been ill for a moment. Even those among them who are evil ghosts or demons have few sufferings or diseases, and not one of them lacks for anything he wants. And I have attained supreme and perfect enlightenment: could I then have things which are not to my liking?

If I had built Buddha images in the past and yet were now experiencing retribution for evil deeds, would I then fearlessly say to you that making such images destroys all evil?

In the past I have given measureless alms of food and treasure: how is it then that I now beg and search yet get nothing, or eat foul food? If such were really the case, how then could I possibly praise the perfection of charity in all my scriptures, and say that its blessed reward is never empty?

I am one who says what is real and true, not one who speaks falsehoods: if I should lie and deceive, then how much more would other men!

I have severed all evil karma forever: I am able to renounce what is hard to renounce and practice what is hard to practice; and what I have renounced is a bodily life exceeding billions of years.

I have built numberless Buddha images, and I have repudiated all sin: then how could it be that I suffer defamation, and wounds, and disease, and pain, and hunger, and thirst?

All the Blessed Buddhas have an unchanging body, a body of reality: it is to bring beings to perfection that they manifest these things which are not real. My injured foot, my painful back, my begging for milk, my taking medicine, indeed even my passing away into nirvana and the erection of shrines over my relics which are divided and scattered abroad: all this is the skillfulness of He Who Has Come, that all beings may see that the world is painful and transitory.

I am the one who reveals this host of painful things to the world: I proclaim to all beings that the retribution of karma is not lost, that they may fear their sins and cultivate their virtues. Later they will truly understand that my unchanging body, my body of reality, has limitless life, and that its land is pure and stainless.

And when King Prasenajit heard these words, he jumped about for joy, together with numberless hundreds of thousands of beings; and they all awakened their thoughts toward supreme and perfect enlightenment.

And then the bodhisattva Maitreya said to the Buddha:

Blessed One, there are women whose will is narrow; many of them cherish envy in their hearts, and hatred and spite, and sycophancy and falsehood; they show no awareness of kindness and do not repay it. Not one of them is able to be firm and diligent in the search for enlightenment; they are always seeking to deceive.

Blessed One, if a woman such as this should build an image of the Buddha, will her karma too be exhausted and annulled? Will she become a man in the future, steadfast and unwearied in seeking the reward of Buddhahood? Will she gain insight and compassion, and learn to weary of the world?

And the Buddha said to the bodhisattva Maitreya:

Maitreya, if a woman is able to build a Buddha image, then she will never be born as a woman again. And if she should become a woman, then she will be the queen of a universal emperor, first among the noble and honorable, and endowed with the five kinds of virtue whereby she surpasses all other women. And what are these five? (1) Her children are many; (2) her family is noble and honorable; (3) her disposition is chaste and virtuous; (4) her bodily form is superlative; and (5) her beauty is admirable and proper.

Maitreya, there are eight causes whereby a woman is reborn as a woman. And what are these eight? (1) Love for the body of a woman; (2) attachment to the passions of a woman; (3) constant delight in the beauties of a woman; (4) insincerity of heart to hide her wicked deeds; (5) weariness and contempt for her husband; (6) constant thoughts of other men; (7) perverse ingratitude for the kindness of others; and (8) wicked adornment of her body for the sake of deception.

But if she can build a Buddha image and renounce these things forever, then until she herself gains Buddhahood she will always be a man, and she will never be born as a woman again.

Maitreya, there are four causes whereby a man is reborn as a woman. And what are these four? (1) Disrespectfully laughing and shouting at the Buddha, or bodhisattvas, or Worthy Ones; (2) slandering one who is pure in keeping the precepts, saying he does not keep them; (3) flattering and fawning in order to deceive; and (4) envying the happiness of other men.

If a man has done these things, then when his life is over he will surely be reborn as a woman, and experience the measureless suffering of his evil ways. But if he repents what he has done, awakens his faith, and builds a Buddha image, then these sins are all annulled, and he will not experience the retribution of becoming a woman.

Maitreya, there are four causes whereby a man is reborn as a eunuch. And what are these four? (1) Castrating another man; (2) laughingly scorning and slandering a recluse who keeps the precepts; (3) transgressing the precepts himself because of his lustful desires; and (4) not only transgressing the precepts himself but also encouraging others to do the same.

If a man has done these things, but later awakens his faith and builds a Buddha image, then until he himself gains Buddhahood he will never experience the retribution thereof, and he will always be a man with all his faculties intact.

Maitreya, there are four causes whereby a man is reborn as a hermaphrodite, which is the lowest possible state among men. And what are these four? (1) Uncleanness where there should be reverence and respect; (2) lust for the bodies of other men; (3) the practice of lustful things upon his own body; and (4) the exposure and sale of himself in the guise of a woman to other men.

If a man has done these things, but later upbraids himself and deeply repents his transgressions, awakens his faith and builds a Buddha image, then until he himself gains Buddhahood he will never be reborn in this way.

Maitreya, there are four causes whereby a man is born with the lusts and desires of a woman, and enjoys being treated as a woman by other men. And what are these four? (1) Despising other men, or slandering and defaming them even in jest; (2) taking pleasure in dressing and adorning himself as a woman; (3) doing lewd uncleanness with his own clanswoman; and (4) falsely accepting reverence while lacking the true virtue worthy of it.

Through these causes a man will be reborn into all manner of suffering and woe, but if he repents his former transgressions and does no new sins, if he bears in his heart the faithful joy with which he builds a Buddha image, then these sins are all annulled, and these lusts and desires will cease within him.

Maitreya, there are five sorts of stinginess which will bring a man to ruin. And what are these five? (1) Stinginess toward his neighbors, for he will be reborn in the midst of a wilderness; (2) stinginess toward his family, for he will be reborn as a worm, remaining always in excrement and filth; (3) stinginess with the correct and proper modes of beauty, for he will be reborn ugly and evil and unpleasant; (4) stinginess with his wealth, for he will be reborn in poverty, with scant and insufficient food and clothes; and (5) stinginess with the Law, for he will be reborn stupid and dull and bestial.

But if he repents his former deeds and builds a Buddha image in a noble manner, then his stinginess will be gone forever, and he will be without all that he formerly suffered.

Maitreya, there are five causes whereby a man is reborn among the barbarians of the borderlands, or at a time when there is no Law in the world. And what are these five? (1) Not reaping a pure faith in the fertile field of the Law; (2) turning his back on the real, forsaking the true, and falsely practicing the teachings and precepts; (3) grasping the teachings in a way discordant with reason and truth; (4) breaking the harmony of the Community, that it becomes two factions; and (5) arousing contention between two monks, that they become enemies.

But if he casts aside such deeds forever and builds a Buddha image, then he will meet the Buddha in person and ever hear the Law.

Maitreya, there are five causes whereby a man becomes a constant object of hatred and rejection, so that even his closest relatives do not like to see him. And what are these five? (1) Having a double tongue; (2) having a wicked mouth; (3) constantly arguing; (4) always being scornful; and (5) artfully slandering with words that seem like truth.

But if he repents his former deeds and vows to sin no more, awakens his faith, and builds a Buddha image, then the sins which he has done are all exhausted and annulled, and he will become loved and honored by all men.

And why is that? It is because all Buddhas have the measureless limitless blessed virtues of their Buddhahood: measureless limitless great insight, measureless limitless meditation and freedom, and all manner of superlative qualities of meritorious virtue.

Sons of good family, suppose that all the three billion billion worlds were reduced to fine dust, and that each grain of that dust were divided into the number of grains of dust there were in those three billion billion worlds.

Now suppose that a man flew to the eastern quarter by magical power and fetched one grain of dust out of all the grains of dust in those three billion billion worlds: in the first instant that passed, he picked up one of those grains of dust in those three billion billion worlds, and similarly in the second and third and every subsequent instant until he had exhausted, after many eons, all those grains of dust.

Now suppose that each instant there was in all those eons were itself an eon containing all the instants of an eon, and that the number of grains of dust in those three billion billion worlds were calculated as before, so that every instant for all those eons this man put down a grain of dust, returned and fetched another grain of dust, and every instant kept adding to what he had done until he had used up all those grains of dust: and even as I have explained in the eastern quarter, so it was in the southern, and western, and northern quarters, until all the worlds in the four quarters had yielded all their grains of dust.

Now if all beings got together and calculated, then they might know and enumerate the measure of this dust, but they could not know what meritorious virtue there is in one fraction of one pore of the body of the Blessed One.

And why is this? Because the virtue of the Blessed Buddha is without limit or measure, and it cannot even be thought or talked of. And that is why, if a man awakens his faith and builds a Buddha image, every single one of his evil deeds will be exhausted and annulled; and from the store of the Buddhas he gains meritorious virtue without limit or measure, until he himself gains Buddhahood, and himself saves beings from all their suffering and woe forever . . .

2. THE DAILY RITUAL

To be a Buddhist means more than simply to accede to a given set of metaphysical doctrines. A Buddhist is defined by his participation in a special existential relationship with the Buddha and the Law and the Community, a relationship formalized by his taking refuge in these Three Jewels: it is by a ritual that his participation in the sacred is made real; it is by rituals that this participation is continued.

Ritual thus enters the life of the Buddhist at the very beginning and pervades it to the very end: he is born and he dies amid the chanting of the monks. In every Buddhist land, the sponsor of ritual is rewarded not only by religious merit but also by the esteem of his peers. According to his piety, he will perform a greater or lesser number of private rituals—perhaps every day or every fortnight, and certainly during the great annual celebrations of the major events in the life of the Buddha.

The following text sets forth a system of daily worship for the Buddhist layman. The work is relatively late and thus presents a ritual repertoire considerably expanded from that of earlier treatises; it is essentially a contemplative reworking of older ritual themes (the worship of the holy relics, for example, and the offering of food to the hungry ghosts). To these themes it adds the later traditions of the worship of the image, the homage to the master, and the offerings and confessions before the five Buddhas.

Certainly the text presents an ideal system, but rituals such as these are part of daily life throughout Buddhist Asia, differing from each other in detail but having the same intent. To the pious Buddhist, every meal, every daily act becomes a ritual: from waking in the morning to going to sleep at night, every event of life is an act of charity and worship, and every aspect of his life made holy.

Anupamavajra, Ādikarmapradīpa [*The lamp for beginners*], in Bouddhisme: Études et Matériaux, ed. *Louis de la Vallée Poussin (London: Luzac and Company, 1898), pp. 186–204.*

The precepts and the vows

Going for refuge. Now when a son or daughter of good family has awakened his faith in the teachings of the Buddha, he should first of all take refuge in the Three Jewels; and the Blessed One himself has told us the reason for this:

He who takes refuge in the Buddha does not go to evil destinies, for when he casts aside his human body he gains the body of a god. And hence he goes for refuge to the Buddha, and to the Law, and to the Community.

And again the Buddha has said:

Adversity increases day by day; and yet in a single moment you can gain infinite merit, simply by taking refuge in the Buddha and the Law and the Community. Thus rightly go for refuge, if you would destroy your attachment to the world.

And this is the ritual to be followed:

On an auspicious day, the faithful son or daughter of good family makes himself ritually pure and dresses in pure white garments; and in a solitary place he offers the five offerings to an image of the Buddha. He offers up the entire world to the Three Jewels and to the master who will there grant him refuge: he walks three times around him, and with profound faith he prostrates himself to the Three Jewels and to his master's feet.

Then he kneels before his master and three times asks him:

My spiritual guide! Grant me the three refuges and the precepts and vows of a disciple.

And when the master sees that his disciple is possessed of good intention, he says:

As far as it is in my power, I shall grant them to you.

And the master recites the refuges, and the disciple repeats after him:

Venerable one! My master, accept me! I (named such-and-such), from this day forward until I myself sit upon the terrace of enlightenment, go for refuge to the Buddha, the Blessed One, omniscient and all-seeing, the best of men; I go for refuge to the Law, the most excellent of the passionless; and I go for refuge to the Community, the highest of hosts. And a second time . . . And a third time . . .

My master, cleave to me! I have taken the three refuges.

The ten precepts. And then the master gives the disciple the ten precepts of the refuges:

My master, accept me! I (named such-and-such), from this day forward until I myself sit upon the terrace of enlightenment, renounce the taking of life, and the taking of what is not given, and misdeeds of lust; I renounce false speech, and slander, and rudeness, and vain and idle chatter; I renounce covetousness, and malice, and wrong views: I cast them aside and renounce them all. And a second time . . . And a third time . . .

The five vows. And when he has taken these ten precepts, he should take the five vows of a disciple and announce his intention, saying:

My master, accept me! Just as the Noble Ones, the Worthy Ones, cast aside the taking of life, and renounced the taking of life for as long as they lived, so do I cast aside the taking of life and renounce it from this day forward, as long as I shall live.

And by this first vow, I shall practice this precept of the Noble Ones, the Worthy Ones: I shall imitate them, and I shall be guided by them.

And just as the Noble Ones, the Worthy Ones, cast aside the taking of what is not given, and misdeeds of lust, and false speech, and intoxicating drink, and renounced them all for as long as they lived, so do I cast them aside and renounce them from this day forward, as long as I shall live.

And by these vows, I shall practice these precepts of the Noble Ones: I shall imitate them, and I shall be guided by them.

And the master says: Well done! Well done!

And he bestows upon his disciple the books of the Law that he should study: and he blesses him by sprinkling him with water . . .

Morning worship

Awakening and bathing. After the third watch of the night, the disciple should rise from his bed, join his palms together, and bow his head to the earth, saying:

OM! I bow to the feet of all Those Who Have Come: I join my body and speech and mind to theirs, and diffuse the diamond of my body and speech and mind through the whole realm of reality:

OM! I offer myself for service in the worship of all Those Who Have Come: diamond truth of all Those Who Have Come, empower me!

OM! I offer myself for initiation in the worship of all Those Who Have Come: diamond jewel of all Those Who Have Come, initiate me!

OM! I offer myself for employment in the worship of all Those Who Have Come: diamond Law of all Those Who Have Come, use me!

OM! I offer myself for action in the worship of all Those Who Have Come: diamond deeds of all Those Who Have Come, employ me!

And I awaken myself to the diamond of omniscience; and the thought I awaken is the diamond of knowledge of all Those Who Have Come, that I may gain the attainment of true reality, equal to the good which I have done . . .

And the disciple should prostrate himself before the Buddhas, with his five limbs to the earth.

Then, for the welfare of his body, he should brush his teeth and wash himself with water over which he recites:

OM! Law of purity, cleanse away all my sins, dispel my misconceptions *HŪM!*

And he should wash his face with water over which he recites seven times: *OM!* Lotus, lotus, lotus of my eyes, lovely one *HŪM!*

For the texts tell us that this king of mantras is a great teaching: thereby the disciple becomes beloved of all men, that he may spread the Law, and he is free of all diseases of his eyes.

Then he should recite the chanting of names, the epitome of the truths of all the lords of sages; and he should make his earnest wish for enlightenment, and prostrate himself before his masters and before the Buddhas and bodhisattvas.

Water for the hungry ghosts. And as soon as the sun has risen, the disciple should offer up pure water to the hungry ghosts and to Jambhala, the god of wealth, that he may grant the means to allay their sufferings. As it is said:

Carefully the compassionate one perfumes the water in a betel leaf cup in his hand, that he may allay the destinies of living creatures, their unaltering closed circle, their zig-zag trail of becoming . . .

And he visualizes Jambhala in the sky before him:

The red syllable *YAM* appears and transforms into an eight-petaled lotus; above the lotus is the white syllable *A,* which transforms into the disc of the moon; and above the moon the yellow syllable *JAM* appears and transforms into Jambhala himself, seated upon his lotus throne.

And he is in union with his consort Lady Bountiful: on his crown is the golden Buddha Source-of-Gems; he is adorned with all ornaments, his fat belly hanging, and wearing a blue lotus garland.

And upon his own hand the disciple visualizes *OM* upon the wrist, *HŪM* upon the palm, *BLŪM* on the tips of his fingers, and *SAH* at the base of his fingers. And he recites over his hand, saying:

OM! To Jambhala, lord of the waters *SVĀHĀ!*

And with his hand he drinks the water mixed with sugar, saying: *OM HŪM BLŪM SAH!*

Then he first offers one hundred and eight handfuls of water to Jambhala, for the Blessed One has said:

He who offers with a firm mind and a profound faith swiftly becomes as rich as Jambhala himself, and swiftly fulfills his stocks of merit and knowledge.

And then he offers up the water to the hungry ghosts, that he may quench their fiery thirst; and in a ritually pure place he recites the mantra:

OM! This water is for all the hungry ghosts *SVĀHĀ!*

And he gives to them one hundred and eight handfuls of water. This is the ritual for offering water to the hungry ghosts.

Worship of the Buddha's relics. And as soon as he has offered up the water, the disciple should make a small shrine of earth, in the shape of a mound which holds the relics of the Buddha. And this is the ritual for making it:

OM! Homage to the Blessed One, to the king of the splendor of the sun, He Who Has Come, the Worthy One, the perfect Buddha!

OM! Subtle, equal to the unequaled, quiet and calm, inaccessible and untouchable: save us! Famous and mighty: undisturbed nirvana, empowered by the empowerment of all the Buddhas *SVĀHĀ!*

He recites this mantra twenty-one times over a piece of earth or lump of clay, and he makes thereof a small reliquary shrine; and by the power of the mantra he makes a billion times as many shrines as there are atoms in the piece of earth . . .

Then he offers up flowers before the relics of the Buddha, saying:

OM! Homage to the Blessed One, to the king of the light of flowers, He Who Has Come, the Worthy One, the perfect Buddha!

OM! Flowers, great flowers, good flowers, sprung from flowers, cause of flowers, valor of flowers, strewing of flowers *SVĀHĀ!*

And by the power of the mantra he gives a billion flowers for every flower he offers.

Then he prostrates himself before the relics of the Buddha, saying:

OM! Homage to the Blessed One, to the king of the light of jewels, He Who Has Come, the Worthy One, the perfect Buddha!

OM! Jewels, great jewels, victory of jewels *SVĀHĀ!*

And by the power of the mantra he bows a billion times each time he prostrates.

Worship of the Buddha's image. Then the disciple makes the small reliquary mound into an image for worship with the ritual of smiting, that the shrine may open and reveal the Buddhahood within, that the deity may descend into it and consecrate it:

He takes up the earth, saying: *OM* bountiful Lady Earth *SVĀHĀ!* He makes it an image, saying: *OM* to the diamond-born *SVĀHĀ!* He protects it with oil, saying: *OM* clean and pure *SVĀHĀ!* He sets down the image, saying: *OM* womb of the realm of diamond *SVĀHĀ!* He seals it with signs, saying: *OM* womb of the realm of reality *SVĀHĀ!* He smashes the demons, saying: *OM* diamond hammer, smash! *HŪM PHAṬ SVĀHĀ!*

He calls down the deity, saying: *OM* delight of the Law *SVĀHĀ!* He establishes him therein, saying: *OM* well-founded diamond *SVĀHĀ!* He consecrates it, saying: *OM* womb of the realm of reality, filled with a hundred blazing and shining gems of all Those Who Have Come *SVĀHĀ!* He dismisses the deity, saying: *OM* womb of the realm of reality, come, take away! *SVĀHĀ!* And he asks for forebearance toward errors in the ritual he has performed, saying: *OM* womb of the realm of space *SVĀHĀ!*

And the shrine is now an image for worship, touched by the presence of Buddhahood: and the disciple puts it in a pure and unpolluted place. This is the ritual of smiting, which opens the mound for worship.

Then the disciple should worship the image he has made: and thus he worships not only the Buddha but the celestial bodhisattvas and high patron deities as well. And this is the ritual for worship:

He strokes the image with a peacock feather to symbolize the offering of a holy bath; and he recites the bathing mantra:

OM ĀH glory of the vows of imitation of all Those Who Have Come *HŪM!*

Then he offers up the offerings:

OM *ĀḤ* diamond vows *HŪM!* OM *ĀḤ* diamond possessions *HŪM!* OM *ĀḤ* diamond garments *HŪM!* OM *ĀḤ* diamond flowers *HŪM!* OM *ĀḤ* diamond incense *HŪM!* OM *ĀḤ* diamond lamps *HŪM!* OM *ĀḤ* diamond food *HŪM!*

And he may offer up any other offering he wishes, announcing each one in turn with its name and syllables.

Offering up the world to the master. And the disciple should then offer up the entire world to his master. For it is said that the master himself is all the Buddhas; it is said that the Buddha and the Law and the Community all come into being through the master . . .

And this is the ritual for offering up the world:

The disciple protects himself and the place, saying: OM *ĀḤ HŪM!* He washes his hands and rinses his mouth, saying: OM *HRĪM SVĀHĀ!* He empowers his seat, saying: OM *HŪM!* He takes possession of the ground, saying: OM *ĀḤ* diamond ground *HŪM!*

Then he takes cow dung and pure water, reciting: OM! Diamond truth, expel all hindering demons *HŪM PHAṬ!* And he cleanses the ground therewith, and he lays out the diagram of the world.

First he draws the boundaries around the world and empowers them: OM *ĀḤ* diamond fence *HŪM!*

He takes flowers over which he has recited the flower mantra, and offers them within the boundaries he has drawn, saying:

OM! Best of diamond masters, accept my homage and my offerings *HŪM!*

Then he washes his hands, and in the center of the diagram he lays out Mount Meru, square, eight-peaked, and made of the four precious substances: silver in the east, lapis lazuli in the south, crystal in the west, and gold in the north.

And in the middle of the mountain is a lion throne studded with divers gems; and upon the throne he sees his own glorious master, seated in the posture of royal ease upon a full-blown lotus, and adorned with all manner of ornaments.

Then he draws the shapes and colors of the four continents of the world around Mount Meru: Pūrvavideha in the east, white and semicircular; Jambudvīpa in the south, golden and triangular; Aparagodānīya in the west, red and round; and Uttarakuru in the north, blue and square.

And he visualizes each of these continents to be filled with rubies, and sapphires, and lapis lazuli, and emeralds, and diamonds, and pearls, and coral.

Then he takes out the flowers he gave before and offers them once again in the middle of the world diagram:

OM *HŪM!* Homage to my master in the middle!

And he pays homage to his master and to the continents of the world:

OM homage to my diamond master! OM *YAM* homage to Pūrvavideha! OM *RAM* homage to Jambudvīpa! OM *LAM* homage to Aparagodānīya! OM *VAM* homage to Uttarakuru!

And he fills the world for his master with all the royal treasures of a universal emperor:

OM/YA homage to the treasure of the royal elephant! *OM RA* homage to the treasure of the royal minister! *OM LA* homage to the treasure of the royal horse! *OM VA* homage to the treasure of the royal queen! *OM YĀH* homage to the treasure of the royal sword! *OM RĀH* homage to the treasure of the royal gem! *OM LĀH* homage to the treasure of the royal wheel! *OM VĀH* homage to the treasure of the royal wealth!

And he pays homage to the sun and moon upon Mount Meru:

OM AH homage to the moon! *OM ĀH* homage to the sun!

And all of these continents and treasures spring into being as he recites their names and syllables, and he offers them all to his master. He takes flowers between his joined palms; he visualizes the world he has created to be filled with all the precious things that he can think of, and he says:

Homage to you! Homage to you! Homage, homage, homage, homage! I pay you homage with devotion: my master and protector, be gracious unto me!

And he prostrates himself, saying:

OM! I bow to the feet of all Those Who Have Come!

And this is the ritual for offering up the entire world to the master . . .

Worship of the five Buddhas. Then in the sky before him there appear the syllables *HŪM* and *OM* and *TRĀM* and *HRĪH* and *KHAM*: and they transform into the five Buddhas, with their colors and gestures:

In the center is blue Unmoving-One, with the gesture of touching the earth; in the east is white Shining-One, with the gesture of highest enlightenment; in the south is yellow Source-of-Gems, with the gesture of bestowing gifts; in the west is red Infinite-Light, with the gesture of meditation; and in the north is green Unfailing-Success, with the gesture of fearlessness.

And they are all in the form of Buddhas, wearing their monastic robes; and they sit upon sun-thrones and blaze with sunlight, but Shining-One sits upon a moon-throne and blazes with moonlight . . .

And there is no difference between the syllable and the deity; so the disciple should worship each syllable as it appears in the sky before him.

Then he offers up all his sensory delights to the Buddhas, for it is said:

Ever offer the pleasures of your senses to the Buddhas, and attain Buddhahood swiftly with these five offerings.

So he offers up to each Buddha the pleasures of his five senses in manifest form: he offers them music for sound, and lamps for sight, and sandalwood for smell, and milk for taste, and garments for touch . . .

And he empowers the offerings he makes to them:

OM! Mass and multitude of clouds of offerings to all Those Who Have Come: spread wide and fill the sky *HŪM!*

Then he offers up to them even his own body:

Homage to all the Buddhas and bodhisattvas, dwelling in worldly realms in the ten directions, protecting the entire realm of beings: Buddhas and bodhisattvas and your retinue, accept me!

I (named such-and-such) ever and always offer myself to all the Buddhas and bodhisattvas: compassionate ones, receive me! Lord protectors of all the worldly realms, empower me! Protect me, and grant me the highest attainment.

Then he confesses his sins before them:

As the Buddhas, the Blessed Ones, give leave: I awaken my thought of enlightenment, and I confess all my sins, born of lust and hatred and delusion through all of time; for bodhisattvas who awaken their hearts to enlightenment confess their sins.

Then he rejoices in the merit and happiness of others:

As the Buddhas and bodhisattvas give leave: I rejoice with the highest rejoicing at all the stocks of merit and knowledge which purify and protect the realm of beings, at all the merit and knowledge gathered through all of time by all the Buddhas and bodhisattvas, by all the disciples and solitary Buddhas, by all the beings in the world.

Then he recites praises and prayers to his heart's content, and he dedicates the merit of his worship:

As Those Who Have Come, the Worthy Ones, the perfect Buddhas give leave: Those Who Have Come, the Worthy Ones, the perfect Buddhas know my merit with their Buddha-knowledge, and see my merit with their Buddha-eyes; they know how it was born, how it was gathered, its nature and its signs; and I rejoice in that merit, and I dedicate it all to supreme and perfect enlightenment.

And then he joins his palms together and bows down before the Buddhas, saying:

OM! I pay homage with pleasing obeisance to all Those Who Have Come, and to the Blessed One my protector. *JAH HŪM BAM HOH!* Protector: accept the flowers of my hands joined in reverence to you *HĀH!*

Reading of sacred books. Then the disciple should read some holy texts, such as the Perfection of Wisdom.

He first walks around them in respect, then he may read them for as long as he wishes, and he concludes with a special earnest wish that he thereby gain enlightenment.

Food for the hungry ghosts. Then he should give the food offerings of a bodhisattva, and this is the ritual with which he gives them:

Homage to the Three Jewels! Homage to the Blessed One, the beautiful, He Who Has Come, the Worthy One, the perfect Buddha!

OM! Send! bestow! save! save! maintain! remember! satisfy! for all the hungry ghosts *SVĀHĀ!*

He recites this mantra seven times over the food, along with some water; he claps his hands three times; and in a solitary place he offers it to all the hungry ghosts. And then he says:

Depart, you who have gathered here: I have given food to all the hungry ghosts who dwell in all the worldly realms.

And thus each hungry ghost is given as much food as a bushel of rice; and the disciple himself will never be hungry or weak or poor, but in all his lives will be strong and beautiful and wealthy, rich in pleasures, living long and without disease; quickly he will realize supreme and perfect enlightenment. And when he dies he will be reborn in the Heaven of Highest Happiness.

This is the ritual of offering food to the hungry ghosts.

Prayer for the teachings. Then the disciple should pray with a joyous mind that the teachings long abide in the world and that their benefit increase; for it is said that he who prays, however briefly, that the teachings long abide will ever possess life and health and happiness.

And then, after one final prostration, the disciple dismisses the master and the Buddhas he had summoned to receive his morning worship.

Daytime worship

Offerings at meals. When the disciple eats his meals, he should first spend the time of three water-clocks in offering up a portion of his food to all the spirits, to the Three Jewels, and to the Lady Guardian-of-Children.

And he should seat himself in the presence of his patron deity, and eat his food according to the rules.

And when he has finished, he should offer up as well all the pieces of food left over, and rinse his mouth; and then he should recite a verse of the Law, as the highest gift he can give to the spirits who have come to share his food.

Then he washes his bowl, saying:

Homage to the Blessed One, to the king of surrounding splendor, He Who Has Come, the Worthy One, the perfect Buddha! Homage to Sweet-Voice the prince, the bodhisattva, the greatly compassionate!

OM! Strong and victorious and wise: support! promise! cleanse the sacrificial gift *SVĀHĀ!*

For it is said that he who recites this mantra even once can cleanse a bowl as large as Mount Meru.

Daily activities. And the disciple should ever perform the deeds of a bodhisattva, to the best of his ability, and live in the commands of charity and love given him by his glorious master. He should pass the day in serving and sharing the aims of living creatures and in converting them to the true Law: in meditation and study, in reciting mantras, in listening to the Law, and in serving the masters who explain its meaning.

He should pass the day in the deeds of a bodhisattva, and with his heart filled with joy: never should his heart be apathetic, but joyous and careful in all things; for it is said that recitation and austerity are useless where there is neither gladness nor concern.

Evening worship

When evening falls, the disciple should remain awake for the first watch of the night, reciting the true Law.

And when he prepares for bed, he first prostrates himself with his five limbs to the earth and pays homage to all the Buddhas and bodhisattvas. He joins in contemplative union with his own patron deity, and he says:

Homage to the blessed Perfection of Wisdom, returning the love of her devotees, fulfilling all the perfections of Those Who Have Come!

OM! Accomplish! awaken! enlighten! arouse! stand! *HRĪH!* tremble! resound! come! Blessed Lady: do not delay, do not delay *SVĀHĀ!*

He recites this mantra twenty-one times over his own right arm; and he lays his head upon that arm, and goes to sleep in the posture of a lion.

And when he awakens again, he once more performs his morning worship. And the son or daughter of good family who performs these rituals quickly attains to the highest enlightenment . . .

4
lIVING together

1. THE HOLY COMMUNITY

Buddhism began as a Community, and it will end when the Community is gone. Even in modern Japan, where the tradition is experimenting with other organizational forms, the most respected Buddhist leaders are still those few who keep the monastic law: the model is kept alive, and the option is still available.

We tend to be wary of institutions and to see them as monolithic and unresponsive, but the Community has been an adaptive feature of the Buddhist tradition, and has found an ecological niche for itself in the culture of every Buddhist land. Indeed, we might define a Buddhist culture as one wherein the Community has found a place, and where the religious life has become a viable institution.

For twenty-five centuries the Community has held Buddhism together. It is a refuge for the weary and an ideal of renunciation, a source of leadership and a standard of permanence in times of cultural change: it is an institution, and thus always available to those who need it. The religious vocation is given a home, the seeker is given a path, and the life of brotherhood is established as a model for all mankind. It is small wonder that some of our earliest texts praise the Community as an ideal, however it may be flawed in practice; and it is in this ideal Community that every Buddhist takes his refuge.

Khuddaka-pāṭha, *in* Khuddaka-nikāya (*Collection of little texts*), gen. ed. *Bhikkhu J. Kashyap (Bihar: Pali Publication Board, 1959), 1:6-9, Sutta VI* (Ratana-sutta).

> eight holy persons
> praised by the good
> four pairs
> worthy of gifts
>
> (gifts to them
> bear great fruit)
>
> minds
> firm & solid
> greedlessly

65

abide
in his teachings
gain
what can be gained
plunge
into undeath
taste
nirvana
for free

pillars
earthrooted
unswayed
by the winds
called good men
see the truth
perfectly
know the truth
well taught
by him of deep wisdom

(though careless yet
never born
an eighth time)

attain the vision
cast aside three
(belief in self
& doubt
& outward show)

free
of fourfold
evil destiny
free
of sixfold
grievous sin
cannot conceal
sin done
by body speech mind
(who have seen
cannot
:they say)

gone the old
the new unborn
minds detached
from future birth
seeds destroyed

hope ungrowing
wise
& quenched
like lamps

this precious gem
the Community
(& by this truth
good fortune)

2. VAIN AND SELFISH HOPES

The Community of saints, to use Hobbes's phrase, is real, not metaphorical. Whether today or 300 B.C., the holy Community consisted of people in voluntary association, attempting to lead a religious life, helping each other, and getting on each other's nerves.

Every attempt at communal structure in the history of the world has had to deal with the inevitable few who refuse to wash the dishes.

But generations of close contact have given the Buddhist community a good deal of often acute psychological insight into the modes of individual abrasiveness that can wear away the best of good wills. Beyond specific offenses, the Buddhists recognize that there can be simple childishness, and they look upon it with a surprising and subtle humor; they know that people are not perfect, else there would be no need for Buddhas.

The following is probably a fairly early text, but it could have been written at any time in the history of the Community: it could have been written by anyone who lived with other people. And we must remember that the Buddhists, above all else, have always been people.

Anaṅgaṇasutta [*Blemishes*], in Majjhima-nikāya [*Collection of medium discourses*], gen. ed. Bhikkhu J. Kashyap (Bihar: Pali Publication Board, 1958), 1:33–44, Sutta V.

You speak of blemishes, my brother. Now what do you mean by that?
My brother, a blemish is a vain and selfish hope.
For it sometimes happens, my brother, that a monk will think: I have committed an offense; I hope the other monks do not find out about it.
And then it happens that the other monks find out that he has committed an offense. And the monk thinks: They know that I have committed an offense.
Then he becomes angry and discontented, and both his anger and his discontent are blemishes.
And it sometimes happens, my brother, that a monk will think: I have committed an offense; I hope the other monks admonish me in private, and not in the midst of the Community.

And then it happens that the other monks do not admonish him in private, but in the midst of the Community. And the monk thinks: They are admonishing me in the midst of the Community, and not in private.

Then he becomes angry and discontented, and both his anger and his discontent are blemishes.

And it sometimes happens, my brother, that a monk will think: I have committed an offense; I hope it is one of my friends who admonishes me, and not some other monk.

And then it happens that it is not one of his friends who admonishes him, but someone else. And the monk thinks: It is some other monk who is admonishing me, and not one of my friends.

Then he becomes angry and discontented, and both his anger and his discontent are blemishes.

And it sometimes happens, my brother, that a monk will think: When the master teaches the Law to the monks, I hope that he will address all his questions to me, and not to any of the other monks.

And then it happens that when the master teaches the Law to the monks he does not address all his questions to him, but to someone else. And the monk thinks: He is addressing all his questions to some other monk, and not to me.

Then he becomes angry and discontented, and both his anger and his discontent are blemishes.

And it sometimes happens, my brother, that a monk will think: When the monks go into the village for alms, I hope they choose me to lead them, and not any of the other monks.

And then it happens that when the monks go into the village for alms they do not choose him to lead them, but someone else. And the monk thinks: They chose some other monk to lead them, and not me.

Then he becomes angry and discontented, and both his anger and his discontent are blemishes.

And it sometimes happens, my brother, that a monk will think: I hope that the best seat, the best water, the best food in the dining hall is given to me, and not to any of the other monks.

And then it happens that he does not get the best seat, the best water, the best food in the dining hall, but someone else does. And the monk thinks: The best seat, the best water, the best food in the dining hall is being given to some other monk, and not to me.

Then he becomes angry and discontented, and both his anger and his discontent are blemishes.

And it sometimes happens, my brother, that a monk will think: I hope that I am the one to say the thanks after the meal, and not any of the other monks.

And then it happens that he is not the one who says the thanks after the meal, but someone else does. And the monk thinks: Some other monk is saying the thanks after the meal, and not me.

Then he becomes angry and discontented, and both his anger and his discontent are blemishes.

And it sometimes happens, my brother, that a monk will think: I hope that I am the one to teach the Law in the lecture hall, and not any of the other monks.

And then it happens that he is not the one who teaches the Law in the lecture hall, but someone else does. And the monk thinks: Some other monk is teaching the Law in the lecture hall, and not me.

Then he becomes angry and discontented, and both his anger and his discontent are blemishes . . .

And this monk may abide in the forest, and beg his food, and make his robes of rags, but his brothers in the religious life will neither honor nor revere him, for they see that he has not cast aside these vain and selfish hopes . . .

3. THE RULES OF CONDUCT

Buddhist monastic law is casuistic: it enunciates no broad principles from which individual rules are derived, but rather seeks to make an exhaustive listing of individual cases, each traditionally decided by the Buddha himself, to cover every conceivable contingency of conduct. It is thus a written code of traditional law, which grew through the daily interactions of real people seeking solutions to the real problems of living the religious life in harmony; and it mixes the most fundamental rules of ethics with the details of monastic etiquette, the restraints against desire with descriptions of acceptable sandals, and the curbs on lust with the precise measurements of a meditation hut in the forest.

The most serious offenses (murder, theft, sexual intercourse, and lying about spiritual attainments) lead to expulsion from the Community: if the offense is conceded, the offender is simply no longer a monk, and that is the end of the matter. Lesser offenses may require only a simple confession, or perhaps also the forfeiture of a personal possession not allowed by the rule (an extra bowl, for example, or an improperly elegant robe). The aim is always the religious welfare of the offender, that he may not hug the chains of his possessions or hide the putrefying sore of his misconduct. It is virtuous to remonstrate with an offender, or even accuse him before the Community, so that he may have a chance to confess and cleanse his guilt.

Certain offenses are rather more serious than those requiring only confession, yet not quite serious enough to warrant immediate expulsion: these include sexual misconduct short of actual intercourse, false accusations against other monks, and various sorts of serious troublemaking in the Community. Such offenses require a formal meeting of the Community and an appropriate legal decision handed down in proper form. The following selection consists of the first of the thirteen rules regarding these offenses.

Each rule sets forth in detail the paradigmatic case on which the original decision was based, even specifying the name of the original offender. Many of these offenders may indeed have been real persons, but by the time the law was codified they had become archetypes. Thus Seyyasaka is found in many rules, always as the typical poor soul, easily swayed by his companions, and constantly in trouble for his gullibility. Udāyin is the model of the frustrated monk, who is never quite able to bring his impulses under control, and to whom the very presence of a woman is an unbearable temptation. He always manages to make a fool of himself and then to be sorry for it: sheer horniness is never really attractive, but somehow Udāyin turns out to be rather a sympathetic character. These monks (and the others who appear in the rules) may be types, but they eventually seem to project human personalities, and they demonstrate the psychological insight that accumulates over generations of watching people behave under the difficult conditions of true community.

The paradigmatic case is followed by the rule itself, with a minute analysis of its contents, and often a list of exceptions generated by special circumstances. And we may note that the intentionality of the act is always the paramount consideration; an unintentional offense is no offense at all. The motive of the rule is always the spiritual well-being of the individual.

Even today, all of the approximately two hundred and fifty rules of conduct are read out loud every two weeks in every Buddhist monastery, so that every monk may know them and have the opportunity to confess his sins. This recitation of the rule has bound the Community together for more than two thousand years and has maintained a remarkable integrity of conduct in the most diverse cultural and political environments. It remains to be seen what will happen to the tradition in what has often been called a post-traditional society.

Bhikkhu-vibhaṅga [*Analysis of the rules for monks*], gen. ed. Bhikkhu J. Kashyap (Bihar: Pali Publication Board, 1958), 1: 150–90.

The Case of the Monk Seyyasaka

. . . Now at one time the venerable Seyyasaka was practicing the religious life, but he was dissatisfied; and so he was haggard and miserable and emaciated, his color poor and pale, his veins showing all over his body.

Then the venerable Udayin saw that the venerable Seyyasaka was haggard and miserable and emaciated, his color poor and pale, his veins showing all over his body, and he said to him:

"My brother Seyyasaka, why are you so haggard and miserable and emaciated? Can it be, my brother, that you are dissatisfied with practicing the religious life?"

"That is so, my brother."

"Well then, my brother, you should eat as much as you like, sleep as much as you like, and bathe as much as you like: and if, though you eat and sleep and bathe as much as you like, you are still dissatisfied, and lust assails your heart, then you should masturbate."

"But my brother, is it proper to do such a thing?"

"Indeed it is, my brother. I do it all the time."

So then the venerable Seyyasaka ate as much as he liked, slept as much as he liked, and bathed as much as he liked: and when, though he ate and slept and bathed as much as he liked, he was still dissatisfied, and lust assailed his heart, he masturbated. And thus in a short time his color returned, his senses were gladdened, his complexion cleared up, and his skin was smooth.

And the monks who were the venerable Seyyasaka's friends said to him: "Our brother Seyyasaka, once you were haggard and miserable and emaciated, your color poor and pale, the veins showing all over your body; but now your color has returned, your senses are gladdened, your complexion has cleared up, and your skin is smooth. Are you using some sort of medicine?"

"I am not using any medicine, my brothers. I eat as much as I like, sleep as much as I like, and bathe as much as I like: and when, though I eat and sleep and bathe as much as I like, I am still dissatisfied, and lust assails my heart, then I masturbate."

"But our brother: do you eat the alms given you in faith with the same hand you use to masturbate?"

"That is so, my brothers."

Now there were monks who were unassuming and modest, conscientious and scrupulous and anxious for training; and they were offended and upset and annoyed at this, and they said: "How could the venerable Seyyasaka masturbate like that?"

And these monks rebuked the venerable Seyyasaka in many ways, and told the Blessed One what had happened.

The Primary Promulgation of the Rule

So for that reason the Blessed One called a meeting of the Community, and he asked the venerable Seyyasaka: "Is it true what they say, Seyyasaka, that you masturbate?"

"It is true, Blessed One."

And the Buddha, the Blessed One, rebuked him and said: "Foolish person, this is neither proper nor pleasing nor fitting; it is unbecoming to a recluse; it is not allowed; it is not to be done. Foolish person, how could you masturbate?

"Foolish person, I have taught the Law for the sake of purity, not for the sake of lust; I have taught the Law for the sake of freedom, not for the sake of bondage; I have taught the Law for the sake of renunciation, not for the sake of grasping.

"Foolish person, I have taught the Law for the sake of purity, yet you strive after lust; I have taught the Law for the sake of freedom, yet you strive after bondage; I have taught the Law for the sake of renunciation, yet you strive after grasping.

"Foolish person, have I not taught the Law in many ways, that you might calm your passion, subdue your pride, destroy your thirst, uproot your attachment, sever your becoming, demolish your craving? Have I not taught the Law for the sake of purity, for the sake of cessation, for the sake of nirvana?

"Foolish person, have I not in many ways told you to cast aside your lust for pleasure, to understand your conception of pleasure, to destroy your thirst for pleasure, to uproot your constant thoughts of pleasure, to quench the fires of pleasure?

"Foolish person, this does not convert the unconverted, nor increase the faith of the converted; but rather it offends the unconverted and causes the converted to waver."

And thus the Blessed One rebuked the venerable Seyyasaka: in many ways he spoke in dispraise of being insufferable and arrogant and discontented and greedy and lazy; in many ways he spoke in praise of being polite and satisfied and contented and austere and careful and gracious and energetic. He gave reasoned discourse on what is proper and pleasing for a monk, and he said:

"Thus, monks, this rule of training should be set forth: *The intentional emission of semen is an offense requiring formal action by the entire Community.*"

And thus the Blessed One promulgated this rule of training to the Community.

The Case of the Dreaming Monk

... Now at one time there were some monks who had eaten abundantly, and who then fell asleep, careless and unmindful; and while they were sleeping, careless and unmindful, one of them emitted semen because of a dream he had.

And they were remorseful and worried, and they said: "The Blessed One has set forth a rule of training, which says that the intentional emission of semen is an offense requiring formal action by the entire Community, and now one of us has emitted semen while he was dreaming. Is this to be considered intentional? What if we have committed an offense requiring formal action by the entire Community?"

And they told the Blessed One what had happened.

The Revised Promulgation of the Rule

And the Blessed One said: "Monks, the intention was present, but this is a special case.

"Thus, monks, this rule of training should be set forth: *The intentional emission of semen is an offense requiring formal action by the entire Community, except when it happens during a dream.*"

And thus the Blessed One promulgated this rule of training to the community.

Analysis of the Rule

Intentional means a transgression committed knowingly and consciously and deliberately.

Semen means any of the ten kinds and colors of semen.

Emission means ejaculation, or any moving from place.

Except during a dream means that a dream is excepted.

Requiring formal action by the entire Community means that the Community places the monk on probation for his offense, sends him back to the beginning of his probation, imposes the mandatory six-day discipline upon him, and then reinstates him; and not just one person does so, nor even several persons, but the entire Community; and thus it is said to require formal action by the entire Community . . .

5
the stages on the path

1. IN PRAISE OF SOLITUDE

It is the ideal of the Community to free the monk from all concern over his material needs: it can shelter him from the distractions of the world and offer him moral support and the opportunity for study. This ideal has often worked in practice; yet it is, finally, the individual—whether officially monk or lay—who must go forth in solitude to walk the path of wisdom. Indeed, what may be one of the oldest Buddhist poems still extant (known as the "Song of the Rhinoceros") repeats but one refrain almost forty times before it is finished, and the refrain is simply this: wander alone.

It was perhaps inevitable that this joy in solitude found its finest expression in Tibetan poetry. The high ranges of the Himalayas have always been the abode of hermits. Nowhere in the world is there such variety and magnificence of scenery, from wooded meadows to awesome rushing cataracts, from vast bleak plains to the eternal snows of the mountains, and nowhere in the world can solitude so press upon the wanderer, or loneliness grant him such freedom. The songs created upon these peaks are sung today; their sweet, sad tunes express the peace and sorrows of the solitary search and the Tibetans' love for their harsh and beautiful native land.

The cotton-clad Mila (1040–1123 A.D.) was one of the first of the great wandering poet-saints of Tibet. His poetry is filled with a love of nature, and he constantly sings of his happiness as he walks alone in the high hills. He founded a lineage of wanderers, and they so prospered that they built great centers and gathered lands and caravans. Within five hundred years they had become embroiled in politics, and a monk named White Lotus (1527–92 A.D.) yearned for the mountains once more.

White Lotus was a central historical figure in the development of Tibetan institutions, an omnivorous scholar, and a man of temporal power. He would run away to the hills to meditate and be fetched back again to govern a people whose chief delight was—and still is—political intrigue. In his songs we find Mila's own joy in loneliness, tempered by an all too acute awareness of the ways of the crowded world and the unsteadiness of the human heart, including his own.

Mi-la ras-pa, Rje-btsun mi-la ras-pa'i rnam-thar rgyas-par phye-ba mgur-'bum zhes bya-ba [*The biography of cotton-clad Mila*], ed. *Sangs-rgyas rgyal-mtshan (1452–1507* A.D.*), (manuscript copy: dbu-can script, 486 folios), chap. 7 (Yol-mo gangs-ri'i skor), folios 49b–56b and Chap. 38 (G.yag-ru'i skor), folios 288a–299b.*

> this mountain land is a joyful place
> a land of meadows & bright flowers
>
> the trees dance in the forest
> a place where monkeys play
>
> where birds sing all manner of song
> and bees whirl & hover
>
> day and night a rainbow flashes
> summer and winter a sweet rain falls
> spring and autumn a mist rolls in
>
> and in such solitude as this
> the cottonclad Mila finds his joy
>
> for I see the clear light
> & contemplate the emptiness of things
>
> happy when things appear before me
>
> the more they are the happier am I
> for my body is free of evil deeds
>
> happy as things swirl about me
>
> the more they come & go the happier am I
> for I am free of the rise & fall of passion
>
> happy in the midst of visions
> for I am free of passion
>
> happy am I as my sorrow turns to joy
> & in the exercise of my body's strength
>
> in my leaping and my running dance
> in the victorious songs I sing

in the sounds I hum
as they turn into words . . .

for happy is the realm where the strong mind ventures
& happy is my spontaneous strength

as all manner of things appear before me
                              *
                        *   *
I am a yogin who wanders on the glacier peaks
reaching out to the spreading horizon

healthy and cleansed of arrogant evil
I lack no joy for I am content

and I have lost my taste for crowds
to gain my freedom in solitude

have given up bother
to be happy in loneliness

have given up family
to possess nothing at all

I do not seek wisdom in books
content to leave my mind alone

nor seek to better myself through talking
content to leave my mouth alone

nor know how to cheat and lie
content to leave the world alone

nor proudly scratch for fame
content when no one speaks of me

any place I stay is all right
whatever happens I am happy

any clothes I wear are all right
whatever you do I am happy

any food I eat is all right
whatever occurs I am happy

I am the old cottonclad Mila
by the grace of my guru
I think nirvana and the world are perfect

I am a yogin who is happy any old time

Pad-ma dkar-po, Dpal pad-ma dkar-po'i rdo-rje'i glu'i phreng-ba snga-ma zhes bya-ba [*The diamond songs of White Lotus*], *(manuscript copy: dbu-can script, 76 folios), folios 2b–4b.*

search within appearances: emptiness
look within knowing: no foundation
where do you get this looked & looking
what do you get from arguing good & bad

for I know the important thing
(tasting : unweighed with books and logic)
& like a great eagle skysoaring
mind careful   White Lotus   contemplate

nurture the knowledge which comes
unleash the genuine within the senses
contemplate nothing save that which happens
what do you get from busywork mindclinging

for I know the important thing
(thinking undoing : unscattered)
& like a stream everflowing
mind careful   White Lotus   contemplate

look on the naked face of defilement
trample hope and fear
nothing good which isn't in the way
what do you get from worrying do & don't

for I know the important thing
(unpassioned union : unslandered act)
& like a mad elephant lustcharging
mind careful   White Lotus   contemplate

the meditator wanders the world
upon this mountain

field of my lord Heruka's sport
ground of my mother Demon's dance
forest of my experience & understanding
lampwick of my lineage

I feel the joy and happiness & I sing
(three jewels I offer you my song)
            *
        * *
thought   no busywork
          no busywork   turn inward

busywork: & you heed the appearances of pleasure

the thirst for joy & sorrow was my friend so long
that my enemy defilement knows the beguiling of my mind

> his army: thoughts   many and savage
> his spies: distraction   clever and tenacious
> my ally: mindfulness   sluggish
> my indolence: apathy   blocking my advance
> my thought: jabbering   just wandered off

and he may break through the ramparts of my calm
White Lotus   look inward

mind   no binding
         no binding   unleash

binding: & it runs off in ten different directions

it is in wandering that I come to rest
it is in nurturing the unmoving that I know my corruption

> swindled by wringing contemplation
> I unleash the genuine
> bear sensory appearances straight before me
> bring down the cave of lying convention
> know all the corruption of erring counsel

and my enemy vanquished has become my friend
I have cleansed the depths of vindictiveness from the whole world

*
* *

when the wise are burdened with worldliness
& contemplators cling to the mountains of the world
when the evil time is filled with wickedness

then rare indeed is he who follows the Law

when we make our vows & yet are servants to desire
& yogins chase the female contemplators
when the time is near to the waning of the Law

then rare indeed is he who truly meditates

when we pass our days in shams of truth
& the holy are scattered and abused in adversity
when all we do becomes but waste

then rare indeed is he who strives for good

when the conceited are bound in hopes of fame
& the poor are trampled in the pit of debt
when the bourgeois bustle in their useless work

then rare indeed is he who makes the most of his humanity

when in the marketplace we ever sound the news
that all these worldly things are doomed to pass away
& all we gather are the husks of words

then rare indeed is he whose mouth & mind agree

I tell no tales of others' faults
but people are annoyed when I speak the truth
just do the opposite
& you'll be doing what the Sage said

of low position wearing tattered rags
reduced to want in food & clothes & fame
the important thing is to meditate in solitude
& practice onepointedness from your heart

this little song of the five rarities
was sung by the monk White Lotus
to the yogin Dorje Sempa
hoping for his benefit

2. THE STAGES OF MEDITATION

Buddhist meditation has much in common with the systems promulgated by other contemporary sects of wandering contemplatives, and there is little doubt that these sects borrowed freely from each other. Thus Buddhist meditation has constantly enriched itself with new techniques and has created a complex repertoire of contemplative methods; but at the same time it sought to achieve a formal character of its own, a basic structural framework within which these various methods could be organized and coordinated.

The following text is one of the earliest statements of the fundamental structure of Buddhist meditation, and the system it sets forth became the standard to which innovative techniques adapted themselves, some with more success than others. Here is the concept of the contemplative path, a gradual refinement of perception and experience, a sequentially ordered process of discipline and control. In some ways, the entire history of Buddhist meditation can be seen as a series of renovations of this ordered process, and of rebellions against it.

The text gives two basic techniques in meditation. There is reason to believe that the two came from very different sources, and were originally

applied to very different experiential ends; for *calm* is a process of enstatic withdrawal from sensory experience, while *insight* is an ecstatic penetration into the true nature of events. The first seems based on the premise that salvation is transcendent and apart from the world, while the second seems to assert the immanence of enlightenment within the world. Part of the genius of early Buddhist meditation was to create a structure wherein these different processes could reinforce each other and combine into an efficient instrument for the realization of Buddhist truths. The tension between immanence and transcendence would not always be so elegantly resolved.

Thus the meditator first purifies himself in virtue and learns to concentrate his mind without distraction. Even the extraordinarily pleasant sensations that come of mental fixedness are progressively cast aside, until there is nothing left save pure attention upon the object of meditation. The four trances are a sequence of exclusion, of withdrawal from the world, of enstatic isolation from sensory input. This is the process of calm.

Then, in contrast, this pure attention is turned outward upon events, and the meditator sees both objective and subjective occurrences with the eye of his contemplation. For the first time he can see things as they truly are, because for the first time he looks upon them without passion or the prejudice of desire. It is this power of ecstatic penetration into the meaning of events that grants freedom from them and power over them, as step by step the meditator sees more deeply into the true nature of reality.

And this insight is turned, finally, to his own previous lives, to the laws of karma within the world, and to the four noble truths. With this fundamental description of the nature of reality he repeats the process of the Buddha's enlightenment. He knows the world as it truly is: he internalizes the intellectual categories of his contemplation as a flash of realization, and he knows that he is free.

Sāmaññaphala-sutta [*The rewards of being a recluse*], in Dīgha-nikāya [*Collection of long discourses*], gen. ed. Bhikkhu J. Kashyap (Bihar: Pali Publication Board, 1958), Sutta II, 1: 41–73.

Wandering Forth

Suppose that He Who Has Come appears in the world, a Worthy One, a perfect Buddha, endowed with knowledge & conduct, well-gone, knowing the world, a tamer of men, a teacher of men & gods, a Buddha, a Blessed One.

And he has realized wisdom for himself; & he knows the world, with its gods & demons, recluses & brahmans, princes & people.

And he teaches the Law, good in the beginning, good in the middle, good in the end, the letter & the spirit; & he proclaims the religious life, completely pure & fulfilled in its entirety.

And there is a householder, or a householder's son, or a man born in one or another caste, who hears that Law; & he gains faith in He Who Has Come, and he thinks:

The household life is a confined & dusty path; wandering forth is the open air. It is not easy for a householder to practice the religious life, completely pure & fulfilled in its entirety & polished like mother-of-pearl. Then let me cut off my hair & beard, put on the yellow robes, & wander forth from home to homelessness.

And before long he renounces his small portion of wealth, or his large portion of wealth; he renounces his small family, or his large family; he cuts off his hair & beard, puts on the yellow robes, & wanders forth from home to homelessness.

Moral Purity

And when he wanders forth, he dwells bound by the restraints of the monastic law, endowed with good conduct, & seeing danger in even an atom of what he should avoid; he undertakes the rules of conduct, & trains himself therein; he is endowed with good action in his body & his speech, & his livelihood is pure.

And he practices virtue & guards the gates of his senses: he is mindful & aware, & he is contented.

Virtue. And how does the monk practice virtue?

He casts aside the taking of life & renounces the taking of life: he lays down his stick & he lays down his sword: he is modest & filled with sympathy, kind & compassionate to all living creatures. This he possesses in his virtue.

He casts aside the taking of what is not given & renounces the taking of what is not given; he takes only what people give to him & depends upon their charity; he dwells with purity as his only wealth. This he possesses in his virtue.

He casts aside unchastity & becomes celibate: he abides far from evil & does not indulge in the vulgar. This he possesses in his virtue.

He casts aside false speech & renounces false speech: he is a speaker of truth, faithful & trustworthy, not deceiving the world. This he possesses in his virtue.

He casts aside slander & renounces slander: what he hears elsewhere he does not tell here to provoke a quarrel; what he hears here he does not tell elsewhere to provoke a quarrel; but rather he reconciles those who quarrel & encourages friendship; he is a maker of peace, a lover of peace, delighting in peace, a speaker of words of peace. This he possesses in his virtue.

He casts aside rudeness & renounces rudeness: he speaks words which are gentle & pleasant, loving, touching the heart, pleasing to the people, delightful to hear. This he possesses in his virtue.

He casts aside vain & idle chatter & renounces vain & idle chatter: he speaks with a purpose, at the right time, & as things truly are; he speaks the Law & he speaks the discipline; and the words he speaks are worth treasuring, for they are timely & cogent, discriminating & to the point. This he possesses in his virtue.

He renounces untimely food: he eats but one meal a day & does not eat after noon . . . He renounces attendance at shows of dancing, or singing, or music . . . He renounces adorning & decorating himself, & wearing garlands, or scents, or perfumes . . . He renounces high beds & large beds . . . He renounces the acceptance of gold or silver. And all this he possesses in his virtue.

And the monk thus practices virtue, & he sees no danger from any side, for he is restrained by his virtue.

A consecrated king, whose enemies are destroyed, sees no danger from his enemies; and in the same way, a monk who thus practices virtue sees no danger from any side, for he is restrained by his virtue.

And as he practices this noble mass of virtue, he experiences a faultless happiness within himself; and thus the monk practices virtue.

Restraint of the senses. And how does the monk guard the gates of his senses?

When his eyes see a visible object, he does not label it, nor grasp at its details; but rather he sets himself to restrain what might be an occasion for evil & impure states, for desire & regret to attack his sight, were it not restrained; and thus he guards his sight & restrains his eyes.

And when his ear hears sounds, or his nose smells odors, or his tongue tastes flavors, or his body touches a tangible object, or his mind perceives a mental event, he does not label it, nor grasp at its details; but rather he sets himself to restrain what might be an occasion for evil & impure states, for desire & regret to attack his mind, were it not restrained; and thus he guards his perceptions & restrains his mind.

And as he practices this noble restraint of his senses, he experiences an untainted happiness within himself; and thus the monk guards the gates of his senses.

Mindfulness & awareness. And how is the monk mindful & aware?

He is aware when going out or coming in; he is aware when he looks toward or looks away; he is aware when he draws in his limbs or stretches them out; he is aware when he puts on his robe or carries his bowl; he is aware when he is eating or drinking or chewing or tasting; he is aware when he urinates or defecates; he is aware when he goes or stands or sits, when he sleeps or wakes, when he speaks or keeps silent.

And thus the monk is endowed with mindfulness & awareness.

Contentment. And how is the monk contented?

He is content with robes enough to protect his body & with alms enough to sustain his stomach; and wherever he may go, he goes taking his robe & his bowl with him.

Wherever a winged bird may fly, he flies bearing his wings with him; and in the same way, the monk is content with robes enough to protect his body & with alms enough to sustain his stomach; and wherever he may go, he goes taking his robe & his bowl with him.

And thus the monk is content.

Calming the Mind

Place & posture. And the monk is endowed with this noble mass of virtue, with this noble restraint of his senses, with this noble mindfulness & awareness, & with this noble contentment; and he resorts to dwelling in solitude.

And so he goes to a forest, or the foot of a tree, or a mountain, or a valley, or a hillside cave, or a cemetery, or a jungle, or a heap of straw out in the open.

And he returns there from his begging round; and he sits down with his legs crossed, holds his body straight, & sets up mindfulness before him.

Casting aside the hindrances. And there he casts aside his desire for the world; and he dwells with his mind free of desire; & he purifies his heart of lust.

And he casts aside his hatred; and he dwells with his mind free of hatred, with kindness & with care for all living creatures; & he purifies his heart of malice.

And he casts aside his sloth & torpor; and he dwells with his mind free of sloth & torpor, his ideas shining, mindful & aware; & he purifies his heart of lethargy.

And he casts aside his worry & distraction; and he dwells with his mind free of worry & distraction, his spirit tranquil within him; & he purifies his heart of apprehension.

And he casts aside his doubt; and he dwells with his mind free of doubt, no longer wondering what is good; & he purifies his heart of perplexity.

Suppose a man took out a loan to start in business; and his business fared so well that he repaid his debt, & had enough left over to support a wife. He would think: I had to take out a loan to start in business; but now my business has fared so well that I have repaid my debt, & have enough left over to support a wife.

And because of that he would be delighted, & he would be exceedingly glad.

Or suppose a man were sick & in pain & grievously ill, so that he could not digest his food, & there was no strength in his body; and after a time he was cured of that disease, so that he could digest his food once more, & his body regained its strength. He would think: I was sick & in pain & grievously ill, so that I could not digest my food, & there was no strength in my body; but now I am cured of that disease, so that I can digest my food once more, & my body has regained its strength.

And because of that he would be delighted, & he would be exceedingly glad.

Or suppose a man were bound in prison; and after a time he was freed from that prison, safe & unharmed, & with none of his property confiscated. He would think: I was bound in prison; but now I am freed from that prison, safe & unharmed, & with none of my property confiscated.

And because of that he would be delighted, & he would be exceedingly glad.

Or suppose a man were a slave, not his own master, subject to someone else, unable to go where he wanted; and after a time he was freed from that bondage, & became his own master, subject to no one else, a free man able to go where he wanted. He would think: I was a slave, not my own master, subject to someone else, unable to go where I wanted; but now I am freed from that bondage, & am become my own master, subject to no one else, a free man able to go where I want.

And because of that he would be delighted, & he would be exceedingly glad.

Or suppose a man were rich & wealthy, traveling a wilderness road, full of danger, where there was no food; and after a time he crossed the wilderness safely, & reached the borders of his village, secure & unharmed. He would think: I traveled a wilderness road, full of danger, where there was no food; but now I have crossed the wilderness safely, & have reached the borders of my village, secure & unharmed.

And because of that he would be delighted, & he would be exceedingly glad.

And in the same way, the monk sees it as a debt, as a disease, as a prison, as slavery, as a wilderness road, until he has cast these five hindrances from him.

But when he casts aside these five hindrances, he sees it as freedom from debt, as health, as release from prison, as freedom, as safety.

And when he sees that he has cast aside these five hindrances, he becomes exceedingly glad: and in his gladness, there springs forth enthusiasm; and in his enthusiasm, his body becomes still; and in his stillness, he feels pleasure; and in his pleasure, his mind becomes concentrated.

The first trance. And he is detached from desire & detached from impure states; and he enters & dwells in the first trance, with discursive thought & reasoning, & with the enthusiasm & pleasure born of detachment.

And the enthusiasm & pleasure born of detachment pervade his entire body, permeating & filling & suffusing it, so that there is no place in his whole body which is not suffused with the enthusiasm & pleasure born of detachment.

Suppose a skillful masseur or his apprentice scattered bath powder in a bronze vessel, and sprinkled it all through with water & kneaded it together, so that the ball of soap was filled with water, drenched with water, & suffused with water inside & out, yet it did not drip.

And in the same way, the enthusiasm & pleasure born of detachment pervade the monk's entire body, permeating & filling & suffusing it, so that there is no place at all in his whole body which is not suffused with the enthusiasm & pleasure born of detachment.

The second trance. And then he calms his discursive thought & reasoning; and he enters & dwells in the second trance, with inner tranquility & concentration of mind, without discursive thought or reasoning, & with the enthusiasm & pleasure born of concentration.

And the enthusiasm & pleasure born of concentration pervade his entire body, permeating & filling & suffusing it, so that there is no place in his whole body which is not suffused with the enthusiasm & pleasure born of concentration.

Suppose there were a deep pool, whose waters welled up from a spring, and it had no inlet from the east or the west, nor from the north or the south, nor did the gods supply it with showers of rain; yet cool water would spring up out of the ground, and cool water would pervade the entire pool, permeating & filling & suffusing it, so that there was no place in the whole pool which was not suffused with cool water.

And in the same way, the enthusiasm & pleasure born of concentration pervade the monk's entire body, permeating & filling & suffusing it, so that there is no place in his whole body which is not suffused with the enthusiasm & pleasure born of concentration.

The third trance. And then his enthusiasm fades away, & he abides in equanimity, mindful & aware; and he enters & dwells in the third trance, his body feeling the pleasure of which the Noble Ones declare: Surely he of equanimity & mindfulness abides in pleasure.

And this tranquil pleasure pervades his entire body, permeating & filling & suffusing it, so that there is no place in his whole body which is not suffused with this tranquil pleasure.

Suppose there were blue & red & white lotuses in a lotus pond, and they were born in the water, grew in the water, drew up the water into themselves, & were nourished by the water in which they were immersed; and the cool water pervaded them from their tips to their roots, permeating & filling & suffusing them, so that there was no place in any blue or red or white lotus which was not suffused with cool water.

And in the same way, this tranquil pleasure pervades the monk's entire body, permeating & filling & suffusing it, so that there is no place in his whole body which is not suffused with this tranquil pleasure.

The fourth trance. And then he renounces pleasure & renounces pain, & all his former happiness & sorrow pass away; and he enters & dwells in the fourth trance, in the total purity of equanimity & mindfulness, without pleasure & without pain.

And there he sits, pervading his entire body with this pure & translucent attention, so that there is no place in his whole body which is not suffused with this pure & translucent attention.

Suppose a man sat wrapped up to his head in a white garment; there would be no place at all on his whole body that was not touched by the white garment.

And in the same way, the monk sits, pervading his entire body with his pure & translucent attention, so that there is no place in his whole body which is not suffused with it.

Insight Meditation

And when his mind is thus concentrated in the fourth trance, pure & translucent, clear & undefiled, dextrous & supple, firm & unshakable, then he can turn & apply his mind to knowledge & to insight.

And he considers: This body of mine is made of matter, composed of the four elements, produced by a father & mother, nourished by food, and subject to impermanence, to decay & destruction & dissolution; and this awareness of mine depends upon it, & is bound to it.

Suppose there were a precious gem, bright & beautiful, well cut into eight facets, clear & limpid, unflawed & perfect, with a string threaded through it, blue or yellow or red or white or orange; and a man with eyes to see took it in his hand. He would see that it was a precious gem, threaded with a string.

And in the same way, the monk considers his body: he sees that it is impermanent, & that his awareness depends upon it, & is bound to it; and he attains to insight.

The Six Superknowledges

The magical powers. And when his mind is thus concentrated, pure & translucent, clear & undefiled, dextrous & supple, firm & unshakable, then he can turn & apply his mind to the various magical powers.

He multiplies his body & then becomes one again: he becomes visible & invisible; he passes unhindered through walls & fences & mountains as through empty space; he dives in & out of the earth as in water; he walks unsinking upon the water as upon the earth; he travels cross-legged in the sky, like a winged bird. The sun & moon may be great & powerful, but he seizes them with his hand & touches them: his body wields power as far as the world of the gods.

Suppose there were a skillful potter or his apprentice, or a skillful ivory carver, or a skillful goldsmith: he could make any vessel he wished from well-prepared clay, or from ivory, or from gold.

And in the same way, the monk turns & applies his mind to the various magical powers, and he performs any magical deed he wishes.

The divine ear. And when his mind is thus concentrated, pure & translucent, clear & undefiled, dextrous & supple, firm & unshakable, then he can turn & apply his mind to the divine ear.

And with that pure divine ear, surpassing that of men, he hears sounds both human & heavenly, whether far or near.

Suppose a man stood on the highway, and he heard the sounds of drums & tambourines & conch-shell trumpets. He would think: This is the sound of a drum, & this of a tambourine, & this of a conch-shell trumpet.

And in the same way, the monk turns & applies his mind to the divine ear, and he hears & recognizes sounds both human & heavenly, whether far or near.

The knowledge of the thoughts of others. And when his mind is thus concentrated, pure & translucent, clear & undefiled, dextrous & supple, firm & unshakable, then he can turn & apply his mind to the knowledge of the thoughts of others.

And his thoughts penetrate to the thoughts of other beings & of other persons. He is aware of their lustful thought as lustful thought: he is aware of their lustless thought as lustless thought. He is aware of their hate-filled thought as hate-filled thought: he is aware of their hateless thought as hateless thought. He is aware of their deluded thought as deluded thought: he is aware of their undeluded thought as undeluded thought . . .

Suppose a young man or woman, fond of ornaments, looked at the reflection of his own face in a bright mirror, or in a clear bowl of water. He would know if he had a mole upon his face, or if he did not.

And in the same way, the monk turns & applies his mind to the knowledge of the thoughts of others; and his thoughts penetrate into their hearts.

The knowledge of his former births. And when his mind is thus concentrated, pure & translucent, clear & undefiled, dextrous & supple, firm & unshakable, then he can turn & apply his mind to the knowledge of his former births.

And he remembers his various former births: one birth, or two, or three, or four, or five; ten births, or twenty, or thirty, or forty, or fifty; a hundred births, or a thousand, or a hundred thousand; births through many eons of dissolution, through many eons of evolution, through many eons of dissolution & evolution. And he thinks: In such a place, such was my name; such was my caste & family, such was my food, such was my experience of pleasure or of pain, such was the length of my life. And then I passed away from there & was reborn elsewhere . . . And then I passed away from there & was reborn here. Thus he remembers his various former births, in all their kinds, & with all their details.

Suppose a man went from his own village to another village, & from that village to another village, & from that village he returned home again. He would think: I went from my own village to that village; and thus I stood, & thus I sat; and thus I spoke, & thus I kept silent. And then I went from that village to another village . . . And then I returned home again.

And in the same way, the monk turns & applies his mind to the knowledge of his former births; and he remembers his various former births, in all their kinds, & with all their details.

The divine eye. And when his mind is thus concentrated, pure & translucent, clear & undefiled, dextrous & supple, firm & unshakable, then he can turn & apply his mind to the knowledge of the passing away & rebirth of beings.

And with his pure divine eye, surpassing that of men, he sees beings pass away & be reborn: he sees beings that are lowly or exalted, ill-born or well-born, in good destinies or in evil destinies, according to the deeds they have done.

And he thinks: Truly, these beings (endowed with evil conduct in body & speech & mind) speak ill of the Noble Ones: possessed of wrong views, they collect the karma of their wrong views; and after their bodies break up & after they die, they are reborn in an evil destiny in hell.

But these beings (endowed with good conduct in body & speech & mind) speak no ill of the Noble Ones: possessed of right views, they collect the karma of their right views; and after their bodies break up & after they die, they are reborn in a good destiny in heaven.

Suppose there were a terrace in the midst of a crossroads: a man standing there with eyes to see could watch the people entering a house, & leaving it, and walking upon the roads & streets, & sitting in the square. He would think: These people are entering a house, & these leaving it; and these are walking upon the roads & streets, & these are sitting in the square.

And in the same way, the monk turns & applies his mind to the knowledge of the passing away & rebirth of beings; and with his pure divine eye he sees them pass away & be reborn, according to the deeds they have done.

The knowledge of the destruction of drunkenness. And when his mind is thus concentrated, pure & translucent, clear & undefiled, dextrous & supple, firm & unshakable, then he can turn & apply his mind to the knowledge of the destruction of drunkenness.

He is aware as it really is: "This is suffering"; he is aware as it really is: "This is the origin of suffering"; he is aware as it really is: "This is the cessation of suffering"; he is aware as it really is: "This is the way which leads to the cessation of suffering."

He is aware as it really is: "This is drunkenness"; he is aware as it really is: "This is the origin of drunkenness"; he is aware as it really is: "This is the cessation of drunkenness"; he is aware as it really is: "This is the way which leads to the cessation of drunkenness."

Thus knowing & thus seeing, his mind is freed of the drunkenness of lust; his mind is freed of the drunkenness of existence; his mind is freed of the drunkenness of ignorance.

He is liberated, & he knows that he is free, and he is aware: My birth has been destroyed, I have fulfilled the religious life, I have done what was to be done, & I have no further life in this world.

Suppose there were a pool of water in a mountain glen, clear & calm & pure: a man with eyes to see, standing on its banks, could watch the oyster-shells & gravel & schools of fish as they darted about or lay within it. He would think: This pool is clear & calm & pure; and within it are oyster-shells & gravel & schools of fish, darting about or lying still.

And in the same way, the monk turns & applies his mind to the knowledge of the destruction of drunkenness; and he is liberated, & he knows that he is free.

And this is the fruit of the life of a recluse, in this very life: and there is no fruit of the life of a recluse, in this very life, which is better or higher than this.

3. MINDFULNESS

Calm and insight are coordinated techniques of a single process; yet, as we have mentioned, originally they seem to have been two separate modes of meditation. There existed a tension between enstatic withdrawal from the world and intellectual penetration into its true nature: the first denied the importance of sensory input, and the second imbued events with meaning projected from the meditator. The basic structure viewed progressive isolation as a prelude to the realization of things as they are, for the alert awareness of insight is beset on every side by the snares of desire and distraction, and long training in calm must precede any attempt to view the world without prejudice.

But the tension remained, and was a creative force in the development of new techniques of meditation and new philosophical systems to account for meditative experience. Very early texts seem to reflect an original pattern in which the two modes of meditation were kept separate: these are the techniques that later commentators, such as Buddhaghosa in the fourth century A. D., found difficult to fit comfortably into the established contemplative structures.

We may look upon the following text as reflecting the anomaly in its particular emphasis upon insight. It is, in effect, an expansion of the short insight section of the preceding selection; but it is also, in its own words, a method for realizing nirvana in and of itself, based almost entirely upon the intellectual and experiential components of the standard structure. It eschews practically the whole notion of trance and withdrawal, and as such it stands in opposition to other meditative treatises—which we shall examine in Part Three—that view progressive trance alone as the means to salvation. Our text does not seek isolation from the world so much as a freedom amid the events of the world: nirvana is here a disentanglement not from events but from mislabeling and desire. As the events themselves continue to appear before the meditator, he becomes a spectator at the kaleidoscope of reality, freely and spontaneously recognizing every event, and leaving every event alone.

With this intellectual emphasis upon recognizing the true nature of events, our text sets out in full the most basic formulations of Buddhist doctrine, but does so in the context of meditation rather than abstract speculation. Here the meditator applies to every event that passes before his eyes the doctrinal formulations that describe its essence, and thus penetrates into the true nature of the world. Nor is this text simply a historical curiosity: its teachings have been revived in the twentieth century by a dedicated group of Burmese monks, and the meditation it presents is now—next to Zen—the most widespread discipline in the Buddhist world. The Buddhist tradition has never lacked the strength to renew itself periodically by a return to its roots.

Mahāsatipaṭṭhānasutta [*Mindfulness*], in *Dīgha-nikāya* [*Collection of long discourses*], gen. ed. Bhikkhu J. Kashyap (Bihar, Pāli Publication Board, 1958), Sutta IX, 2: 217–36.

There is but one path for the purification of beings, for passing beyond sorrow & grief, for destroying pain & misery, for attaining the way, for realizing nirvana: and this is the four-fold establishment of mindfulness.

What are the four? A monk overcomes his desire & regret about the world: & he dwells observing his body, ardent & aware & mindful. He overcomes his desire & regret about the world: & he dwells observing his feelings, ardent & aware & mindful. He overcomes his desire & regret about the world: & he dwells observing his thoughts, ardent & aware & mindful. He overcomes his desire & regret about the world: & he dwells observing events, ardent & aware & mindful.

Observing the Body

Breathing. How does a monk dwell observing his body? He goes to a forest, or the foot of a tree, or an empty room; he sits down with his legs crossed, holds his body straight, & sets up mindfulness before him.

Mindful he breathes in, & mindful he breathes out. He is aware when he breathes in a long breath, "I am breathing in a long breath"; he is aware when he breathes out a long breath, "I am breathing out a long breath"; he is aware when he breathes in a short breath, "I am breathing in a short breath"; he is aware when he breathes out a short breath, "I am breathing out a short breath."

He trains himself to be conscious of his whole body when he breathes in; he trains himself to be conscious of his whole body when he breathes out. He trains himself to calm the state of his body when he breathes in; he trains himself to calm the state of his body when he breathes out.

As a skillful lathe-operator or his apprentice is aware when he makes a long turn, "I am making a long turn"; as he is aware when he makes a short turn, "I am making a short turn": in the same way the monk is aware when he breathes in, & when he breathes out; he trains himself to be conscious of his whole body, & he trains himself to calm the state of his body as he breathes.

Thus he dwells observing his body internally; he dwells observing his body externally; he dwells observing his body internally & externally. He dwells observing the events which occur in his body; he dwells observing the events which pass away in his body; he dwells observing the events in his body which occur & which pass away. And he establishes the mindfulness that "This is a body" just sufficiently for a bare awareness & a bare mindfulness of it; and he dwells in freedom & does not cling to anything in the world.

Thus a monk dwells observing his body.

Posture. And the monk is aware when he is going, "I am going"; he is aware when he is standing, "I am standing"; he is aware when he is sitting, "I am sitting"; he is aware when he is lying down, "I am lying down." However his body may be disposed, he is aware of it.

Thus he dwells observing his body internally; he dwells observing his body externally; he dwells observing his body internally & externally. He dwells observing the events which occur in his body; he dwells observing the events which pass away in his body; he dwells observing the events in his body which occur & which pass away. And he establishes the mindfulness that "This is a body" just sufficiently for a bare awareness & a bare mindfulness of it; and he dwells in freedom & does not cling to anything in the world.

Thus a monk dwells observing his body.

Awareness. And the monk is aware when going out or coming in; he is aware when he looks toward or looks away; he is aware when he draws in his limbs or stretches them out; he is aware when he puts on his robes or carries his bowl; he is aware when he is eating or drinking or chewing or tasting; he is aware when he urinates or defecates; he is aware when he goes or stands or sits, when he sleeps or wakes, when he speaks or keeps silent.

Thus he dwells observing his body . . .

Repulsiveness. And the monk considers his own body, upward from the soles of his feet & downward from the top of his head, covered with skin & filled with all sorts of filth, and he thinks: "In this body there is hair, body-hair, nails, teeth, skin, flesh, sinews, bones, marrow, kidneys, heart, liver, membranes, spleen, lungs, stomach, bowels, intestines, feces, bile, phlegm, pus, blood, sweat, fat, tears, grease, saliva, mucus, fluids, & urine."

Suppose there were a double-mouthed sack filled with all sorts of grain, with rice & paddy & beans & peas & sesamum & husked rice, and a man with eyes to see opened it & considered it, thinking: "This is rice, this paddy, this beans, this peas, this sesamum, & this husked rice." In the same way, the monk considers his own body, upward from the soles of his feet & downward from the top of his head, covered with skin & filled with all sorts of filth, and he reviews all the repulsive things which are within his body.

Thus he dwells observing his body . . .

Elements. And the monk considers his own body, however it is placed or disposed, with regard to the elements of which it is made, and he thinks: "In this body there is earth & water & fire & air."

Suppose a skillful butcher or his apprentice slaughters a cow & cuts it up into pieces where he sits by the crossroads. In the same way the monk considers his own body, however it is placed or disposed, and he reviews the elements which make it up.

Thus he dwells observing his body . . .

Decay. And should the monk see a corpse cast away in the cemetery, dead for one day or two days or three days, swollen & purple & rotting, he applies the sight to his own body, and he thinks; "This body of mine is the same as that one; it will become like that one, & it will not escape."

Thus he dwells observing his body . . .

And should he see a corpse cast away in the cemetery, ripped by crows & kites & vultures, gnawed by dogs & tigers & jackals, eaten by worms, he applies the sight to his own body, and he thinks: "This body of mine is the same as that one; it will become like that one, & it will not escape."

Thus he dwells observing his body . . .

And should he see a corpse cast away in the cemetery, rotted to a chain of bones with pieces of flesh & blood sticking to them, held together by their tendons; or rotted to a chain of fleshless bloodsmeared bones; or rotted to a chain of fleshless bloodless bones; or rotted to bones no longer held together but scattered here & there, in one place the bones of the hand, in another the bones of the foot, in one place the leg, in another the thigh, in one place the spine, in another the skull . . . he applies the sight to his own body, and he thinks: "This body of mine is the same as that one; it will become like that one, & it will not escape."

Thus he dwells observing his body . . .

And should he see a corpse cast away in the cemetery, rotted to shell-white bones; or a mere heap of bones a year old; or moldering bones crumbled to dust, he applies the sight to his own body, and he thinks: "This body of mine is the same as that one; it will become like that one, & it will not escape."

Thus he dwells observing his body internally; he dwells observing his body externally; he dwells observing his body internally & externally. He dwells observing the events which occur in his body; he dwells observing the events which pass away in his body; he dwells observing the events in his body which occur & which pass away. And he establishes the mindfulness that "This is a body" just sufficiently for a bare awareness & a bare mindfulness of it; and he dwells in freedom & does not cling to anything in the world.

Thus a monk dwells observing his body.

Observing the Feelings

How does a monk dwell observing his feelings? He is aware when he experiences a pleasant feeling, "I am experiencing a pleasant feeling"; he is aware when he experiences a painful feeling, "I am experiencing a painful feeling"; he is aware when he experiences a neutral feeling, "I am experiencing a neutral feeling."

He is aware when he experiences a pleasant worldly feeling, "I am experiencing a pleasant worldly feeling"; he is aware when he experiences a pleasant spiritual feeling, "I am experiencing a pleasant spiritual feeling." He is aware when he experiences a painful worldly feeling, "I am experiencing a painful worldly feeling"; he is aware when he experiences a painful spiritual feeling, "I am experiencing a painful spiritual feeling." He is aware when he experiences a neutral worldly feeling, "I am experiencing a neutral worldly feeling"; he is aware when he experiences a neutral spiritual feeling, "I am experiencing a neutral spiritual feeling."

Thus he dwells observing his feelings internally; he dwells observing his feelings externally; he dwells observing his feelings internally & externally. He dwells observing the events which occur in his feelings; he dwells observing the events which pass away in his feelings; he dwells observing the events in his feelings which occur & which pass away. And he establishes the mindfulness that "This is a feeling" just sufficiently for a bare awareness & a bare mindfulness of it; and he dwells in freedom & does not cling to anything in the world.

Thus a monk dwells observing his feelings.

Observing the Thoughts

How does a monk dwell observing his thoughts? He is aware of a lustful thought as a lustful thought; he is aware of a lustless thought as a lustless thought. He is aware of a hate-filled thought as a hate-filled thought; he is aware of a hateless thought as a hateless thought. He is aware of a deluded thought as a deluded thought; he is aware of an undeluded thought as an undeluded thought. He is aware of an attentive thought as an attentive thought; he is aware of a distracted thought as a distracted thought. He is aware of a lofty thought as a lofty thought; he is aware of a gross thought as a gross thought. He is aware of an ordinary thought as an ordinary thought; he is aware of a supreme thought as a supreme thought.

He is aware of a concentrated thought as a concentrated thought; he is aware of a confused thought as a confused thought. He is aware of a liberated thought as a liberated thought; he is aware of an unliberated thought as an unliberated thought.

Thus he dwells observing his thoughts internally; he dwells observing his thoughts externally; he dwells observing his thoughts internally & externally. He dwells observing the events which occur in his thoughts; he dwells observing the events which pass away in his thoughts; he dwells observing the events in his thoughts which occur & pass away. And he establishes the mindfulness that "This is a thought" just sufficiently for a bare awareness & a bare mindfulness of it; and he dwells in freedom & does not cling to anything in the world.

Thus a monk dwells observing his thoughts.

Observing Events

The hindrances. How does a monk dwell observing events? He dwells observing events with regard to the five hindrances. He is aware when there is a sense-desire within him, "There is a sense-desire·within me"; he is aware when there is no sense-desire within him, "There is no sense-desire within me." He is aware when a sense-desire occurs which has not occurred before; he is aware when he casts aside a sense-desire which has occurred; he is aware when a sense-desire he has cast aside does not occur again.

He is aware when there is hatred within him . . . He is aware when there is sloth & torpor within him . . . He is aware when there is worry & distraction within him . . . He is aware when there is doubt within him, "There is a doubt within me"; he is aware when there is no doubt within him, "There is no doubt within me." He is aware when a doubt occurs which has not occurred before; he is aware when he casts aside a doubt which has occurred; he is aware when a doubt he has cast aside does not occur again.

Thus he dwells observing events internally; he dwells observing events externally; he dwells observing events internally & externally. He dwells observing the events which occur; he dwells observing the events which pass away; he dwells observing the events which occur & which pass away. And he establishes the mindfulness that "This is an event" just sufficiently for a bare awareness & a bare mindfulness of it; and he dwells in freedom & does not cling to anything in the world.

Thus a monk dwells observing events with regard to the five hindrances.

The aggregates. And the monk dwells observing events with regard to the five aggregates by which he clings to existence, and he thinks: "Such is form, such is the arising of form, & such is the passing away of form. Such is feeling, such is the arising of feeling, & such is the passing away of feeling. Such is idea, such is the arising of idea, & such is the passing away of idea. Such is motive, such is the arising of motive, & such is the passing away of motive. Such is perception, such is the arising of perception, & such is the passing away of perception."

Thus he dwells observing events with regard to his fivefold clinging to existence . . .

The senses & their objects. And the monk dwells observing events with regard to the six senses & their external objects. He is aware of his eyes, & he is aware of visible objects: he is aware of the bondage which occurs dependent on them both. He is aware when this bondage occurs which has not occurred before; he is aware when he casts aside the bondage which has occurred; he is aware when the bondage he has cast aside does not occur again.

He is aware of his ears, & he is aware of sounds . . . He is aware of his nose, & he is aware of smells . . . He is aware of his tongue, & he is aware of tastes . . . He is aware of his body, & he is aware of tangible objects . . . He is aware of his mind, & he is aware of mental events: he is aware of the bondage which occurs dependent on them both. He is aware when this bondage occurs which has not occurred before; he is aware when he casts aside the bondage which has occurred; he is aware when the bondage he has cast aside does not occur again.

Thus he dwells observing events with regard to the six senses & their objects . . .

The factors of enlightenment. And the monk dwells observing events with regard to the seven factors of enlightenment. He is aware when there is mindfulness within him as a factor of enlightenment, "There is mindfulness within me"; he is aware when there is no mindfulness within him, "There is no mindfulness within me." He is aware when mindfulness occurs which has not occurred before; he is aware when he cultivates & perfects the mindfulness which has occurred.

He is aware when there is the investigation of events within him . . . He is aware when there is striving within him . . . He is aware when there is enthusiasm within him . . . He is aware when there is serenity within him . . . He is aware when there is meditation within him . . . He is aware when there is equanimity within him as a factor of enlightenment, "There is equanimity within me"; he is aware when there is no equanimity within him, "There is no equanimity within me." He is aware when equanimity occurs which has not occurred before; he is aware when he cultivates & perfects the equanimity which has occurred.

Thus he dwells observing events with regard to the seven factors of enlightenment . . .

The noble truths. And the monk dwells observing events with regard to the four noble truths. He is aware as it really is, "This is suffering"; he is aware as it really is, "This is the origin of suffering"; he is aware as it really is, "This is the cessation of suffering"; he is aware as it really is, "This is the way which leads to the cessation of suffering."

The truth of suffering. And what is the noble truth of suffering? Birth is suffering, old age is suffering, death is suffering; sorrow & lamentation & pain & misery & despair are suffering; not getting what one wants is suffering; the fivefold clinging to existence is suffering.

What is birth? It is when a being is born in one destiny or another: his conception & production & gestation, the appearance of his aggregates, the acquisition of his senses.

What is old age? It is when he grows old in one destiny or another: his decay & decrepitude & growing grey & getting wrinkled, the failing of his life, the loss of his faculties.

What is death? It is when he passes away from one destiny or another: his departure & dissolution & disappearance & dying & death, the finishing of his time, the destruction of his aggregates, the casting aside of his body, the cutting off of his life.

What is sorrow? It is the sorrow & woe & affliction & inward grief & hidden heartache of one who is visited by some misfortune, of one who is touched by some painful event.

What is lamentation? It is the mourning & wailing & weeping & crying & complaining & lamenting of one who is visited by some misfortune, of one who is touched by some painful event.

What is pain? It is bodily pain & bodily suffering, the feeling of pain & suffering which comes of bodily contact.

What is misery? It is mental pain & mental suffering, the feeling of pain & suffering which comes of mental contact.

What is despair? It is the dejection & despair & despondency & distress of one who is visited by some misfortune, of one who is touched by some painful event.

What is not getting what one wants? It is when creatures who are subject to birth begin to wish, "Alas! if only we were not subject to birth, if only a new birth were not to come!": but they do not get this by wishing for it. And it is when creatures who are subject to old age & disease & death, to sorrow & lamentation & pain & misery & despair begin to wish: "Alas! if only we were not subject to these things, if only these things were not to come!": but they do not get this by wishing for it.

What is the five-fold clinging to existence? It is the aggregate of form by which one clings to existence, the aggregate of feeling, of idea, of motive & of perception by which one clings to existence.

And this is called the noble truth of suffering.

The truth of origin. And what is the noble truth of the origin of suffering? The origin is craving, bound to pleasure & lust, taking its delight here & there, causing rebirth: the craving of the senses, the craving for existence, & the craving for nonexistence.

But where does this craving occur, & where does it dwell? It occurs where there are dear & pleasant things in the world, & it dwells among them.

What are dear & pleasant things in the world? The eye & ear & nose & tongue & body & mind are dear & pleasant things in the world: and there this craving occurs, & there it dwells.

And visible objects & sounds & smells & tastes & tangible objects & mental events are dear & pleasant things in the world: and there this craving occurs, & there it dwells.

And eye perceptions & ear perceptions & nose perceptions & tongue perceptions & body perceptions & mental perceptions are dear & pleasant things in the world: and there this craving occurs, & there it dwells.

And sensory contact is dear & pleasant, and the feelings which come of sensory contact are dear & pleasant, and ideas about sensory objects are dear & pleasant, and the will toward sensory objects is dear & pleasant, and the craving for sensory objects is dear & pleasant, and the thought of sensory objects is dear & pleasant, and the constant concern for sensory objects is a dear & pleasant thing in the world: and there this craving occurs, & there it dwells.

And this is called the noble truth of the origin of suffering.

The truth of cessation. And what is the noble truth of the cessation of suffering? The cessation is the absolute elimination of craving, abandoning it & renouncing it, being detached from it & free of it.

But where is this craving cast aside, & where does it cease? It is cast aside where there are dear & pleasant things in the world, & it ceases among them.

What are dear & pleasant things in the world? The eye & ear & nose & tongue & body & mind are dear & pleasant things in the world: and there this craving is cast aside, & there it ceases.

And visible objects & sounds & smells & tastes & tangible objects & mental events are dear & pleasant things in the world: and there this craving is cast aside, & there it ceases.

And eye perceptions & ear perceptions & nose perceptions & tongue perceptions & body perceptions & mental perceptions are dear & pleasant things in the world: and there this craving is cast aside, & there it ceases.

And sensory contact is dear & pleasant, and the feelings which come of sensory contact are dear & pleasant, and ideas about sensory objects are dear & pleasant, and the will toward sensory objects is dear & pleasant, and the craving for sensory objects is dear & pleasant, and the thought of sensory objects is dear & pleasant, and the constant concern for sensory objects is a dear & pleasant thing in the world: and there this craving is cast aside, & there it ceases.

And this is called the noble truth of the cessation of suffering.

The truth of the path. And what is the noble truth of the way which leads to the cessation of suffering? It is the noble eight-fold path: right view & right aspiration & right speech & right conduct & right livelihood & right effort & right mindfulness & right meditation.

What is right view? It is to know suffering, to know the origin of suffering, to know the cessation of suffering, & to know the way which leads to the cessation of suffering.

What is right aspiration? It is to aspire to renunciation, to aspire to love, & to aspire to harmlessness.

What is right speech? It is to abstain from false speech, to abstain from slander, to abstain from rudeness, & to abstain from vain & idle chatter.

What is right conduct? It is to abstain from the taking of life, to abstain from the taking of what is not given, & to abstain from misdeeds of lust.

What is right livelihood? It is when a noble disciple renounces wrong livelihood & supports himself with right livelihood.

What is right effort? It is when a monk rouses his will & makes an effort & awakens striving & applies his mind & exerts himself to prevent the occurrence of evil & impure states which have not yet occurred; when he rouses his will & makes an effort & awakens striving & applies his mind & exerts himself to cast aside the evil & impure states which have occurred;

when he rouses his will & makes an effort & awakens striving & applies his mind & exerts himself to bring about good states which have not yet occurred; & when he rouses his will & makes an effort & awakens striving & applies his mind & exerts himself to maintain & sharpen & nurture & increase & cultivate & perfect the good states which have occurred.

What is right mindfulness? It is when a monk overcomes his desire & regret about the world; & he dwells observing his body, observing his feelings, observing his thoughts, & observing events, ardent & aware & mindful.

What is right meditation? It is when a monk is detached from desire & detached from impure states; and he enters & dwells in the first trance, with discursive thought & reasoning, & with the enthusiasm & pleasure born of detachment. And it is when he calms his discursive thought & reasoning; and he enters & dwells in the second trance, with inner tranquility & concentration of mind, without discursive thought or reasoning, & with the enthusiasm & pleasure born of concentration. And it is when his enthusiasm fades away, & he abides in equanimity, mindful & aware; and he enters & dwells in the third trance, his body feeling the pleasure of which the Noble Ones declare: "Surely he of equanimity & mindfulness abides in pleasure." And it is when he renounces pleasure & renounces pain, & all his former happiness & sorrow pass away; and he enters & dwells in the fourth trance, in the total purity of equanimity & mindfulness, without pleasure & without pain.

And this is called the noble truth of the way which leads to the cessation of suffering.

Thus he dwells observing events internally; he dwells observing events externally; he dwells observing events internally & externally. He dwells observing the events which occur; he dwells observing the events which pass away; he dwells observing the events which occur & which pass away. And he establishes the mindfulness that "This is an event" just sufficiently for a bare awareness & a bare mindfulness of it; and he dwells in freedom & does not cling to anything in the world.

Thus a monk dwells observing events with regard to the four noble truths.

Whoever practices this four-fold establishment of mindfulness for seven years can expect one of two results: perfect knowledge in this very life or (if there be a residue of clinging to existence) the state of never returning to this earth.

Let alone seven years, whoever practices this four-fold establishment of mindfulness for six years, or five years, or four years, or three years, or two years, or one year ... Let alone one year, whoever practices this four-fold establishment of mindfulness for seven months can expect one of two results: perfect knowledge in this very life or (if there be a residue of clinging to existence) the state of never returning to this earth.

Let alone seven months: whoever practices this four-fold establishment of mindfulness for six months, or five months, or four months, or three months, or two months, or one month, or half a month ... Let alone half a month, whoever practices this four-fold establishment of mindfulness for one week can expect one of two results: perfect knowledge in this very life or (if there be a residue of clinging to existence) the state of never returning to this earth.

And this is why we said that there is but one path for the purification of beings, for passing beyond sorrow & grief, for destroying pain & misery, for attaining the way, for realizing nirvana: and this is the four-fold establishment of mindfulness.

4. THE MEDITATIONS OF A BODHISATTVA

The religious fervor of the Great Vehicle was a major force in renovating the traditional structure of meditation. The concept of the path was extended to include an entire sequence of bodhisattva stages to enlightenment: the foundation of the path became compassion rather than personal virtue, and compassion led inevitably to the awakening of the thought of enlightenment, the vow to achieve Buddhahood for the sake of all beings.

The sequence of calm and insight remained the same, but insight meditation became the vehicle of the new metaphysics, the basis for the reaffirmation of the value of action in the world. The alert awareness of the meditator turns toward events in the world with a concern for ontology: he achieves his freedom metaphysically rather than psychologically, and in the metaphysics of his freedom lie the seeds of universal salvation. Skillful means must accompany his wisdom, as part of the ever increasing emphasis upon the immanence of enlightenment within the world.

Thus the structure of the path does not change, but rather than labeling events with the labels of suffering and impermanence, reality and unreality, the meditator wanders free in the unlabeled dream of the world. Dedicating himself to the salvation of all living creatures, he plunges into the swamp of the world, rather than letting the world go by. The experiential basis for this return to the world is the same ecstatic mode of intellectual penetration into reality, the same freedom and disentanglement amid events as in our previous selections; but the mood has changed from peace and tranquility to action and concern, from the joys of repose in the torrent of events to the joys of participation in a cosmic drama of redemption. Kamalásíla's text on meditation, written in the eighth century A. D., remains the standard guidebook on this ordered contemplative process in the Great Vehicle.

Kamalaśīla, Bhāvanākrama [*The stages of meditation*], in Minor Buddhist Texts, *ed. Giuseppe Tucci (Rome: Istituto Italiano per il Medio ed Estremo Oriente, 1958), 2: 187–282.*

Compassion

The necessity of compassion. He who wishes to gain omniscience swiftly must strive in three things: in compassion, in the thought of enlightenment, and in meditation. And he should practice compassion from the very outset, for we know that compassion alone is the first cause of all the qualities of Buddhahood. As we read in scripture:

> Blessed One, a bodhisattva should not practice too many things at once: for if a bodhisattva can master and truly understand just one thing, then he will hold all the qualities of Buddhahood in the palm of his hand. And what is this one thing? It is great compassion: Blessed One, it is through compassion that a bodhisattva holds all the qualities of Buddhahood in the palm of his hand.
>
> Blessed One, it is like the bright chariot wheel of a universal emperor: wherever it may roll, all the hosts of his army follow; and when a bodhisattva has great compassion, all the qualities of Buddhahood follow close behind. Blessed One, it is like life itself: only when there is life can the other faculties occur, and only when there is great compassion can the other qualities of a bodhisattva occur as well.

And again we read:

> The great compassion of a bodhisattva does not perish. And why is that? Because it precedes all else. Just as a man's breath precedes his ability to live, the great compassion of a bodhisattva precedes his endowment with all the merit and knowledge of the Great Vehicle.

And again we read:

> What is the beginning of a bodhisattva's practice, and what is its abode? Great compassion is the beginning of a bodhisattva's practice, and it abides among living beings.

Thus a bodhisattva is impelled only by a desire to help others, with no regard for himself; and he sets out upon a long and arduous path, ever exerting himself to acquire merit and knowledge. As we read in scripture: "When his compassion aims to bring all beings to maturity, there is no happiness at all which he will not renounce."

When a bodhisattva sets out on this arduous path, swiftly and inevitably he will make perfect his merit and knowledge, and attain to omniscience; for compassion is the root of all the qualities of Buddhahood. The Buddhas, the Blessed Ones, attained to their omniscience by embracing compassion; and they so rejoice in the welfare of the world that they remain therein, nor do the Blessed Ones abide in nirvana, because of their compassion.

Meditation upon compassion. Now this compassion grows through an increasing concern for beings who suffer; and thus he should meditate upon these beings, that throughout the triple world they are ever tormented with the three-fold suffering of their condition.

Thus the Blessed One has shown us that those in hell are sunk in unremitting and burning pain; he has shown us, too, that the hungry ghosts feel pain both sharp and keen, their bodies withered with the ache of unbearable hunger and thirst, who cannot find in a hundred years even a wretched piece of filth to eat. And we ourselves can see how animals suffer many pains, maiming and slaughtering each other in mutual rage; how some are bound and beaten, their noses split for rings, their bodies castrated, tormented on all sides; how they weary, their reluctant bodies exhausted in bearing their hard and heavy loads . . .

And we can see, too, how men can suffer the pains of hell, for thieves have their limbs cut off, are impaled and hanged, and endure the sufferings of hell; the poor and powerless suffer the hunger and thirst of hungry ghosts; slaves suffer the bondage and beatings of animals, owned by the strong, belonging to others, tormented. For men endure immeasurable pain: they seek each other out to torture and betray; they are separated from their loved ones and forced to serve those that they despise.

Even those called rich and happy will meet with death: sunk in the abyss of their evil ways, they gather the sinful deeds which will be for them their pain in hell; they stand above a dizzy precipice; and they truly suffer, who stand in the cause of suffering.

Even the gods themselves in the realm of desire have minds which blaze with the fires of sharp lust, darkened and distracted: they find not a moment for peace or calm. How can we call them happy, who are destitute of the happiness of peace? How can we call them happy, who are ever oppressed with the terror of death, of losing their lofty place . . . ?

And thus he understands that the entire world is licked by the blazing flames of suffering; and he meditates upon compassion for all beings, for he knows that they abhor their pain as he does his own.

He meditates first, then, upon those whom he loves: he sees how they must bear the many sufferings we have described; they are all the same as he, and he sees no difference among them.

Then he meditates upon those to whom he is neutral: he considers that in the beginningless world there is no being who has not been his kinsman a hundred times, and he awakens compassion for them as for those he loves.

Then he meditates upon his enemies also, and he realizes that they are all the same as he is, and he awakens compassion for his enemies even as for those he loves.

And thus gradually he meditates upon all beings in the ten directions: he awakens his compassion for all beings equally, that they are as dear to him as his own suffering children, that they are his own family, and he wishes to lead them out of pain. Then is his compassion made perfect, and it is called great compassion . . .

The Thought of Enlightenment

The yearning for Buddhahood. It is thus through his constant habit of compassion, his intention to lead all beings out of pain, that he spontaneously and effortlessly awakens the thought that he will achieve enlightenment for their sake; and he begins to yearn for supreme and perfect Buddhahood. As we read in scripture:

> He sees that beings are without protection or refuge or sanctuary; and his mind is established in compassion, and he awakens the thought of supreme and perfect enlightenment.

Now a bodhisattva, a great being, may awaken this thought of enlightenment at the urging of someone else; but the Blessed One has shown us that it is far more excellent if he awakens it himself, through the impulse of his own compassion.

And the Blessed One has shown us, too, that this thought of enlightenment, this yearning for Buddhahood, has great fruits in the world, even when it is unaccompanied by any religious practice. As we read in scripture:

> Even a flawed diamond is better than the finest golden ornament: it is still called a diamond, and it is still able to relieve all poverty. In the same way, this diamond of awakening your mind to omniscience, even when flawed in practice, is better than any golden ornament of a disciple's or solitary Buddha's virtues: it is still called the thought of enlightenment, and it is still able to relieve the poverty of being in the world.

He who is unable to practice all the perfections, all the time, in all ways, should just awaken this thought of enlightenment, for it has great fruits when it is skillfully embraced. As we read in scripture:

> Great king, you are very busy, and you have much to do; and you are unable to practice all the perfections, from charity to wisdom, all the time, in all ways. And so, great king, you should hope for perfect enlightenment, believe in it, long for it, yearn for it; and when you go or stand or sit, when you lie down or when you awaken, when you eat or when you drink, bear it always in mind, think upon it, meditate upon it.
>
> Add together all the merit of all the Buddhas and bodhisattvas, noble disciples and solitary Buddhas, ordinary people and yourself, in the past and present and future: add it all together and rejoice in it with the highest rejoicing.
>
> Honor with your worship all the Buddhas and bodhisattvas, noble disciples and solitary Buddhas; share the merit thereof with all beings; and three times a day dedicate your merit to supreme and perfect enlightenment, that all beings may gain omniscience and fulfill all the qualities of Buddhahood.
>
> And thus, great king, you will conquer and hold sovereign sway; nor will you neglect your royal duties. And by the ripening of the merit which comes of this thought of perfect enlightenment, you will be born many times as a god, and you will be born many times as a man, and among gods and men you will ever bear the rank of royalty.

The vow of enlightenment. But it is when this thought of enlightenment is accompanied by religious practice that its fruits are truly great. As we read in scripture:

> If the merit of this thought of enlightenment were matter, then it would fill the entire realm of space, and there would be more left over. For a man might fill with precious gems Buddha fields as many as the sands of the Ganges, and give them all to the Lords of the World; but it is an infinitely better worship for him to make a single act of homage, as he turns his thought to enlightenment.

And again we read: "The thought of enlightenment is the seed of all the qualities of Buddhahood."

And thus this thought of enlightenment is of two sorts: the intention, and the setting forth. As we read in scripture:

> It is hard to find beings in the world who intend to achieve supreme and perfect enlightenment; and it is even harder to find beings who actually set forth to find supreme and perfect enlightenment.

Now the intention is the initial yearning for Buddhahood: "Oh, that I might be a Buddha, for the sake of all beings!" And the setting forth is the actual making of a vow to become a Buddha, and the actual accumulation of the stocks of merit and knowledge.

And the bodhisattva makes his vow in the presence of a master who himself holds the vow, and who is capable of conferring it on others; and, if this is not possible, then he may awaken this thought of enlightenment in the presence of all the Buddhas and bodhisattvas, whom he has visualized before him.

And the bodhisattva who has thus awakened his thought of enlightenment should himself give charity, and strive in all manner of religious practice: for he who is himself untrained in religious practice can never succeed in training those who follow him.

Religious Practice

The necessity of practice. And thus enlightenment is not attained without religious practice. As we read in scripture: "Enlightenment is for bodhisattvas who undertake religious practice, and not for those who do not."

And again we read:

> Therefore train yourself, saying: I shall undertake religious practice. And why is that? Because for him who undertakes religious practice, supreme and perfect enlightenment is not hard to gain.

Now the religious practice of a bodhisattva, as the scriptures show us, is found in the six perfections, the four immeasurable contemplations, the four means of attraction, and so on: thus he should train himself not only in the meditation which transcends the world, which goes without saying, but also in the arts and crafts of the world itself: for how else can he serve all the different aims of beings?

Wisdom and means. In brief, then, the religious practice of a bodhisattva consists in wisdom and in means, and neither in wisdom alone nor in means alone. As we read in scripture: "Wisdom without means, and means without wisdom: these are a bodhisattva's bondage."

And this implies, of course, that wisdom with means, and means with wisdom, are a bodhisattva's liberation. As we read in scripture:

> Two are the paths of a bodhisattva: endowed with these two paths, a bodhisattva swiftly realizes supreme and perfect enlightenment. And what are those two? They are wisdom and means.

The means used by a bodhisattva are all the perfections except the perfection of wisdom: charity, and virtue, and forebearance, and striving, and meditation; and they include all his means of conversion and attraction to the Law, even to the creation of magical bodies to train the beings who surround him, in the purity and pleasure of his own magical heaven.

His wisdom, on the other hand, is what allows him truly to analyze the nature of the means he employs. As we read in scripture: "His means are knowing how to attract: his wisdom is knowing how to analyze."

And again we read: "What is skill in means? It is his universal attraction. What is wisdom? It is his universal accuracy."

And both wisdom and means must be cultivated all the time, and not wisdom alone nor means alone, even by those who have entered upon the bodhisattva stages; for the scriptures tell us that a bodhisattva practices all the perfections on all ten stages, and not just the one perfection particular to the stage he is on . . . As we read in scripture:

> Maitreya, a bodhisattva practices the six perfections for the sake of enlightenment. Yet there are foolish people who say a bodhisattva should train himself in the perfection of wisdom—what use are the other perfections? And thus they think to slander the other perfections, the perfections of means. What do you think? When I was the king of Benares, I gave my own flesh to a hawk, to save the life of a dove: was that stupid of me?
>
> Maitreya said: No, Blessed One, it was not.
>
> The Blessed One said: Maitreya, when I was coursing in the practice of a bodhisattva, I gathered the merit of the six perfections: did this merit harm me?
>
> Maitreya said: No, Blessed One, it did not.
>
> The Blessed One said: Unconquered One, you yourself have practiced all the perfections from charity to wisdom, each one for sixty eons; and still there are foolish people who say that emptiness is the only way to attain enlightenment.

And again we read:

> Compassion is the root of omniscience: the thought of enlightenment is its cause, and means are its fulfillment.

And thus a bodhisattva should ever cultivate both wisdom and means.

The middle way. For it is by so doing that he attains to the unfixed nirvana of the Blessed Ones; he does not abide in nirvana, for he has gained the fruit of his means, the retinue and pleasures of a body of form in his own magical heaven; nor does he abide in the world, for his wisdom has cast aside all error, and error is the root of the world.

And thus he holds to the middle way, for his is the way of wisdom and of means, the way which shuns both affirmation and denial; for his wisdom shuns the extreme of affirmation, and his means shun the extreme of denial. As we read in scripture:

> He delights in the attainment of a body of form, with all its marks and signs; he does not delight only in the attainment of the Body of Reality.

And again we read:

> Know that Those Who Have Come are born of wisdom and of means, and are possible only because of them.

The growth of wisdom. . . . Thus the bodhisattva should cultivate both his wisdom and his means; for it is only when charity, and virtue, and forebearance, and striving, and meditation are embraced with wisdom that they are truly called perfect; and he should strive to make them thus pure, and seek to gain wisdom.

He should first awaken the wisdom which comes of study and learning; for it is with this wisdom that he begins to understand the meaning of scripture.

And then, with the wisdom which comes of consideration, he penetrates even more deeply into the meaning of scripture, both explicit and implicit; for it is only through this wisdom that he may be certain of meditating upon what is real, and not upon what is unreal. For erroneous meditation will not dispel his doubt, and then true knowledge will not appear; and then his meditation would be without profit, like that of the non-Buddhists. As we read in scripture:

> Reflect upon events which have no self, and when you have reflected, meditate upon them. For this is the cause of gaining the fruit of nirvana, and there is no other cause for peace.

And thus, when he has reflected upon reality with the wisdom which comes of consideration, and with logic and scripture as his guide, he meditates upon the true nature of reality, already certain through logic and through scripture that the true nature of things is absolute nonoccurrence . . .

Meditation

The necessity of meditation. And thus he should awaken the wisdom which comes of meditation, that he may directly experience reality for himself. For the scriptures teach us that even by much study and much consideration he cannot experience reality directly: if the light of manifest knowledge does not begin to shine, he cannot cast aside the darkness of his obscurations; and it is through meditation that the light of manifest knowledge shines even upon objects which are not really real, such as the impurities and the devices and so on: how much more upon what is really real!

For the scriptures say that meditation bears fruit: and the fruit is clear and manifest knowledge:

> I shine through! he says: I understand! For as a man concentrates more and more, his mind sinks deep within the object, as he directs his mind, and as he concentrates it.

And thus he who wishes to see reality face-to-face should set out to meditate.

Calm. First he should practice calm, that he may steady his mind: for the mind is as wavering as water, and is not steady without the support of calm; and he cannot know things as they really are with a mind unconcentrated. As the Blessed One has said: "It is a concentrated mind which understands things as they really are."

And he can attain to this calm quite swiftly if he be but indifferent to gain, and steady in his practice; if he can withstand suffering in search of virtue, if he is willing to strive mightily. And this is why the scriptures say that charity, and virtue, and forebearance, and striving lead ever higher and higher.

He who stands prepared by his virtue, therefore, should go to a pleasant spot and there bow down to all the Buddhas and bodhisattvas; he should confess his sins and rejoice in the merit of himself and others; he should awaken his great compassion in the hope of leading the entire world out of its suffering; he should sit on a comfortable seat with his legs crossed and his body straight, and he should turn himself to meditation.

And he first fixes his mind upon a simple theme which can be applied to any meditative object: for example, the theme might be simply the division between the material and the immaterial; and he should apply this simple theme to the object he is meditating upon, that he may avoid the distractions of complexity which can hinder a beginner.

As he gradually masters his power of attention, he can meditate with more and more complex and detailed themes, such as the five aggregates, or the six senses and their objects, and so on. Thus scripture speaks of all different sorts of contemplative themes, such as the eighteen kinds of emptiness, which he may apply to the meditative object: and the Blessed One has taught us simple themes (such as the division between the material and the immaterial), intermediate and complex themes, to suit the capacity of every meditator.

He should very carefully enumerate all the component items of the representative theme he has chosen, such as the five aggregates, or the six senses and their objects, that he may avoid both the affirmation and the denial of the object he is meditating upon; and when he is quite certain of them, he should bind his mind continuously upon the theme.

Now should his mind be distracted outward, say, by lust, he should recognize it as a distraction and calm it by meditating upon the impurities of the object of lust; and he should bring his mind back to the meditative object once again.

Should he find that his mind no longer takes pleasure in meditation, he should refresh himself by considering the virtues of his practice; and he should calm discontent by considering the evils of distraction.

Should his mind become depressed, and overcome by drowsiness and torpor, which keep him from clearly grasping the meditative object, he should calm his depression with a less abstract meditation, concentrating perhaps on such a pleasing theme as the virtues of the Buddhas and bodhisattvas; and he should then grasp the meditative object all the more firmly.

Should he find that his mind is becoming a bit giddy through remembering past laughter and delight, he should calm its giddiness by concentrating upon something sobering, such as impermanence; and he should then exert himself upon the meditative object, with his mind flowing evenly and naturally.

And when he finds that his mind is detached from depression and giddiness, and is flowing smoothly and spontaneously, he should relax all effort; for to make any effort when his mind is flowing smoothly would only distract it.

And when his mind is thus flowing evenly and naturally upon the meditative object, he can continue as long as he wishes: and he should know that his calm is then made perfect. For the essence of calm is simply one-pointedness of mind: and this is the defining characteristic of all states of calm, regardless of the meditative object.

This is the way of calm which the Blessed One has taught us in scripture.

The nurturing of calm. Now scripture gives us nine terms for a state of calm: the mind, it says, is fixed, and founded, and fast, and firm; it is trained, and calmed, and quieted, and unified, and concentrated.

"Fixed" means that the mind is bound to the meditative object; "founded" means that it continues to hold to the meditative object; "fast" means that it casts aside any distraction which occurs; and "firm" means that it fixes itself upon the meditative object once again, when the distraction has been cast aside.

"Trained" means that the mind delights in meditation; "calmed" means that it calms discontent by considering the evils of distraction; "quieted" means that it calms any drowsiness and torpor which occur; "unified" means that it flows evenly and naturally upon the meditative object; and "concentrated" means that it flows smoothly and spontaneously upon it . . .

Now there are six defects to any state of meditation: and these are sloth, and fading away of the meditative object, and giddiness, and depression, and lack of effort, and too much effort.

And he should cultivate as antidotes to these the eight conditions which suppress them: and these are faith, and hope, and exertion, and serenity, and mindfulness, and awareness, and investigation, and equanimity.

The first four of these are all antidotes to sloth. For a bodhisattva's faith is defined as his complete confidence in the virtues of meditation: hence he begins to wish to possess these virtues; hence he sets out with energy; hence his body and his mind become supple; and with this serenity of body and of mind he wards off sloth. Thus he should cultivate his faith, and his hope, and his exertion, and his serenity, that sloth may be suppressed thereby.

Mindfulness is the antidote to the fading away of the meditative object, and awareness is the antidote to both giddiness and depression. But when giddiness and depression have been calmed, he may then meditate with insufficient effort; and he should cultivate investigation as its antidote. And when the mind is flowing serenely, he may then meditate with too much effort, and he should cultivate equanimity as the antidote to that.

A state of meditation endowed with these eight conditions is the most supple, and it produces all the magical powers. As we read in scripture: "Endowed with suppression, he cultivates the magical powers."

The four trances. As he thus makes his one-pointedness of mind ever more supple, using the particular virtues of the different meditative objects, the bodhisattva attains to what are called trances, and formless meditations, and gates of deliverance, and so on.

Thus he becomes filled with a feeling of equanimity, with discursive thought and reasoning: and this is called a state of approach. And he becomes detached from sensual craving, and filled with enthusiasm and pleasure and inner tranquility: and this is called the first trance. (When this first trance is free of discursive thought, it is called a special trance.)

And then he becomes detached from craving for the level of the first trance, free of discursive thought and reasoning, yet still filled with enthusiasm and pleasure and inner tranquility: and this is called the second trance.

And then he becomes detached from craving for the level of the second trance, filled with pleasure and equanimity, mindful and aware: and this is called the third trance.

And then he becomes detached from craving for the level of the third trance, without pleasure and without pain, filled with equanimity and mindfulness: and this is called the fourth trance . . .

Insight meditation. When his mind is thus firmly fixed upon the meditative object, he must examine it with wisdom: for it is only where the light of knowledge dawns that the seeds of delusion are wholly cast aside; and meditation by itself cannot destroy defilement, as we can see by looking at the non-Buddhists. As we read in scripture: "He who cultivates meditation, yet does not examine his concept of the self, will again be shaken by defilement."

And here our scripture briefly outlines the process by which he cultivates his wisdom:

> He ascends to mind alone and does not think that external objects really exist; but with reality before him, he transcends mind alone; he transcends nonappearance, and he abides in nonappearance, seeing the Great Vehicle; and in the effortless state, tranquil, made pure by his vows, where nothing appears, he sees not-self, the highest knowledge.

And this is what it means:

He should first examine all those material events which other people think are really external objects: are they something external to their perception? Or are they perhaps just the perception itself, appearing to be external, as in a dream? He should examine these objects which are supposedly external to their perception; he should divide them into their component atoms, and these atoms into their parts, and realize the anomalies of postulating an external world; and he should think: All this is nothing but mind; there is no such thing as an external object.

And thus we read: "He ascends to mind alone and does not think that external objects really exist." And this means that he renounces all thought that material things are real, and imposes upon reality no construct "material things:" for they may be defined by their perceptibility, but they do not exist.

And when he has thus uncovered material events for what they are, he should similarly uncover the immaterial, and he should consider: If all is mind alone, then there is no object; and where there is no object, there cannot be a subject, for the subject presupposes the object. Hence the mind is devoid of either subject or object; the mind is nondual; and reality is defined by its nonduality.

And thus we read: "But with reality before him, he transcends mind alone." And this means that he transcends the postulation of a subject and abides in the knowledge of nonduality, where no duality appears.

And when he has thus transcended mind alone, he should similarly transcend this nonappearance, this knowledge where no duality appears; and he should consider: Things which occur are not born from themselves, nor from other things: both subject and object are falsehoods. And if they do not exist, then the knowledge of their nonduality cannot exist either, for it is inconceivable without them. And thus he casts aside all insistence that this knowledge of nonduality is a real thing, and abides in the knowledge where no knowledge of nonduality appears.

Thus he abides in the realization that all events are without essence: abiding there he enters into the highest reality, the state of meditation wherein he imposes no constructs at all upon reality, whether of existence or of nonexistence. And when he thus abides in the knowledge where no knowledge of nonduality appears, he abides in the highest reality, and he sees the Great Vehicle: for what we call the Great Vehicle is nothing but this vision of the highest reality.

And this vision of the highest reality is a nonvision, which dawns with the light of true knowledge, when he sees all events with the eye of wisdom. As we read in scripture: "What is the vision of reality? It is the nonvision of all events."

The union of calm and insight . . . Now the Blessed One has shown us the way to bring about the union of this insight with the calm of meditation, that we may cast aside all obscuration; for it is these two together which bring about true knowledge, wherein no constructs at all are imposed upon reality:

> Established in virtue, he gains the state of meditation: in the state of meditation he cultivates wisdom: his wisdom makes pure his knowledge: and his pure knowledge fulfills his virtue.

Thus, when his calm firmly fixes his mind upon the meditative object, he examines it with his wisdom; and then the light of knowledge dawns, to cast aside his obscuration, as a light illuminates the darkness. For his calm and insight both work together to bring about true knowledge, as his eye sees with the aid of light . . .

And it is said that in this state of meditation he understands reality as it really is: for in this state he examines things with his wisdom, and he sees no event as being real. This then is the highest nonseeing: and his condition is called the effortless state, for there is nothing for him to see beyond it; and it is called tranquil, for he has calmed all the busy work of his mind, which imposes upon reality the constructs of existence and of nonexistence.

For when he examines the world with his wisdom, he sees no essence of any existing thing, nor does he impose any construct of existence upon reality; and thus he imposes no construct of nonexistence. For he looks with his eye of wisdom into the past, and the present, and the future, and he does not see any thing which exists: then how can he negate this and impose the construct of nonexistence?

And no other constructs will occur then, for all constructs are included within the universal categories of existence and nonexistence; and when the universals do not exist, the particulars do not exist either. And this is then the highest yoga, which imposes no constructs upon reality . . .

This is the process by which the bodhisattva should contemplate reality. And should giddiness or depression occur, he should calm them as above. And when his knowledge takes the essencelessness of all events as its meditative object, and flows evenly and spontaneously upon it, free of giddiness or depression, then he has made perfect the way which brings about the union of his insight with his calm; and he should abide therein with deep conviction as long as he is able, for this is the stage of Practicing with Conviction.

The return to the world. Then, when he wishes to arise from this state of meditation, he should not yet uncross his legs, but he should consider: All these events, from the absolute point of view, have no essence; yet they are still here in conventional reality. As we read in scripture:

> How is a bodhisattva skilled in selflessness? He looks upon form with true wisdom, and he looks upon feeling, and idea, and motive, and perception: and when he looks upon form, he does not see its occurrence, he does not see its existence, he does not see its cessation; and when he looks upon feeling, and idea, and motive, and perception, he does not see its occurrence, he does not see its existence, he does not see its cessation. And thus it is from the absolute point of view, with the wisdom which abides in nonoccurrence; but it is not so in every-day life.

People with the minds of children wrongly insist that things are real, so they wander in this world, and experience all its many sufferings; and the meditator should awaken his great compassion and consider: When I attain to omniscience, let me awaken them to the true nature of things.

And he should praise and worship all the Buddhas and bodhisattvas, and undertake all the vows of beneficent conduct; and he should set out to gather all the knowledge and all the merit of charity, and virtue, and forebearance, and striving, and meditation, for these are the womb of wisdom and compassion. As we read in scripture:

> A bodhisattva, seeing reality as it really is, sets forth in great compassion for all beings, and he thinks: I should cause all beings to open this door of meditation, this vision of all events as they really are.
>   And moved by his great compassion, he fulfills the three-fold training of virtue and meditation and wisdom, and he realizes supreme and perfect enlightenment.

This then is the way of the bodhisattvas, which brings about the union of wisdom and means: for though he sees the highest reality, he does not cut himself off from conventional reality; not cut off from their reality, he sets out to serve the aim of beings, led by his great compassion, and without delusion.

Now when a bodhisattva abides in transcendent wisdom, he need not resort to the use of means; but when he employs his means he must resort to his wisdom, like a magician, knowing the absolute truth of what he does and what he sees, prepared by his practice in transcendent and unmistaken knowledge. And this is the way which brings about the union of wisdom and means . . .

As we read in scripture:

> How is a bodhisattva skilled in the Great Vehicle? He trains himself in all training: but he does not see the training, he does not see the way he is trained, he does not see in what he is trained: and for that reason, and for that cause, he falls not into the extreme of denial.

And again we read:

What is the religious practice of a bodhisattva? All the activity of his body, and all the activity of his speech, and all the activity of his mind: all of it is undertaken out of regard for beings, because it is preceded by his great compassion; it is under the sway of compassion, and it springs from his hope for the welfare and happiness of all beings. And he who hopes for the welfare of the world thinks to himself: Let me undertake religious practice, that I may bring welfare and happiness to all beings.

And he sees the aggregates as like a magic show, but he does not wish to disown the aggregates; he sees the senses as like a poisonous serpent, but he does not wish to disown the senses; he sees sensory awareness as like an empty village, but he does not wish to disown sensory awareness, as he works for the welfare of the world.

And he sees form as like a heap of foam, but he does not renounce the magical creation of bodies of form; he sees feeling as like a bubble, but he still sets forth to attain the pleasures of meditation; he sees ideas as like an illusion, but he still conceives of attaining the knowledge of a Buddha; he sees motives as like a hollow reed, but he is still motivated to attain the qualities of Buddhahood; he sees perceptions as like a magic show, but he still seeks to attain the activity of body and speech and mind which springs from knowledge.

And in countless scriptures we are taught the religious practice which combines wisdom and means.

The Stages of the Bodhisattva Path

And as the bodhisattva thus strives for a long time, his wisdom and his means grow gradually ever more developed; and there are twelve different states, which we call stages, as he abides in ever higher and higher virtues, ranging from the stage of Practicing with Conviction to the stage of Buddhahood itself.

The Path of Preparation

Practicing with Conviction. At first the bodhisattva has not himself directly realized the selflessness of persons and of events; but his firm conviction thereof cannot be shaken even by the Evil One, and with the strength of this conviction he contemplates reality: and this is called the stage of Practicing with Conviction.

Now the bodhisattva abiding at this stage is still an ordinary person; but he has already transcended the failures of the foolish, for he is endowed with the immeasurable virtues of his meditation and his supernormal knowledge.

Here, too, there are four different states, called the *four modes of penetration,* according as his realization is weak, or average, or strong, or very strong.

Thus, as he contemplates the selflessness of all events, the light of knowledge may begin to shine, but dimly: and this is the mode of penetration into reality which is called *warmth.* In the Great Vehicle we call it the meditation wherein the light appears.

When the light of knowledge shines through more brightly, this is the mode of penetration into reality which is called *climax,* or the meditation wherein the light increases.

When the light of knowledge shines so brightly that external objects no longer appear, this is the mode of penetration into reality which is called *acceptance,* for he then accepts that nothing exists save sensory awareness itself: and it is called the meditation wherein he enters into unity, for he enters into the nonseeing of the external world.

And when there appears the knowledge of nonduality, free of both subject and object, this is the mode of penetration into reality which is called *the highest event in the world*: and it is called the meditation of immediate succession, for immediately afterward he passes into the vision of true reality.

And everything up to this point is the stage of *practicing with conviction.*

The Path of Vision

The joyful stage. The remaining eleven stages, briefly, are entered upon according to the fulfillment of eleven criteria.

Thus, when the bodhisattva realizes the truth of the selflessness of persons and of events, he fulfills the criterion for entering upon the first of these stages: immediately after he experiences the highest event in the world, there dawns in him a manifest and transcendent knowledge, wherein his mind is free of all its busy work, and he stands face-to-face with the essencelessness of all events; and he enters into a state of faultless understanding, for the Path of Vision begins; and he enters upon the first stage.

And the bodhisattva is joyful, for he has realized for the first time a truth which he had not attained before: and hence this stage is called *the joyful.* And here too he casts aside the 112 defilements removed by his vision of reality (he casts aside the remaining sixteen worldly defilements, removed by his contemplation of reality, on the remaining stages, which constitute the Path of Contemplation).

On this stage the realm of reality approaches and arouses the bodhisattva to action, that he works for others as for himself: so here the perfection of charity is predominant.

And the bodhisattva has realized the truth, but still he may slip unaware into minor faults: and as long as that is the case, he remains on the first stage.

The Path of Contemplation

The stainless stage. And when he becomes aware of even the most minor faults, he fulfills the criterion for entering upon the second stage.

On this stage he never slips into even the most subtle and inadvertent fault: so here the perfection of virtue is predominant. And he is free of all the stains of unvirtuous conduct: and hence this stage is called *the stainless.*

And the bodhisattva abides in the awareness which keeps him from slipping into any minor fault, but still he is unable to enter into all the different meditations upon the world, or to hold fast all that he has learned: and as long as that is the case, he remains on the second stage.

The luminous stage. And when he is able to do so, he fulfills the criterion for entering upon the third stage.

On this stage he holds fast all that he has learned, and enters into all the different meditations upon the world; and he endures all manner of suffering that he may do so: so here the perfection of forebearance is predominant. And when he attains to these meditations, there dawns in him the infinite and transcendent brightness of knowledge: and hence this stage is called *the luminous.*

And the bodhisattva attains to all the meditations upon the world; but still he is unable to maintain continually all the qualities conducive to enlightenment which he has gained, or to maintain equanimity toward all his meditative states: and as long as that is the case, he remains on the third stage.

The flaming stage. And when he is able to do so, he fulfills the criterion for entering upon the fourth stage.

On this stage he abides every moment with all the qualities conducive to enlightenment, that he may transcend the foolish chatter of his body and speech and mind: so here the perfection of striving is predominant. And here there blaze the flames of the qualities conducive to enlightenment, to consume the fuel of all his defilements: and hence this stage is called *the flaming.*

And the bodhisattva abides every moment with all the qualities conducive to enlightenment, but still he is unable so to contemplate the noble truths that he turns his mind from this world to nirvana, or to cultivate the qualities conducive to enlightenment as assisted by his means: and as long as that is the case, he remains on the fourth stage.

The hard-to-conquer stage. And when he is able to do so, he fulfills the criterion for entering upon the fifth stage.

On this stage he continually contemplates the different aspects of the four noble truths: so here the perfection of meditation is predominant. And the cultivation of the qualities conducive to enlightenment as assisted by his means is very difficult to practice and conquered only with difficulty: and hence this stage is called *the hard-to-conquer.*

And the bodhisattva ever abides in the cultivation of the qualities conducive to enlightenment as assisted by his means, but still he is unable to enter into a state which is free of all labeling, for his mind still despairs at seeing the ways of this world: and as long as that is the case, he remains on the fifth stage.

The face-to-face stage. And when he is able to do so, he fulfills the criterion for entering upon the sixth stage.

On this stage he abides in the contemplation of dependent co-arising: so here the perfection of wisdom is predominant. And because the perfection of wisdom predominates, he stands face-to-face with all the qualities of Buddhahood: and hence this stage is called *the face-to-face.*

And the bodhisattva abides in a state which is free of all labeling, but still he is unable to enter into this state continuously and without a break: and as long as that is the case, he remains on the sixth stage.

The far-going stage. And when he is able to do so, he fulfills the criterion for entering upon the seventh stage.

On this stage he realizes that no labels really label anything, yet he does not turn away from labels: so here the perfection of means is predominant. And he goes as far as he can to embrace the effortless way: and hence this stage is called *the far-going.*

And the bodhisattva abides in a state which is free of all labeling, continuously and without a break, but still he is unable to enter into this state effortlessly and spontaneously: and as long as that is the case, he remains on the seventh stage.

The immovable stage. And when he is able to do so, he fulfills the criterion for entering upon the eighth stage.

On this stage he effortlessly embraces all that conduces to virtue: so here the perfection of the vow is predominant. And he never sways from his effortless nonlabeling: and hence this stage is called *the immovable.*

And the bodhisattva abides effortlessly and spontaneously in a state which is free of all labeling, but still he is unable to master the teaching of the whole of the Law, in all its aspects, and with all its different definitions and etymologies: and as long as that is the case, he remains on the eighth stage.

The good stage. And when he is able to do so, he fulfills the criterion for entering upon the ninth stage.

On this stage he attains to a special awareness which allows him to teach to all beings, and he embraces the special power of wisdom: so here the perfection of power is predominant. And he attains to a special faultlessness, for he is skilled in the exposition of the Law in all its aspects: and hence this stage is called *the good.*

And the bodhisattva has attained to the four-fold special awareness, but still he is unable to manifest magical creations, heavens and retinues, or to train all beings in the bliss of the perfect Law: and as long as that is the case, he remains on the ninth stage.

The cloud of the Law. And when he is able to do so, he fulfills the criterion for entering upon the tenth stage.

On this stage he possesses the special knowledge needed to train beings through magical creations: so here the perfection of knowledge is predominant. And with his clouds of teaching he lets fall a rain of the Law over all the worlds: and hence this stage is called *the cloud of the Law.*

And the bodhisattva has attained to mastery over magical creations, but still he is unable to bring forth the knowledge which knows everything that can be known, unattached, and unhindered, and omniscient: and as long as that is the case, he remains on the tenth stage.

The Path Beyond Learning

The stage of Buddhahood. And when he is able to do so, he fulfills the criterion for entering upon the stage of Buddhahood itself. As we read in scripture: "There is no other state beyond the stage of Buddhahood, for it is the very limit of all manner of excellence and superiority."

Even the Buddhas themselves are unable to express all the different virtues of this stage of Buddhahood, in all their aspects, for the virtues of Buddhahood are infinite: how then could one like myself think to speak of them? As we read in scripture: "The Self-sprung One cannot reach the end or limit of his qualities; though long examined, the virtues of Buddhahood are inconceivable."

But we may, briefly, say this: the Buddhas, the Blessed Ones, fulfill all the worthy aims of themselves and others, and cast aside every single fault; and they enter into the Body of Reality; and with bodies of bliss, and magical bodies, they magically serve the aim of all beings, as long as this world shall last . . .

6
the vision and the word

1. THE VISION OF PARADISE

Yet another strand in the complex weave of Buddhist meditation—and one that seems to have received little scholarly attention—is the magical and visionary mode of consciousness. The ecstatic vision of the poet-seer was the model for the Buddha's enlightenment, and had its roots in the most ancient Vedic literature, wherein the shining realm of the gods was opened by the drinking of soma, and the vision of the priest expanded to the very ends of the universe. This vision was an ecstatic penetration into the divine meaning of the cosmos, homologized to the holy patterns of the sacrifice and expressed not in intellectual categories but in mythic and visual terms. And the vision was always associated with magic power, for the recitation of the sacred words of the hymns and the formulas of the ritual granted control over all things seen, and coerced even the gods.

Whatever the nature of soma (and there is considerable evidence that it was in fact the psychotropic mushroom *Amanita muscaria*), the glittering vision it granted, and the sense of power in the resonance of the sacred word, remained the ideal state of visionary meditation. Long after the secret of soma was lost, the heavens of the Buddhists were still filled with jeweled trees and nets of pearls, glittering crystal waters and diamond earth: all hard points of sharp and brilliant light, an expanded vision of a divine and magic world.

For Buddhist meditation had incorporated the processes of visualization, the deliberate contemplative creation of shining realities that required no ecstatic projection of meaning from the meditator, because they were replete with symbolic significance in the very process of their creation. Just as ecstasy balanced enstacy in the earlier standard structure of contemplation, so both states could be synthesized in a new visionary mode, a reality as dreamlike, as real and unreal as our own, but endowed by its symbolism with magical meaning and power.

The following text is considered one of the foundations of the Pure Land sects of devotionalism, and is often treated as an adjunct to more descriptive and less contemplative works. But it is important to stress that faith is but part of a larger visionary whole: the *NAMO AMITA BUDDHA* so faithfully recited throughout East Asia is a magic formula, with its source in the symbolically potent vision of the Heaven of Highest Happiness. As our text points out, to gain the vision of the Buddha is to become the Buddha: the vision is a reality of its own.

Thus the meditation set forth in our text is the studied construction of an alternative reality, as the meditator manipulates the magical creation of heaven. It is the contemplative equivalent of the vision granted by soma, but here under full and conscious control. This visionary mode is as much a part of the Buddhist tradition as is withdrawal from the world, or the projection of meaning upon the events of the world we know: its sudden appearance during the first centuries of our millennium was a resurgence of an ancient mode of being in the world, an archaic technique that gained new life from the reconstruction of reality in the Great Vehicle.

Kuan wu-liang-shou fo-ching [Amitāyur-dhyāna-sūtra], [*The meditation upon the Buddha of everlasting life*], in Taishō Shinshū Daizōkyō, gen. eds. Takakusu Junjirō and Watanabe Kaigyoku (Tokyo: Taishō Issaikyō Kankōkai, 1924–29), 12, no. 365.

. . . Then the Blessed One said: Do you not realize that the Buddha of Everlasting Life is never far from you? You need only concentrate, and visualize the land where all pure virtues ripen.

I shall now teach you these things with many metaphors, that all the people in time to come may practice these pure virtues, and gain rebirth in the Western Land of Happiness.

The Pure Virtues

Whoever wishes to be reborn in that land must practice three virtues. First, he should honor and support his parents, serve and respect his teachers, be loving and compassionate, and cultivate the ten paths of good conduct.

Second, he should take the three refuges, observe all the precepts, and neglect none of the ritual observances.

Third, he should awaken his thought of enlightenment, believe in the efficacy of karma, study the Great Vehicle, and encourage others to do the same.

These three things are called the pure virtues. Do you not realize that these three virtues are the direct cause for all the good done by all the Buddhas throughout all of time?

And the Blessed One said: Listen and hear me; think well upon it; for He Who Has Come is telling you of the pure virtues, for the sake of all the future beings who will suffer at the hands of the thief passion. It is good; I have been asked of this just in time.

The Granting of the Vision

And you should take my words and openly tell the multitudes what the Buddha has said; for He Who Has Come is telling you and all future beings how you may see the Western Land of Happiness.

It is by power of the Buddha that you will gain the vision of that Pure Land, as clearly as you see the reflection of your face in a bright mirror.

And when you have seen that land and its highest happiness, your heart will rejoice; and you will realize that no event in this world is truly real.

You are still an ordinary person, and your concentration is weak: you have not gained the divine eye, and you cannot see what is far off. But all the Buddhas have skill in means, that you may be granted the vision.

And then the Buddha was asked: Blessed One! It is by the power of the Buddha that people such as I can see that land; but after the Buddha has passed away, all beings will be evil, and without virtue, suffering the five sufferings: how can they see this Land of Happiness?

The Meditation on the Sun

And the Buddha said: You and all beings should concentrate your minds to a single point, and meditate upon the western direction. How should you meditate upon it? All beings not born blind have eyes to see, and they have seen the setting sun: and it is upon this that you should meditate.

Sit down facing the west, and visualize the place where the sun sinks down; fix your mind upon it, that you will not be distracted; gaze upon the sun as it sets, resembling a drum hanging in space.

When you have thus seen the sun, you will be able to make it appear before you whether your eyes are open or closed.

This is the meditation on the sun, the first visualization.

The Meditation on the Water

Next, meditate upon the water: look at some water, clear and pure; let it appear before you; let it not fade away from your mind.

When you have thus seen the water, you should meditate upon it becoming ice: look at the ice, dazzling and transparent.

When you have thus seen the ice, you should meditate upon it as crystal: look at this crystal ground, dazzling and transparent.

Beneath it is a diamond pillar of the seven precious gems, which supports the crystal ground. The pillar has eight facets in the eight directions: each facet has a hundred gems; each gem shines with a thousand bright rays of light; each ray of light has eighty-four thousand colors; and the colors are refracted through the dazzling crystal ground, like a thousand million suns so bright you cannot see them all.

Above this crystal ground are ropes of yellow gold, intertwined as ornaments, divided by the seven gems, each part clear and bright. Each gem shines with rays of five hundred colors, and the rays of light are like flowers, like the stars and moon: and there the rays hang in empty space, and become a bright tower a million storeys high, made of a hundred gems.

On both sides of the tower of light are a hundred million pillars of flowers, adorned with innumerable musical instruments; and from the bright rays there blows a cool breeze, which plays upon the instruments;

and they sound forth the song of the Law, and they say: Suffering . . . Emptiness . . . Impermanence . . . No self . . .

This is the meditation on the water, the second visualization.

The Meditation on the Land

When you have thus meditated upon the water, you should visualize all the items one by one, that they do not fade away, whether your eyes are open or closed: except when you sleep, these things should be ever before you.

He who has thus meditated is said to have seen the Land of Happiness, but only roughly: it is beyond the power of words to describe his meditative vision, when finally every part of this land becomes distinct and clear before him.

This is the meditation on the land, the third visualization.

And you should take the words of the Buddha and teach all future beings how to visualize this land, who wish to be free of suffering: whoever visualizes this land shall be exempt from the sins which lead to rebirth for eighty million eons; and when his body dies, surely he will be reborn in the Pure Land, where his heart will find peace.

To do this visualization is called right meditation: to do otherwise is called wrong meditation.

The Meditation on the Trees

When you have thus meditated upon the land, you should visualize the jeweled trees. Visualize the jeweled trees one by one; then meditate upon them in seven rows: each tree is eight thousand miles high; all the trees have flowers and leaves of the seven gems; and all of them are perfect.

Each flower and leaf has the color of a gem: golden rays of light shine from lapis lazuli leaves; red rays shine from crystal leaves; diamond rays shine from agate leaves; blue-pearl rays shine from beryl leaves; and coral and amber and all the gems are dazzling ornaments upon them.

Nets of pearls are spread upon the trees: each tree is covered with seven nets; and between the nets are five hundred million flowery mansions, like the royal palaces of the highest gods.

And these mansions are the homes where all the children of heaven dwell: each of the children wears five hundred million divine and magic gems as ornaments; the rays of the gems shine for a thousand miles, as if a hundred million suns and moons were blazing forth together.

And the jeweled trees stand in the midst of all these colors, row upon row, leaf upon leaf: between the leaves grow wondrous flowers, and upon the flowers are miraculous fruits, made of the seven gems.

Each leaf is twenty-five miles long and wide: the thousand-colored leaves have a hundred veins like a divine necklace; and their host of wondrous flowers are the color of river gold, like wheels of fire spinning among the leaves, where fruits well up as from the bounty of the gods.

There is a great shining light, which transforms into banners and flags, and numberless jeweled canopies; and amid these jeweled canopies appear the deeds of all the Buddhas in the vast universe, and all their magical heavens in the ten directions.

When you have thus seen the trees, you should visualize all their parts one by one, that you may clearly and distinctly see their trunks and branches, their leaves and flowers and fruits.

This is the meditation on the trees, the fourth visualization.

The Meditation on the Wondrous Waters

Next you should meditate upon the waters: for in that Land of Happiness there are waters in eight lakes, and the waters in each lake are made of the seven gems, melted and liquid; they flow from a great wish-granting gem and divide into fourteen streams; each stream has the wondrous color of the seven gems and flows in a channel of yellow gold, its bed covered with a sand of multicolored diamonds.

In the midst of each lake are sixty million lotus flowers, all of them twelve miles in diameter; and the jeweled water flows amidst the flowers, up and down among the trees.

And the murmuring and wondrous waters sing in praise of all the signs of the Buddhas, and sound forth the song of the Law. And the great wish-granting gem shines with a bright and wondrous golden ray of light, which transforms into singing birds the color of a hundred gems, their soft sweet songs praising the remembrance of the Buddha, and the Law, and the Community.

This is the meditation on the wondrous waters, the fifth visualization.

The Summary Meditation

In every quarter of that jeweled land are five hundred million jeweled pavilions, and in each pavilion are innumerable deities playing heavenly music. And there are musical instruments hanging in empty space like the jeweled banners of heaven: unstruck, they sing by themselves, and all their sounds sing in praise of the remembrance of the Buddha, and the Law, and the Community.

He who has thus meditated is said to have seen the Land of Happiness with its jeweled trees and jeweled ground and jeweled waters, but still only roughly: yet whoever has seen this shall be exempt from the most heinous sins for innumerable eons; and when his body dies, surely he will be reborn in that land.

This is the summary meditation, the sixth visualization.

To do this visualization is called right meditation: to do otherwise is called wrong meditation.

Listen and hear me; think well upon it, for I am telling you in detail how to free yourself from suffering; bear it ever in your mind and tell the multitudes what I have said.

And as soon as the Blessed One had spoken these words, the Buddha of Everlasting Life appeared in the sky, with the two great bodhisattvas standing to his right and to his left; and they shone with such brilliant and dazzling light that they could not be clearly seen, a hundred thousand times incomparably more blazing than the color of river gold . . .

And then the Buddha was asked: Blessed One! It is by the power of the Buddha that I have gained this vision; but how can future beings see the Buddha of Everlasting Life and the two bodhisattvas?

The Meditation on the Lotus Throne

And the Buddha said: Whoever wishes to see that Buddha should first visualize his lotus throne, resting upon that ground of seven gems: each petal has the color of a hundred gems and eighty-four thousand veins like the writing of the gods; and each vein shines with eighty-four thousand rays of light, so distinct and clear that you can see each one.

The lotus has eighty-four thousand petals, and each petal is two hundred and fifty miles long and wide; between the petals are a hundred million pearls as dazzling ornaments; each pearl shines with a thousand bright rays of light, like a canopy of the seven gems spreading over the ground.

There is a tower of divine and magic gems, and this lotus tower is adorned with eighty thousand diamonds and rubies and gems and truly wondrous nets of pearls.

Upon the tower are four miraculous pillars, each pillar as high as a thousand million Mount Merus; upon the pillars are jeweled draperies encrusted with fifty million wondrous pearls, like the royal palaces of the highest gods; each pearl shines with eighty-four thousand rays of light; and each ray of light glows with eighty-four thousand golden colors.

Each golden color spreads over the whole jeweled land and transforms into a different shape in every place: here it is a diamond tower, there a net of pearls, and there a cloud of multicolored flowers; in all the ten directions it transforms and appears as it wishes, and performs the deeds of a Buddha.

This is the meditation on the lotus throne, the seventh visualization.

This wondrous lotus flower was formed by the power of the vow made by the monk Dharmākara. Whoever wishes to think upon the Buddha of Everlasting Life should first meditate upon his lotus throne; and when you perform this meditation you should not visualize the lotus vaguely, but visualize all the items one by one: each leaf and each pearl and each ray of light, each tower and each pillar should be as clear and distinct as when you see the reflection of your face in a mirror.

Whoever has thus meditated shall be exempt from the sins which lead to rebirth for fifty thousand eons; and most surely he will be reborn in the Land of Happiness.

To do this visualization is called right meditation: to do otherwise is called wrong meditation.

The Meditation on the Buddha's Form

When you have seen these things, you should next meditate upon the Buddha: for the body of every Buddha is the body of reality itself, and it is already within the mind of every being.

Thus when you meditate upon the Buddha, it is your own mind which has all the signs and minor signs of Buddhahood: your mind becomes the

Buddha; your mind is the Buddha in reality. The ocean of the true and perfect knowledge of all the Buddhas springs from the meditation of your mind; and hence you should concentrate your mind to a single point, and visualize the Buddha, the Worthy One, the supremely and perfectly enlightened.

When you meditate upon the Buddha, you should first meditate upon his form: whether your eyes are open or closed, you should see his shining form, like the color of river gold, seated upon his lotus throne.

And when you have seen his seated form, the eye of your mind opens: clearly and distinctly you see the whole of the Land of Happiness, its array of the seven gems, its jeweled ground and jeweled waters, its rows of jeweled trees, its heavenly jeweled banners, its jeweled nets in empty space; and you see these things clearly and distinctly, as you might see the palm of your hand.

When you have seen these things, you should next meditate upon two great lotus flowers on either side of the Buddha, and the two great bodhisattvas seated upon these lotus thrones.

And the forms of the Buddha and bodhisattvas shine with bright golden rays, illumining all the jeweled trees; and under each tree there are also three lotus flowers, with the forms of the Buddha and bodhisattvas upon them, throughout the entire land.

And as you meditate upon them, you will hear the song of the Law sung by the murmuring waters, by the rays of light, by the jeweled trees, by the ducks and swans and wild geese. Always you will hear the wonderful Law; and what you hear you should ever bear in mind, and not forget, even when you arise from meditation. And it should agree with the teachings, for if it does not agree it is a false meditation: but if it agrees with the teachings, it is said to be a true vision of the Land of Happiness.

Whoever has practiced this visualization shall be exempt from the sins which lead to rebirth for incalculable millions of eons; and in this very life he will attain to meditation in the remembrance of the Buddha.

This is the meditation on the Buddha's form, the eighth visualization.

The Meditation on the Bodily Signs of the Buddha

When you have thus meditated, you should next visualize the bodily signs and the shining light of the Buddha of Everlasting Life.

His body is a hundred billion times brighter than the color of the river gold in the palaces of the gods, and its height is six hundred thousand billion miles, measured in miles innumerable as the sands of the Ganges.

The white tuft of hair between his brows twists to the right, as tall as five Mount Merus; his eyes are like the waters of the four great oceans; the pupils and the whites are clear and distinct.

Brilliant rays of light shine from every pore of his body: his shining halo is as large as a hundred million universes. And in the midst of that shining halo are a hundred thousand billion magical Buddha bodies, innumerable as the sands of the Ganges, and each of these Buddhas has innumerable magical bodhisattvas to be his retinue.

The Buddha of Everlasting Life has the eighty-four thousand signs of a great person; each sign has the eighty-four thousand minor signs of a great person; and each of the minor signs shines with eighty-four thousand brilliant rays of light.

And this light shines out over the ten directions of the world, embracing and protecting every being who meditates upon the Buddha.

No words can describe the brilliant rays of light, the signs and minor signs, the magical Buddha bodies; but the eye of your mind sees them in meditation. And in seeing these things you see all the Buddhas in the ten directions; and thus you attain to meditation in the remembrance of the Buddha.

For to see these things is to attain a vision of the body of the Buddha; to see the body of the Buddha is to know the mind of the Buddha; and his mind is great compassion, with which he embraces every creature that lives.

Whoever has performed this visualization shall surely be reborn in the presence of all the Buddhas, and he will realize that no event in this world is truly real.

Therefore the wise man concentrates his mind upon visualizing the Buddha of Everlasting Life: he begins with just one sign or minor sign and visualizes the tuft of hair between the Buddha's brows, as clearly and distinctly as he can.

And when he can see this sign before him, then all the eighty-four thousand signs and minor signs will spontaneously appear.

Whoever thus sees the Buddha of Everlasting Life attains a vision of all the innumerable Buddhas in the ten directions; and in their presence he receives a prophecy of his own Buddhahood.

This is the meditation on the bodily signs of the Buddha, the ninth visualization.

To do this visualization is called right meditation: to do otherwise is called wrong meditation . . .

Rebirth in the Land of Happiness

And when you have seen these things, you should imagine that you yourself are born in the Western Land of Happiness: you are sitting within a lotus, and the lotus has enclosed you, but now it unfolds its petals.

And as the lotus opens, five hundred colored rays of light shine upon your body; you open your eyes, and you see the Buddhas and bodhisattvas filling the sky; and you hear the sounds of the murmuring waters, and the birds, and the trees, and all the Buddhas preaching the wonderful Law.

Even when you arise from this meditation, you should remember it always, and never forget it; for to see these things is to attain a vision of the Land of Happiness of the Buddha of Everlasting Life . . .

The Recitation of the Name

Suppose there were a man who did wicked deeds, the five grievous sins and all manner of evil, so that because of his wickedness he would fall into evil destiny and feel endless pain for many eons.

And suppose that at the very moment of his death this wicked man should meet a good and learned friend, who consoles and comforts him, and tells him of the wonderful Law, and teaches him to think upon the Buddha; but that man would feel such pain that he could not keep the Buddha in his mind.

And his good friend tells him: Even if you cannot think upon the Buddha, still you can call his name; so call upon the Buddha of Everlasting Life, and repeat *NAMO AMITA BUDDHA* . . .

And because he utters the name of the Buddha, at each recitation he is exempt from the sins which lead to rebirth for eighty million eons.

And when he dies he sees a golden lotus, shining like the sun before him: and within that lotus he is born in the Land of Happiness, and the lotus encloses him for twelve great eons.

And then the petals unfold, and the two great bodhisattvas speak to him with great compassion: they teach him the true nature of things and the way to purge his sins; and he rejoices as he hears it, and awakens his heart to enlightenment . . .

For whoever practices this meditation will attain this vision of the Buddha of Everlasting Life. If a son or daughter of good family but hears the name of the Buddha, he is exempt from the sins which lead to rebirth for incalculable millions of eons: how much more he who himself recites the name!

Know that whoever recites the name of the Buddha is a white lotus among men; the two great bodhisattvas shall be his friends; he shall sit upon the terrace of enlightenment and be born in the house of the Buddhas . . .

2. THE WORSHIP OF THE FIERCE LORD

The visionary mode in India was early joined to devotionalism and to the summoning of the shining gods to receive the worship of their followers. Visionary theism was undergoing a renaissance in the early centuries of our era, joining ancient visionary techniques to the speculations of the philosophers. The immanence of deity and the participation of the holy in all things became the foundation of what could finally be called Hinduism, and became an important strand in the Buddhist religious revival called the Great Vehicle.

From that point on, Buddhist and Hindu religious ritual was based upon the vision and the word, the summoning and appearance of the deity before the worshipper. This ritual found fertile ground in Tibet, where it supported and enriched a deep shamanic heritage. Here the vision drew upon the most ancient Indian symbols of power and omnipotence, images of death and procreation made immanent as blood and semen, power made manifest as weapons of ferocity and dripping human heads. Symbolically potent deities took form from the realm of emptiness, to act within the world: worship was the creation of the god from his primal source, then offerings and praises and prayers to the holy power of the sacred which entered into all things. Thus, as in this text by White Lotus, the ferocity of sacred truth unleashed within the darkness of events is kindled, and approached with reverence and awe.

Pad-ma dkar-po, Mgon-po mchod-pa [*The worship of the fierce lord*], *(manuscript copy: dbu-can script, 6 folios), folios 1–6.*

Evocation

ALL is

      primordial sound (brightness
        of reality : the unfixed center)

     to create the great mandala
          of the world (to kill
       all harm with beams of light
         from $H\bar{U}M$ and chopper) gather
       all the power of the Buddhas

                & be the body

BLACK in color (unbearably
      dark) & garlanded with flame
        covered with smoke

            (swirls):

    one face
        (terrible : wrathful)
            three red eyes
    heroism : sensuousness : terror

         CROWN of dried skulls

(& the six bone ornaments) hanging down
      a necklace : fifty dripping heads

     (wet freshflayed skin
         human skin) elephant
    skin (tigerskin
         for clothes) & coiled
    poisonous snakes

DELIGHT in trampling
     hero's haughtiness upon
         the four Evils (shrivelling
   at his roar of $H\bar{U}M$) & holds

    four hands : a coconut (a sword
       made of the tongue of a living corpse) a skull
       filled with blood (a staff
         with curling ribbons) &

EMACIATED is Blazing Lady
        (ever by his side) in divers forms : and thin
            blueblack (furious
countenance) holding a sword
          bow & arrow : an enemy's
head

               FIERCE : wrathful
there is a man of dwarfish shape
  and the daughters of Evil
      She-who-Slays She-who-Rages
        (She-who-Saves)
  and the Raven-faced
    clacking his beak (raging
        at his enemies)

          & the triple world shakes : trembles
          fearful of his feet

                  GREEN too
is the demoness (with bloody matted hair)
    & Frog (defilement is : addiction
        the three poisons born of desire)
demon darkness who destroys the world (&
Lion-faced : power of flesheating demons

HE is

    surrounded by gatekeepers (naked
      women) dancing swiftly : darting
        like fish
a hundred living corpses (a thousand
    black men) a hundred thousand
    flesheating demons : ten thousand demonesses
      (seventyfive glorious protectors)

             INDEED
I say to you
        you are the protector : guarding
    this land (in accordance with the Law)
      this auspicious eon
        of Those Who Have Come
(& the time has come) to ply your power
    destroy the five impurities

          (be not indifferent): &
          come

JABBERING demons were under the Tree
    (in the last life of the Lord)
    & you were the chief of the army of heroes
      wreaked havoc upon them
        (with flowery arrows)

    so I invite you to this place
      that I may pass beyond corruption

(KEENING birds
    above you : with followers about you)
      I pray to you before the hosts of your servants
with devotion I invite you : with offerings beseech you

            come

    LIONS support your throne (& press
  upon the gods) : remember your promise of the past
humbly I bow before you
        (for it is you who guard the teachings)

MARKED by Great Bliss : and sealed in nonduality
  you are initiated with the flask of five nectars
      by the five families (highest sons of wisdom)
    to gain dominion
      over all powers

Offerings

NOW I stretch forth to you the perfumed waters
    (the female lineage) the blood
      the ocean of great red blood
        which cuts the root of the world
    (the male lineage) the semen
      the conch-white semen
        to wash your face & feet

    OFFERING flowers (untouched by frost)
  fumes of burning incense : lamps
      scented water
        food (created by my mind
    to have all the qualities you desire)
      that you may rejoice in them

PAPER of ignoble effigy : red ink cast upon it
food for you
(damming up a lake of blood
piling up a mountain of flesh & bone)
to be your offering
killing it with the magic substances
(of meditation : mantra : gesture)

QUICK : and eat my offerings
eight intoxicants : five nectars
food for you
offerings of meat & drink (washed with *OM*
kindled with *ĀH* : increased with *HŪM*)
& melted into nectar with my *HOH*!

RED: hot (my navel flames
with the fire of knowledge
with Blazing Lady)
to awaken Heruka within my head
& trickle down . . .

and with the portions of joy where they meet
I fill myself to the sky

(& offer it to you)

SUMMON with *JAH* the four mandalas (wherein
with *HŪM* I bind the noose of the four initiations) with *BAM*
fasten myself upon the tantric path

with *HOH* attain the Diamond Stage

OM VAJRAKĀYĀYÁ AVAPĀŚĀYA MAHĀKĀLA HŪM HŪM PHAT!

TAKING my beads : reciting
(clearly : distinctly) making firm my gesture
& face your offerings (are you) : confess

for I have not been cured of my sins
& I make sacrifice to your mind
in expiation : and repent
my failings

Praise

UNCONSCIOUS they fell
the haughty ones
hard to tame
for you tamed them
(with a host of Protectors) spreading
to the ends of the earth (with the power
of all the Buddhas)
you tamed them
& they awoke from their madness
became your slaves

VOICING the Middle Way
forbidding wrong belief : you
blast the Self (& speak your mantra) to delight
with sixty sweetnesses of speech

WHATEVER event
is pure : you see (in an instant) with all your thoughts
& know it is
the only realm of Buddhahood (yet
one taste with all events)

X & not-x (miracle manifest : actionless action) everywhere
opposites reconciled
nirvanaless nirvana worldless
world & pathless path

(reverence & praise
to the inconceivable)

YOU answer with benefit
when I plan harm : when I have contempt
for my Lord you have forgiveness (my praise
is a crown : I am a thorn) & the time has come
to save me (be not indifferent to me)

Prayer

ZEALOUS in your promise : prepare your deeds
for the ocean of your servants
(I exhort you) act
as you vowed when the white gods praised you
(when the white gods spread like a cloak
over the assemblies of the Law)

ALL the flesheating demons
follow behind you : the eight classes of demons
make thunder (whistling through their teeth)
& the hosts of your armies
pervade the earth & sky : frightening
their enemies (disguising
themselves) everywhere (with magic)

BLAST the maledictions of my enemies : trample upon
the curses of the earth (& press
upon the curses of the water) burn the curses
of fire (turn about the curses of the wind)
avert the black makers of malediction
make them into yourself

CLEAR at last : I see the hindering demons
are the same as nectar (all that appears
is your body) & all that is heard
is your speech : and all that I think
is the sport of your wisdom (& everything
is diamond song & dance)

DONE all reverence : all praise : all hymns
(by all the Buddhas) & I ask of you
the energy of faith
(of all the beings of all the world) the power
to perform all rituals

EVEN from today (until I gain
enlightenment) may my sacrificial offerings
protect me : may the Protector & all his retinue
dissolve into me : and into

all beings

3. A CHARM AGAINST SNAKES

The magical use of the sacred power of the word is as old as any aspect of Buddhism: the use of protective spells is found throughout the tradition and played an important practical part in the religion from the very beginning. Indeed, there was early made a collection of such spells from the canonical writings, grouped under the rubric of *paritta*, or "protection"; in Ceylon today, these *pirit* rituals are still performed when building a new house, or when there is sickness or death.

The following brief passage is taken from the code of Buddhist monastic law, and is without doubt one of the earliest written examples of Buddhist magic. We may note that from the outset the employment of magic was part of an essentially meditational process, as here, where the spell is presented as given life and power by the contemplative construction of a shield of love.

Cullavagga [*Small group*], gen. ed. Bhikkhu J. Kashyap (Bihar: Pali Publication Board, 1956), khandhaka 5 (Khuddakavatthu-khandhaka), section 3 (Ahirājaparitta), pp. 198–99.

Now at one time a certain monk was bitten by a snake and died. And they told the Blessed One what had happened, and he said:
This monk did not have love in his heart for the four royal families of snake: for had he permeated the snake with love he would not have died, though the snake bit him . . .

Monks, I allow you to permeate snakes with love, and to make a magic spell to guard and protect yourselves. And this is how it should be done . . .

> my love to the footless
> my love to the twofooted
> my love to the fourfooted
> my love to the manyfooted
>
> let the footless not harm me
> let the twofooted not harm me
> let the fourfooted not harm me
> let the manyfooted not harm me
>
> all beasts all creatures
> all beings every one
> let all see good things
> let no evil come
>
> infinite is the Buddha
> infinite is the Law
> infinite is the Community
>
> finite are creeping things
> snakes scorpions centipedes
> spiders lizards rats
>
> I have made a protection
> I have made a magic spell
> so let the creatures depart . . .

4. DO MAGIC SPELLS REALLY WORK?

The Questions of King Milinda seems to have been composed in northern India, perhaps around the turn of our millennium or within a few centuries thereafter. There is reason to believe that it was first written in a northern Indian dialect, and later translated into Pali, a language that had by that time achieved a canonical status. But the text practically disappeared from its place of origin: its primary influence was in Ceylon, and thence it extended to the countries of Southeast Asia. It became a standard handbook of Buddhist philosophy, giving authoritative answers to all the doctrinal doubts of its putative interlocutor.

King Milinda was in fact a real person, a Greek monarch named Menandros who ruled over the state of Bactria in northwestern India during the second century B.C., an inheritor of a small piece of the vast empire conquered by Alexander the Great. It is doubtful that the conversations recorded in this book ever took place: probably the memory and name of a Greek king interested in philosophy and indigenous religion (after all, Alexander had been a pupil of Aristotle) became the nucleus for the collection of debates on official Buddhist doctrine.

The defense of magic that follows is typical of these dialogues: the doubts of the rationalist king are laid to rest by the unanswerable arguments of the wise monk Nāgasena. What is even more important, however, is the establishment of the recitation of spells as fully orthodox, and even as a necessary part of medical and religious practice.

Milinda-pañha [*The questions of King Milinda*], ed. V. Trenckner (London: Williams and Norgate, 1880), pp. 150–54.

"Venerable one, the Blessed Buddha has said that neither in the sky, nor in the midst of the sea, nor in a cleft of the mountain can one find a place to escape the snare of death; but the Blessed One has also taught us magic spells in his scriptures.

"Now if there is neither palace nor hut nor cave nor cavern wherein one can escape from death, then these magic spells are useless; and if one can escape from death with a magic spell, then the saying is wrong. This question that I put to you has teeth at both ends, knottier even than a knot, and it is up to you to resolve it for me."

"Great King, the Blessed One has said that saying, and he has taught us magic spells; but they are for those who have a portion of life remaining, who are in the prime of life, who are free of evil karma: there is neither ritual nor means to prolong the life of one whose life is exhausted.

"It is like a dead tree, withered and dry and sapless, whose life has ceased, from which life has departed: you could pour a thousand pots of water upon it, yet it will not grow green nor put forth shoots. Even so there is neither ritual nor means, neither medicine nor magic spell to prolong the life of one whose life is exhausted.

"All the herbs and medicines in the world are useless for him; but magic spells can guard and protect those who have a portion of life remaining, who are in the prime of life, who are free of evil karma: and it is for that reason the Blessed One has taught us magic spells.

"It is like a farmer who keeps the water from his grain when it is ripe and dead at harvest time, but makes it grow with water when the crop is young and dark and full of life. Even so we put aside both medicine and magic spells for one whose life is exhausted, but recite our magic spells for those who have a portion of life remaining, who are in the prime of life, who are free of evil karma: for they can profit by the magic spell."

"But, venerable one, if he whose life is exhausted dies, and he who has a portion of life remaining lives, then the magic spell is equally ineffective."

"Great King, have you ever seen a disease turned back with medicines?"

"Indeed, venerable one, I have seen it many hundreds of times."

"Then it is just as wrong to say that magic spells are ineffective."

"But, venerable one, the doctors applied medicines, potions and ointments, and it was these that turned back the disease."

"And likewise the sick man hears the sound of the magic spells recited: his tongue is dry, his heart sinks, his throat is hoarse, but the recitation allays all his disease, and all his ills depart.

"Great King, have you ever seen a man bitten by a snake, and the poison removed by a mantra, the poison oozing out and purged above and below?"

"Indeed, venerable one, that is common in the world even today."

"Then it is wrong to say that magic spells are ineffective. For when a man recites a magic spell, the snake that threatens him does not strike, and the upraised sticks of thieves are lowered; the charging elephant is calmed, and the surging mass of blazing fire is put out. The deadly poison becomes his food, the waiting assassin becomes his slave, and the yawning pit cannot hold him.

"Great King, have you ever heard of the peacock who recited a magic spell, so that for seven hundred years the hunter could not catch him in his net, and then caught him on the very day he did not recite the magic spell?"

"Indeed, venerable one, I have heard of it, for the story is known throughout the world."

"Then it is wrong to say that magic spells are ineffective. And have you ever heard of the demigod who put his wife in a box to guard her, and swallowed the box, and carried her around in his belly; and a magic spirit went in through his mouth and made love to her; and when the demigod found out he vomited up the box, and opened it, and the magic spirit escaped from him when he opened the box?"

"Indeed, venerable one, I have heard of it, for that story too is known throughout the world."

"Well, did not the spirit escape capture by the power of a magic spell?"

"Yes, that is so."

"Then there must be strength in magic spells. And have you ever heard of the other magic spirit, who got into the harem of the King of Benares and did wicked things with the queen; and when he was captured recited a mantra, and instantly became invisible?"

"Indeed, venerable one, I have heard of that also."

"Well, did not the spirit escape capture by the power of a magic spell?"

"Yes, that is so."

"Then there must be strength in magic spells."

"But venerable one, do magic spells thus protect everyone?"

"They protect some people, Great King, but not others."

"Then magic spells are not always effective."

"Great King, does food protect the lives of everyone?"

"It protects the lives of some people, venerable one, but not of others."

"And why is that?"

"Well, some people eat too much food and die of cholera."

"Then food does not always protect life?"

"There are two reasons, venerable one, why food can destroy life: through overeating, and through a weak digestion. And even life-giving food can destroy life through witchcraft."

"Even so, Great King, magic spells protect some people and not others. And there are three reasons why a magic spell does not work: through evil karma, through sin, and through lack of faith. Magic spells are a protection for living creatures, but lose their power through what creatures do themselves.

"It is like a mother who lovingly nourishes the child in her womb and gives him birth with care; and when he is born she cleans away his filth and mucus and anoints him with the finest ointments. And should anyone scold him or hit him, then her heart trembles, and she drags that man before the magistrate.

"But if her son is naughty and stays out late, then she herself spanks him, or hits him with a stick; and does his mother then get seized and dragged before the magistrate?"

"No, venerable one."

"And why is that?"

"Because the child himself was in the wrong."

"And even so, Great King, magic spells are a protection for living creatures, but are made barren through the wickedness of creatures themselves."

"Very good, venerable one. The question is answered, the thicket is cleared, the dark is made light, the net of falsehood is disentangled—and by you, best of teachers!"

5. RED COPPER BEAK

While magic has been part of Buddhism from the very beginning, it was not until relatively late that there began the full-scale production of texts whose sole purpose was to promulgate a powerful spell. Yet these texts have been perhaps the single most influential genre of Buddhist literature. When we dig in the sands of central Asia, and uncover the great oasis cities of the ancient caravan routes by which Buddhism traveled to all of Asia, we find the trail littered with the small manuscripts that contain these magic charms. Indeed, an entire Buddhist sect—the Dharmaguptakas—sprang up in northwestern India and central Asia to serve as professional reciters of these texts, and protect the caravans that passed through the demon-filled wilderness.

Each Buddhist land made its own contribution to the burgeoning corpus of magic spells, and the texts passed down to our own day. The next selection comes from Tibet, and follows what came to be the standard format for the preaching of protective charms: it could be matched by similar texts from China, Japan, or Southeast Asia.

'Phags-pa zangs-kyi mchu dmar-pos gdug-pa'i phyogs thams-cad gnon-par byed-pa zhes bya-ba'i gzungs [*The mantra of Red Copper Beak*], ed. L. A. Waddell, Indian Antiquary *43 (1914), pp. 94–95.*

Thus have I heard: at one time the Blessed One dwelt in the grove of
    reeds, where the banks of the Ganges are covered with a blanket of
        sweet lotuses, with an immeasurable great retinue, with
    a great community of monks
                                And they asked him for
  the evocation of Red Copper Beak, that they might have power over
    fierce rituals, that they might be victorious over the leprosy
        sent by the serpent-kings

for this mantra stops the fall of the rough boiling waves of
        quicksilver: it halts the spread of the eight plagues, the fierce
    harm, the seizing, the turning, the stealing of flesh, the sucking of
        blood, the robbing of warmth

        then cast the magic iron nail, to gather the paralysis
    from the four limits to the earth; take it to the cemetery and cast
  back the disease upon the eight great serpent-kings; cast your lines
    into the sky and cleanse the stupefying wounds of earth.

  For Red Copper Beak has the head of an eagle, a body of copper; he
    feeds overhead; nine hundred and ninety fathoms long is his copper
  beak.

  And he eats the four families of serpent-king for his food; he drinks
      their pus and blood; he binds them with his wrathful red eyes;
        he gnaws their bloody marrow; he crunches their bones.

Swiftly he sends putrefying disease upon them; he tramples the
    minds of the triple world; he spreads the poison of the fearful
    plague among them. He crumbles to powder the hells below; he
  pierces the highest world above. He breaks open the hoard of the six
    thousand plagues; he lays low the thousand families of serpent
        kings   This is the terrifying appearance he has

        and Thunderbolt-in-Hand said to the Blessed One, the
  ascetic: Well-gone One, I pray you grasp with compassion the beings
        in the six destinies; free them of the disease of their passion;
    free them from the disease of their lust. Kill the fire of their
  hatred; smash the rock of their pride; brighten the darkness of their
delusion. Liberate them from the pestilence of harm: liberate
    them from the eighty-four thousand demon evils.

    And the Buddha looked about him with compassion, and he knew
what must be done.

Thunderbolt-in-Hand, they are all injured
in body, tormented with passion and with disease; they have
transgressed their vows and broken their oaths; they are smitten
with disease and bound with the thread of desire. Say to them all:
come! come swiftly here! I shall teach them

and Thunderbolt-in-Hand drew near to the eight classes of
gods and demons:

Hear the words of the Conqueror! Look upon the body of the Conqueror!
You are summoned to come swiftly

and Thunderbolt-in-Hand
said to Vasuta, the serpent-king, the brahman:

Do you not know who I am?

I do not know, nor do I care, for I shall not hear your words, nor
look upon you. For I am strong, and I have power, and strong is my
retinue as well.

And Thunderbolt-in-Hand said to him:

What power do you have?

Let me but breathe upon you, and you shall be rooted to the spot.

And Thunderbolt-in-Hand stood straight before him, and Vasuta, the
serpent-king, breathed upon him; and Thunderbolt-in-Hand felt it
whistle about him   so he considered what to do,
and he said:

Indeed you possess great power and are a king: how then shall I
speak to you?

I am the king of serpent-kings, the precious brahman named Vasuta,
and all poison belongs to me   and this is the mantra
of Red Copper Beak, which alone can defeat me
OM
HRŪM HRĪ HRŪḤ ĀḤ TATHĀGATĀ NĀGAHṚDAYA
TATHĀGATA NAMAḤ DHAMAYĀ
TATHĀGATE RĀJAŚRĪLHANANA BUDYA
BUDYA RĀJA ĪŚALA PARI PARILIRA NĀGAHU
YARBADA POVAMDHA SVĀHĀ GUHA RĀJALA SVĀHĀ HRŪM HRĪ

and Thunderbolt-in-Hand recited this sharp sword of the
noble Red Copper Beak; and he subjugated the six families of Vasuta,
and he smashed them all into atoms

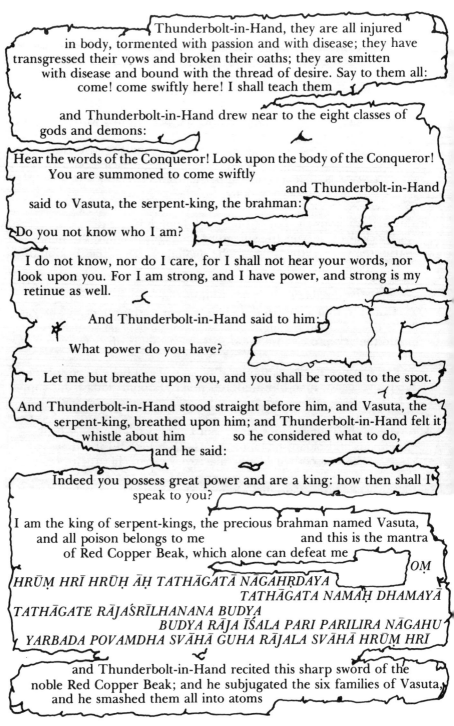

6. A SPELL BOOK

Magic is used throughout the Buddhist world and is an integral part of the complex contemplative whole. Spells such as the one given in the preceding text can be turned to any end, if the practitioner has the meditative and visionary strength to control their power: they can be used to summon and destroy, to protect and nourish, even to coerce divinity itself; and they are the final resource in all the contingencies of daily life, from the most sublime to the most prosaic and practical.

The Buddhist tradition has produced any number of handbooks for the professional practitioner of magic, as well as collections of home recipes for those who lack the meditative training to employ the more potent spells. The following selection—from an Indian text dating possibly from the tenth century A.D.—provides a sampling of the far-reaching uses to which the Buddhists apply their magical tradition.

'Phags-ma sgrol-ma ku-ru-ku-lle'i rtog-pa [Ārya-tārā-kurukullā-kalpa], [*The rituals of the goddess Kurukullā*], in the Peking Bka'-'gyur *Rgyud* CA 30b–45a (Tokyo: Suzuki Research Foundation, 1958), 3, no. 76.

An amulet, of subjugation. Draw a triangle upon a cloth stained with menstrual blood, & therein write the name of the person to be subjugated, the words which impel the deity, & your own name:

MAY SUCH-AND-SUCH A PERSON COME UNDER
THE POWER OF ——!

& add to this the basic mantra of the goddess Kurukulla:

OM KURUKULLE HRĪH HŪM SVĀHĀ!

This amulet should be drawn with colors of liquid lacquer, with the blood of the left-hand ring finger, with saffron or with camphor:

> for with this magical amulet
> & the burnt offering
> you summon & consort with
> all those famed as queens
> dwelling on the ways
> of the triple world:
> you subjugate with your mind
> you subjugate all beings with love
> you impress on them the certainty
> of enlightenment as Buddhas
> this is a ritual of subjugation

To scare away snakes. On the lower step of the threshold, inscribe a triangle, & another triangle upon that, to form a six-pointed star: starting from the east, the wise man writes the six seeds of the mantra at the six corners, with the seeds of the Law in the midst thereof, & the syllable *PHUḤ* between them:

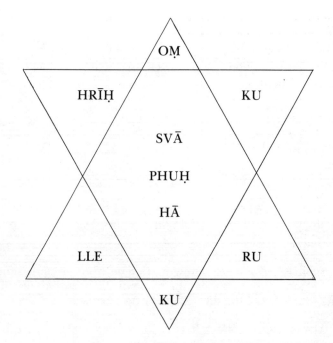

For a woman to subjugate her husband. On white birchbark, or on a cloth stained with menstrual blood, draw a seven-petalled lotus & write the seven syllables *OṂ KU RU KU LLE SVĀ HĀ* on the seven petals; & in the center of the lotus, between two *HRĪḤ*s, write the name of the person to be subjugated; then roll it up into a little ball and fasten it upon the upper arm:

> & the husband becomes the woman's slave
> even a king becomes her servant
> but only a woman who is pure & virtuous
> may apply this mantra

An amulet of protection. Draw a four-petalled lotus flower on a piece of birchbark: on the eastern petal draw an arrow, on the southern petal a bow, on the western petal a hand in the fearless gesture, & on the northern petal a lotus flower. Draw a moon in the center of the four petals & write thereon the name of the person to be protected, surrounded by the seven seeds *OM*

KU RU KU LLE SVĀ HĀ. Draw a garland of lotus flowers all around the amulet and fasten it upon the upper arm; & whether you be a child or an old man or a youth, this magical amulet will protect you.

To gain wealth & power. Make a four-petaled lotus as above & draw a bow in its center; in the middle of the bow, draw the shoot of a lotus flower, having the appearance of precious gems; & in the middle of the heart of the lotus shoot, write the syllable *JRŪ* surrounded by the seven syllables; & all this should be clearly drawn with fine grains of natural gold. Encircle the amulet with a garland of lotus flowers; bathe it from a full flask adorned with the five gems; & make offerings before it for eight or twelve days, reciting the basic mantra one hundred and eight times:

OM KURUKULLE HRĪḤ HŪM SVĀHĀ!

Then place the amulet securely upon the top of your dwelling place, or roll it up into a little ball and fasten it upon the upper arm; & within a year you will rival the god of wealth in your riches & your power.

Cowrie shell practices. If on a Tuesday you find a cowrie shell lying on its back, place it in the palm of your hand & recite the basic mantra eight hundred thousand times: then if you play at dice you will be victorious over your opponents.

Take a cowrie shell, bathe it, & make offerings before it for eight or twelve days, reciting the basic mantra one hundred and eight times; then wrap it up in silk & bind it on your upper arm: thereby you will become a great lord of wealth.

Take that same cowrie shell & hide it inside a vessel: every day you will find therein a weight of gold.

To find treasure. Recite the mantra fifty times & place your feet upon the ground: wherever your feet begin to tremble, you know that there is buried treasure. If the upper part of your foot trembles, you are getting near; if the sole of your foot trembles, you are moving away from it. It is just as clear as if you were told where the treasure is, for he who holds this mantra sees beneath the earth as if it were day.

To walk on water. Take the milk of a black bitch & mix it with fresh butter; spread it gradually upon your boots & you will be able to walk upon the water.

To get rid of grey hair. After every meal, snuff up water through your nose while you recite the mantra & you will never have prematurely grey hair.

To cure frigidity. Grind some conqueror-root together with camphor-water & the fruit of the gold-tree; churn it with your finger & anoint your body therewith. Then, if the woman does not flow during intercourse & wishes to go disrespectfully from her lord, rub her with some of the mixture, secretly, during the preliminary embraces, & light a lamp; then she will be bound there & made to flow; quickly her desire for men will be aroused & you will long dwell within her.

7. THE MEDITATOR BECOMES THE GOD

The Buddhist magical and visionary tradition culminated in the contemplative technique known as Tantra. Here the process of deliberate visualization is fundamental, for it is the means whereby the meditator cleanses himself, guards himself from hindrance, and sets forth to create a new and symbolically potent reality. His vision transforms the world into a divine mansion filled with gods, and within this flashing and shining contemplative reality he magically manipulates the powerful sexual symbols of his transformation. He takes on the body, the speech, and the mind of the deity, that he may plunge at last into the omnipotent emptiness of the deity's wisdom: he returns to the sources of all human experience and emerges master of all realities, including the one we call our own.

Thus the symbols of his meditation are not abstract concepts, but magical keys to the unlocking of divine immanence; for it is the coercive power of the compelling vision and the magic word that combine to summon the god within the meditator. He recreates himself from emptiness to be the deity: he becomes the god and receives the divine initiation and offerings; and in his visionary body he magically controls the power and enlightenment of the god. The deity is the manifestation of Buddhahood within the world: the practitioner gains his freedom in the world by becoming the god, by controlling the Buddhahood that appears in his divine and ecstatic vision.

Pad-ma dkar-po, Snyan-rgyud yid-bzhin nor-bu'i bskyed-pa'i rim-pa rgyas-pa 'dod-pa'i re-skong zhes bya-ba [*The process of generation of the wishing gem of the ear-whispered teachings*], *(Dalhousie: Phun-tshogs chos-'khor gling, n.d.), folios 1–19.*

Preliminary Meditations

Going for refuge. I arise from my bed & wash myself: I sit with my face to the south. And I am in a cemetery, surrounded by dancing skeletons & a host of evil spirits, for they are the passions of the triple world.

And I fix my heart onepointedly upon my hope of benefit & joy for all beings:

I take refuge in the best of men, and in the peaceful Law, and in the highest of hosts; I take refuge in my master, and in my patron deity; I take refuge in my innate mind, where emptiness & compassion are one . . .

And I awaken myself to enlightenment, holy & incomparable: I firmly grasp the disciplines of virtue and take my vow to save all beings: for I shall save the unsaved, and I shall encourage the weary, and I shall lead all beings to nirvana . . .

The cleansing of sin. And the syllable *PAM* appears on the top of my head, & transforms into a white eight-petalled lotus; in the center of the lotus is the syllable *A*, which transforms into the disc of a moon; above the moon is the syllable *HŪM*, which transforms into a white five-pointed vajra marked in the center with *HŪM*.

And light radiates forth from that syllable *HŪM*: and it makes offerings to the Noble Ones & serves the aims of all beings; and it is gathered back, & it dissolves into the syllable.

And the *HŪM* transforms into the Blessed Diamond Being: his body is colored white; he has one head & two arms; he holds a vajra & a bell, and with these he embraces the Mother.

And the Mother is Diamond Pride: she is colored white; she holds a chopper & a skull-bowl, and with these she embraces the Father.

And both are adorned with ornaments of bones & jewels, and they sit with their legs crossed.

On their forehead is *OM*, on their neck is *ĀH*, on their heart is *HŪM*: and light radiates forth from the *HŪM*, and invites all the Buddhas & bodhisattvas, all in the form of Diamond Being, Father & Mother. *JAH HŪM BAM HOH!*

O Blessed One, I beseech you make clean & pure the whole host of my filth: the sins, the obscurations, the faults, the downfalls of myself & the infinite host of all beings:

OM Diamond Being: guard my vows! Diamond Being: let them be firm! Be steadfast for me, be satisfied, be favorable, be nourished for me! Grant me all the magical attainments! Indicator of all my deeds, make glorious my mind *HŪM! HA HA HA HA HOH!* Blessed One, diamond of all Those Who Have Come, do not forsake me: make me diamond! Great being of the vow *ĀH!*

O Lord, through the darkness of my ignorance I have transgressed & disgraced my vows; may the lord master be a refuge for me! I go for refuge to my lord, the great bearer of the diamond, the chief of all beings, whose essence is compassion.

I confess & repent all my transgressions of my vows, major & minor, by body or speech or mind. I beseech you make clean & pure the whole host of my filth: my sins, my obscurations, my faults, my downfalls.

And when I have thus prayed to him, Diamond Being Father & Mother melt into light: & I absorb them into myself, that I may be cleansed of all my sins.

The prayer to the masters. Great bearer of the diamond & my demon mother; & all your sons, my masters, the crest gems of the world; to them I pray: empower me ... & my gracious master; to him I pray: empower me!

For I know that the gods are but your sport, & I will seek no other refuge than you, my honored masters.

And I beseech you awaken (freely : spontaneously) the power of your compassion, to lead all beings from this fearful world.

And may my body be warmed in your initiation, varnished with the gold of freedom, & become the body of a Buddha, the most precious of gems.

The four immeasurable contemplations. ŚRĪ-HERUKA! And I myself become the Blessed Cakrasamvara, Father & Mother, and from my mouth there issues forth:

A Ā I Ī U Ū R R̄ L L̄ A AI O AU AM AH KA KHA GA GHA ṄA CA CHA JA JHA ÑA ṬA ṬHA ḌA ḌHA ṆA TA THA DA DHA NA PA PHA BA BHA MA YA RA LA VA ŚA ṢA SA HA KṢA HŪM HŪM PHAṬ PHAṬ!

And from these syllables there radiates an immeasurable brilliance of white & red light: and it serves the aims of all beings, and it is gathered back & fills all the places of my body.

And I think: O that all beings might find such bliss; & I dwell in a state of love.

And I think: O that all beings might be free of suffering; & I dwell in a state of compassion.

And I think: O that all beings might always have such bliss; & I dwell in a state of sympathetic joy.

And I think: O that all beings might abide on the path of purity; & I dwell in a state of equanimity.

The worship of the masters. The syllable *A* appears in my heart & transforms into a moon; and above the moon is the syllable *HŪM.*

And light radiates forth from that syllable *HŪM*: and the light is the light of the five knowledges, which invites the lineage of my masters to sit above my head, in the upper part of the mandala of the Blessed Cakrasamvara. And I pay homage to them: *NAMAḤ TE HŪM! NAMAḤ ME HŪM! NAMO NAMAḤ HŪM!*

And for the sake of all beings I offer up to them my own body; and thus I cast aside all clinging to I & mine.

And from my own heart there emanate goddesses of offerings for them: *OM ĀḤ* diamond lady of the lute *HŪM HŪM PHAṬ! OM ĀḤ* diamond lady of the flute *HŪM HŪM PHAṬ! OM ĀḤ* diamond lady of the tambourine *HŪM HŪM PHAṬ! OM ĀḤ* diamond lady of the drum *HŪM HŪM PHAṬ!*

OM ĀḤ diamond lady of laughter *HŪM HŪM PHAṬ! OM ĀḤ* diamond lady of sensuality *HŪM HŪM PHAṬ! OM ĀḤ* diamond lady of song *HŪM HŪM PHAṬ! OM ĀḤ* diamond lady of dance *HŪM HŪM PHAṬ!*

OM ĀḤ diamond lady of flowers *HŪM HŪM PHAṬ! OM ĀḤ* diamond lady of incense *HŪM HŪM PHAṬ! OM ĀḤ* diamond lady of lamps *HŪM HŪM PHAṬ! OM ĀḤ* diamond lady of perfume *HŪM HŪM PHAṬ!*

OM ĀḤ diamond lady of form *HŪM HŪM PHAṬ! OM ĀḤ* diamond lady of taste *HŪM HŪM PHAṬ! OM ĀḤ* diamond lady of touch *HŪM HŪM PHAṬ! OM ĀḤ* diamond lady of the realm of reality *HŪM HŪM PHAṬ!*

And my masters enter into inseparable union with the goddesses of offerings, & they are satiated with spontaneous knowledge.

And my master is the Blessed Cakrasamvara himself, and thus I offer him my praises & my prayers:

My master: holding the diamond, by your grace (freely : spontaneously) you bestow great bliss; & I bow to the feet of your gem-like body.

Blessed One, Lord: blazing like the fire which consumes the world, the diadem of your matted hair is tied into a royal crown; your face is fierce & raging; your teeth flash.

I bow to the great body, the majestic body, thousand-armed; holding axe & noose, spear & skull-staff; dressed in terrifying tigerskin; putting an end to hindering demons.

And my Blessed Lady the noble Diamond Sow, invincible in battle in all the triple world, with her great thunderbolt smashing the terror of demons.

Seated on her diamond throne, victorious over the gods: Diamond Sow of wrathful form, my lady of fierce pride.

Victorious over the demonesses, defeating the terrors of Evil, drying them up.

And I bow to her, the goddess of my desires: for she is the diamond demoness & empress of demons, for she is the five knowledges & the three bodies.

Homage to her, refuge of beings; homage & praise to her, for she cuts the bonds of delusion & enters into the deeds of the world.

I confess all my sins & faults before you; I take my vows, cutting off the past; I rejoice in all virtue. I pray you turn the wheel of the Law, that all beings may be led to enlightenment; I beseech you not to pass into nirvana until this world is emptied out. And until I myself am enlightened, I take refuge in the divine hosts of my righteous masters; I awaken my mind for the sake of beings; I cleave to this holy teaching of the great path. And for the sake of all beings, may I attain to Buddhahood!

The empowerment of the disciple. And I myself am the Blessed One, the Lord Cakrasamvara: and my form is Shining One, and my feelings are Diamond Sun, and my ideas are Lotus Lord of Dance, and my motives are Diamond King, and my perceptions are Unmoving One, and my knowledge is Glorious Heruka.

And the element of earth is She-who-casts-down, and the element of water is She-who-slays, and the element of fire is She-who-summons, and the element of air is Goddess-of-dance, and the element of space is She-with-a-lotus-net, and the element of knowledge is the Lady of the Realm of Reality.

And my eyes are Diamond-of-Delusion, and my ears are Diamond-of-Hatred, and my nose is Diamond-of-Envy, and my tongue is Diamond-of-Lust, and my body is Diamond-of-Spite, and my mind is Diamond-of-God.

The protective circle. And from the mouth of my head in the front come the syllables of the mantra OM SUMBHANI SUMBHA HUM HŪM PHAṬ, as large as Mount Meru, surrounded as by a fence with blazing red-black light; and upon them in the east is the Raven-faced Lady.

And from the mouth of my head on the left come the syllables of the mantra OM GRHNA GRHNA HUM HŪM PHAṬ, as large as Mount Meru, surrounded as by a fence with blazing red-black light; and upon them in the north is the Owl-faced Lady.

And from the mouth of my head in the rear come the syllables of the mantra OM GRHNAPAYA GRHNAPAYA HUM HŪM PHAṬ, as large as Mount Meru, surrounded as by a fence with blazing red-black light; and upon them in the west is the Dog-faced Lady.

And from the mouth of my head on the right come the syllables of the mantra *OM ĀNAYA HOḤ BHAGAVAN VAJRA HUM HŪM PHAṬ*, as large as Mount Meru, surrounded as by a fence with blazing red-black light; and upon them in the south is the Sow-faced Lady.

And from the mouth of my head in the front come the syllables of the mantra *OM SUMBHANI SUMBHA HUM HŪM PHAṬ*, as large as Mount Meru, surrounded as by a fence with blazing red-black light; and upon them in the southeast corner of fire is the Lady Steadfast, the Slayer of Death.

And from the mouth of my head on the left come the syllables of the mantra *OM GṚHNA GRHNA HUM HŪM PHAṬ*, as large as Mount Meru, surrounded as by a fence with blazing red-black light; and upon them in the southwest corner of demons is the Lady Messenger, the Slayer of Death.

And from the mouth of my head in the rear come the syllables of the mantra *OM GṚHNAPAYA GṚHNAPAYA HUM HŪM PHAṬ*, as large as Mount Meru, surrounded as by a fence with blazing red-black light; and upon them in the northwest corner of wind is the Lady Fang, the Slayer of Death.

And from the mouth of my head on the right come the syllables of the mantra *OM ĀNAYA HOḤ BHAGAVAN VAJRA HUM HŪM PHAṬ*, as large as Mount Meru, surrounded as by a fence with blazing red-black light; and upon them in the northeast corner of power is the Lady Conqueror, the Slayer of Death.

And all these fierce goddesses have four hands; and they hold in their upper hands an iron hook & a noose; and they hold in their lower hands a diamond hammer & a magic dagger; and their wrathful bodies face outwards in the midst of their blazing red-black fire, pervading as far as the world of the gods.

And that great fence of light transforms itself, and from the mantra *OM diamond earth, diamond receptacle HŪM VAM HŪM!* there appears a diamond ground.

And from the mantra *OM diamond rampart HŪM PAM HŪM!* there appears a diamond fence.

And from the mantra *OM diamond enclosure HŪM YAM HŪM!* there appears a diamond pavilion.

And from the mantra *OM diamond canopy HŪM KHAM HŪM!* there appears a diamond awning.

And from the mantra *OM diamond net of arrows TRAM SAM TRAM!* there appears a diamond net of arrows.

And from the mantra *OM diamond blazing fire HŪM HŪM HŪM!* there appears a blazing diamond fence of fire all about the outside.

Then there appear terrifying pits beneath the feet of the fierce goddesses, and I incite the goddesses, saying:

OM! GHA GHA slay! slay all evil! PHAṬ! stab! stab all sin! PHAṬ! HŪM HŪM HŪM! Bearer of the diamond: command all hindering demons; stab with the diamond of your body & speech & mind! *HŪM PHAṬ!*

And the goddesses seize all the hindering demons & pierce them with their iron hooks & bind them with their nooses; and they cast them down into the pits, & seal them in with their magic daggers.

And I say: *OM diamond hammer, magic dagger, crush! HŪM PHAT!* And the goddesses strike the heads of their magic daggers with their diamond hammers, and the hindering demons are slain & liberated from their vicious natures, & intoxicated with an inexhaustible bliss.

And the goddesses dissolve into light & melt into the fence and the pavilion; and the fence and the pavilion gain thereby the power of the three bodies and the five knowledges.

The Body of the God

Emptiness. And on the top of my head is *HE*, on my neck is *RU*, on my heart is *KA*. And light radiates forth from these syllables: and it touches all beings & awakens in them their innate enlightenment & fixes them in the three gates of deliverance on the path.

For *HE* is the causelessness of all events, *RU* is the impermanence of all events, and *KA* is the abodelessness of all events. And I awaken compassion when I contemplate these things, for I think: It is because they are ignorant of these things that beings fall into the world; when I have become the Lord Heruka, may all beings become aware of them.

OM! Pure of essence are all events, pure of essence am I!

And I & the three syllables transform into *OM*, and above that into *ĀH*, and above that into *HŪM*. And light radiates forth from these syllables: and it makes the whole world of animate & inanimate objects melt into light; & all the light is gathered back & dissolves into the syllables.

And the *OM* dissolves upward into the *ĀH*, and the *ĀH* into the *HŪM*, and the *U*-vowel into the *HA,* and the *HA* into the head-stroke, and the head-stroke into the crescent, and the crescent into the dot; and the dot dissolves into Pure Sound. And from that Pure Sound comes the mantra *OM!* I am the very self whose essence is the diamond of the knowledge of emptiness!

And this mantra appears as the natural expression of the Pure Sound; and it grows fainter & fainter, until all my perceptions become calmed: & there I enter into meditation.

The palace for the god. And in this realm of peace, I suddenly recall my immeasurable contemplations: & instantaneously I erect the protective circle once again, to serve the aim of beings.

In the center thereof appears the syllable *E*, which transforms into a triangle, the Source of All Events, white on the outside & red on the inside. And within this are the syllables *YAM RAM VAM LAM*, which transform into the shapes & colors of the four elements: the black semicircular form of wind, the red triangular form of fire, the white circular form of water, & the yellow square form of earth, all piled one on top of the other.

And upon this foundation of the four elements there appears a green syllable *SUM*, which transforms into Mount Meru; and on the peak of the mountain appears the syllable *PAM*, which transforms into a lotus; and on the lotus is the syllable *HŪM*, which transforms into a crossed vajra with the syllable *BHRŪM* in its center.

And the *BHRŪM* transforms into the Buddha Shining One & his consort: and they melt into light & become a balconied palace of divers jewels, square, with four arched gates, complete with all the proper characteristics & surrounded by eight cemeteries.

Inside the palace, the four directions are four different colors. And in the center is the Circle of Great Bliss: an eight-petaled lotus, noble & jeweled, growing upwards on its stalk; its petals are red in the four directions; & in the intermediate directions its petals are yellow & black & green & blue. The lotus is surrounded by a garland of choppers; and in its center is a sun-throne; & cast down upon it is the demon Creator-of-Terror, black & four-armed & like a corpse, and the demoness Night-of-Time, alive but overthrown upon her back . . .

The creation of the god. Above the central throne are all the vowels, set out twice & going counterclockwise:

A Ā I Ī U Ū R̞ R̞̄ L̞ L̞̄ E AI O AU AM̞ AH̞ A Ā I Ī U Ū R̞ R̞̄ L̞ L̞̄ E AI O AU AM̞ AH̞!

and all the consonants, set out twice, & going clockwise:

KA KHA GA GHA ṄA CA CHA JA JHA ÑA TA ṬHA ḌA ḌHA ṆA TA THA DA DHA NA PA PHA BA BHA MA YA RA LA VA ŚA ṢA SA HA KṢA YA RA LA VA DA ḌHA! KA KHA GA GHA ṄA CA CHA JA JHA ÑA TA ṬHA ḌA ḌHA ṆA TA THA DA DHA NA PA PHA BA BHA MA YA RA LA VA ŚA ṢA SA HA KṢA YA RA LA VA ḌA ḌHA!

And these vowels & consonants transform themselves into a kissing sun & moon, a round orb which is half one & half the other; and in the middle thereof is a *HŪM* like quicksilver & an *A* like vermilion. And light radiates forth from these syllables: and it transforms the world of inanimate objects into a divine palace, & the world of animate objects into the host of deities of the maṇḍala of the Blessed Cakrasamvara; and it is gathered back again, & it dissolves into the syllables, and transforms them into a vajra marked with *HŪM* & a chopper marked with *A*.

And all those are mixed into one & transform into the Blessed Lord Cakrasamvara.

And my body is colored white; I have four heads & twelve arms; my right foot is stretched out, trampling upon the breast of the red Lady Night-of-Time; & my left foot is slightly bent, trampling upon the forehead of the blue Creator-of-Terror. My head in front is white, my head on the left is green, my head in the rear is red, & my head on the right is yellow, and each of my faces has three eyes.

I have matted & piled hair, marked with a jewel, a crossed vajra, & a crescent moon; on each of my heads is a diadem of five dried human skulls; & I have made a necklace of fifty dripping human heads. I am adorned with the six signs of ferocity: wheel & earrings & necklace & bracelets & girdle & ashes of the dead.

Terrifying, I flash my teeth; my lower garment is a tigerskin; & I appear to dance. My body is heroic & sensuous & terrifying; my speech is laughing & raging & reviling; my mind is compassionate & calm & wondrous.

In the first two of my twelve hands I hold a vajra & a bell, and with these I embrace the Mother; in the two hands below, I hold aloft the dripping skin of a freshly flayed elephant; in my third right hand is a skull-drum, in my fourth an axe, in my fifth a chopper, & in my sixth a trident; and in my third left hand is a skull-staff, in my fourth a skull-bowl filled with blood, in my fifth a diamond noose, & in my sixth the four-faced head of the god Brahma.

And upon my lap is the Mother; her body is colored red; she has one head & two hands; & her face has three eyes.

Her left hand holds a skull-bowl filled with entrails, & with this arm she embraces the Father; her right hand holds a vajra aloft to the sky, with a terrifying gesture; on her head is a diadem of five dried human skulls, & she has made a necklace of fifty human skulls; her hair hangs free, & she is adorned with the five signs of ferocity.

And the calves of her legs embrace the thighs of the Blessed One, & we both stand in the midst of the blazing fire of knowledge.

On a moon at the tops of the heads of both Father & Mother is *OM*; on a sun at our necks is *ĀH*; on a sun at our hearts is *HŪM*. And *SVĀ* is at the break of our waists; *ĀH* is on our sexual organs; and *HĀ* is between our thighs.

In the secret place of the Father appears the syllable *HŪM*, which transforms into a white vajra; on its tip appears the syllable *BAM*, which transforms into a red gem; & the hole is blocked by a yellow *PHAT*.

In the Mother's place of space appears the syllable *ĀH*, which transforms into a red lotus; in its center appears the syllable *OM*, which transforms into its white anthers; & the hole is blocked by a yellow *PHAT*.

And the Father & Mother enter into union, and the vajra is within the lotus; and by the sound of the bliss thereof, & by the light which radiates forth from our hearts, we invite all those whose accomplishment of deity is innate, & all those whom we have cleansed & transformed into the mandala of the Blessed Cakrasamvara.

And they all enter into union in the sky before me: they melt into Great Bliss & enter through my mouth; they descend my central channel; they pass through my vajra, and fall & mix into the lotus of the Mother.

And the Father & Mother dissolve into a ball of Bliss, which is as if in the form of quicksilver.

The creation of the mandala. Then all the Buddhas of the ten directions arouse this ball of Bliss by singing this song:

OM! Great Bliss: Diamond Being *JAH HŪM BAM HOH!* You are the deity: appear! *HOH!*

And instantaneously the ball of Bliss becomes the Blessed Lord Cakrasamvara.

And my body is colored blue as sapphire: I have four heads & twelve arms; my right foot is stretched out, trampling upon the breast of the red Lady Night-of-Time; & my left foot is slightly bent, trampling upon the forehead of the blue Creator-of-Terror . . .

In the secret place of the Father appears the syllable *HŪM*, which transforms into a blue vajra; on its tip appears the syllable *BAM*, which transforms into a red gem; & the hole is blocked by a yellow *PHAT*.

In the Mother's place of space appears the syllable *ĀH*, which transforms into a red lotus; in its center appears the syllable *OM*, which transforms into its blue anthers; & the hole is blocked by a yellow *PHAT*.

And the Father & Mother enter into union, and the vajra is within the lotus; and by the sound of the bliss thereof, & by the light which radiates forth from our hearts, we invite from the ten directions all Those Who Have Come.

And they enter me through the juncture of my eyebrows; they arrive in my heart & melt into lust; they descend my central channel; they pass through my vajra, and fall & mix into the lotus of the Mother.

And in the womb of the Mother they assume the roles of the deities who dwell in the mandala of the Blessed Cakrasamvara, and appear as all the deities thereof, as clearly as if their forms were visible to the eye.

And from the womb of the Mother there issues forth a divine palace to be their residence: & this dissolves into the palace for the god.

And from her womb there issue forth the Lord Cakrasamvara Father & Mother: & they dissolve into me.

And all the deities issue forth from her womb and take their places upon the petals of my lotus, and within the divine palace of the mandala . . .

And on the four intermediate petals of my lotus are four flasks filled with semen, which is the thought of enlightenment; and above the flasks are skull-bowls filled with the five nectars . . .

The mandala within the body. In my heart is an eight-petaled lotus, & in its center stands the god himself, the same as I am, but only four fingers tall; on the four petals in the four directions are the four goddesses of the central lotus, & in the intermediate directions are the four offerings. And in the twenty-four places of my body, as I touch each place with the ring finger of my left hand, there appear the twenty-four syllables: *PUM JĀM OM AM GOM RAM DEM MĀ KAM OM TRIM KOM KĀM LAM KĀM HIM PREM GREM SAUM SUM NAM SIM MAM KUM!*

And these syllables melt into light and become the twenty-four great places of pilgrimage in the world: the fields & solitary places, the assembly places & cemeteries. And in this divine pavilion of radiance within my body there appear all the deities of my mandala; and each place of pilgrimage is a stage on the path to enlightenment, and all the gods & goddesses therein are the qualities which lead to enlightenment . . .

And the eight Ladies who guard the gates of the mandala stand at the portals of my mouth & nose & penis & anus & left ear & eyes & right ear.

And my body has become the world, and my whole body is filled with the mandala.

And I grasp the ego of the unchanging body & speech & mind of all Those Who Have Come: *OM ĀH HŪM!* I am the very self whose essence is the diamond of the body & speech & mind of all the gods & goddesses! *OM!* All events are diamond pure, diamond pure am I!

The armor of the god. OM HAH! On the heart of the Lord is Diamond Being: white, with three heads, white & yellow & red; with six hands, the three right ones grasping a vajra & a skull-drum & a head of Brahma, & the three left ones grasping a bell & a skull-bowl & a skull-staff.

NAMA HI! On his forehead is yellow Shining One. *SO HA HU!* On the top of his head is red Source-of-Gems. *BAU SA TE HE!* On his two shoulders is black Heruka. *HŪM HŪM HOH!* On his three eyes is blue Infinite-Light. *PHAŢ HAM!* On all his limbs is green Unfailing-Success . . .

And I empower them by saying: *OM HAH NAMA HI SO HA HU BAU ŞA ŢE HE HŪM HŪM HOH PHAŢ HAM!*

OM BAM! On the navel of the Mother is Diamond Sow: red, with three heads, red & green & yellow; with six hands, the three right ones grasping a chopper & a skull-staff & an iron hook, & the three left ones grasping a skull-bowl & a head of Brahma & a noose.

HA YOM! On her heart is the blue Lady Slayer-of-Death. *HRIM MOM!* On her throat is the white Lady Infatuation. *HREM HRIM!* On her hair is the yellow Lady Agitation. *HŪM HŪM!* On her crest is the green Lady Terror. *PHAŢ PHAŢ!* On all her limbs is the green Lady Blazing . . .

And I empower them by saying: *OM BAM HA YOM HRIM MOM HREM HRIM HŪM HŪM PHAŢ PHAŢ!*

The knowledge of the god. And my body is strengthened & ready to receive the deity himself; & from my heart there radiate iron hooks of light, to invite the entire retinue of the Knowledge Being from his natural abode, & the five families of initiation deities: *PHEM!*

JAH HŪM BAM HOH! They dissolve into me: & we become insepara-bly one.

The initiation of the god. I pray to all Those Who Have Come: grant me the initiation!

And all Those Who Have Come emanate beautiful women from them-selves, holding flasks filled with the five nectars, & singing: All the gods bathed the Buddha when he was born: and so do we bathe & purify your body with this pure divine water.

OM! The glory of the vows of initiation by all Those Who Have Come *HŪM!*

And I am initiated as the deity himself; and from the water they pour upon me there are born the Lords of the Family, to form an ornament upon our heads, Unmoving One upon the Lord & Shining One upon the Mother . . .

The empowerment of the god. And on the top of my head is *OM,* on my neck is *ĀH,* on my heart is *HŪM*: and light radiates forth from these syllables & arouses the body & speech & mind of all Those Who Have Come.

And their body & speech & mind cleanse the three poisons of beings, and return into me with the light, & dissolve into the three syllables.

And the syllables transform into Diamond-of-Body & Diamond-of-Speech & Diamond-of-Mind, together with their consorts; & their light pervades my entire body.

Offerings to the God

The goddesses of offerings. And from my heart there emanate goddesses of offerings to the deity:

I make offering: filling the sky
      with innumerable Ladies of the Lute
and Flute & Tambourine and Drum
      (youthful : satisfying
      with their pleasing appearance)
haughty-bodied : sensuous
      with these four thoughts of Joy

OM ĀḤ diamond lady of the lute *HŪM HŪM PHAṬ! OM ĀḤ* diamond lady of the flute *HŪM HŪM PHAṬ! OM AH* diamond lady of the tambourine *HŪM HŪM PHAṬ! OM ĀḤ* diamond lady of the drum *HŪM HŪM PHAṬ!*

I make offering: filling the sky
      with innumerable Ladies skilled
in song & dance in the pride of youth
      (youthful : satisfying
      with their pleasing appearance)
haughty-bodied : sensuous
      with these four thoughts of Highest Joy

OM ĀḤ diamond lady of laughter *HŪM HŪM PHAṬ! OM ĀḤ* diamond lady of sensuality *HŪM HŪM PHAṬ! OM AH* diamond lady of song *HŪM HŪM PHAṬ! OM ĀḤ* diamond lady of dance *HUM HUM PHAṬ!*

I make offering: filling the sky
      with innumerable ladies bearing flowers
and incense & lamps and perfume
      (youthful : satisfying
      with their pleasing appearance)
haughty-bodied : sensuous
      with these four thoughts of the Joy of Cessation

OM ĀḤ diamond lady of flowers *HŪM HŪM PHAṬ! OM ĀḤ* diamond lady of incense *HŪM HŪM PHAṬ! OM ĀḤ* diamond lady of lamps *HŪM HŪM PHAṬ! OM ĀḤ* diamond lady of perfume *HŪM HŪM PHAṬ!*

I make offering: filling the sky
      with innumerable Ladies of Form
and Taste & Touch and Reality
      (youthful : satisfying
      with their pleasing appearance)
haughty-bodied : sensuous
      with these four thoughts of Spontaneous Joy

OM ĀḤ diamond lady of form *HŪM HŪM PHAṬ! OM ĀḤ* diamond lady of taste *HŪM HŪM PHAṬ! OM ĀḤ* diamond lady of touch *HŪM HŪM PHAṬ! OM ĀḤ* diamond lady of the realm of reality *HŪM HŪM PHAṬ!*

The offering of the five nectars. In front of me are the forms of wind & fire, surmounted by three human heads; & upon the heads is the syllable *A*, which transforms into a skull-bowl; & inside the skull-bowl are the syllables *GO KU NA HA DA*, which transform into the five fleshes (cow & dog & horse & elephant & human flesh), & the syllables *PI MU ŚU MA RA*, which transform into the five nectars (excrement & urine & semen & flesh & blood); and each of these is marked with its own syllable & has the syllable *OM* upon it, to cleanse its impurities.

Then the syllable *ĀḤ* appears and transforms into a moon; above the moon is the syllable *HŪṂ*, which transforms into a diamond skull-staff; and the staff points downward upon the bowl & seals the top.

And the wind kindles the fire; & all the substances within the bowl mix into a single taste & blaze like the surface of the rising sun. And the light thereof invites the gods of the spirits to the surface of the moon upon the bowl: they enter into union, and they melt & dissolve into the nectar of knowledge, & they drip into the bowl.

And my offering becomes an inexhaustible ocean of divine color & taste & odor.

And goddesses come, bearing the offerings of their own bodies, adorned with bones: and silently they offer a skull-bowl filled with this nectar to the Lord & his retinue.

The offering of reality. On a moon at the tops of the heads of both Father and Mother is *OṂ*: on a sun at our necks is *ĀḤ*; on a sun at our hearts is *HŪṂ*. And *SVĀ* is at the break of our waists; *ĀḤ* is on our sexual organs; and *HĀ* is between our thighs.

In the secret place of the Father appears the syllable *HŪṂ*, which transforms into a blue vajra; on its tip appears the syllable *BAM*, which transforms into a red gem; & the hole is blocked by a yellow *PHAṬ*.

In the Mother's place of space appears the syllable *AḤ*, which transforms into a red lotus; in its center appears the syllable *OṂ*, which transforms into its blue anthers; & the hole is blocked by a yellow *PHAṬ*.

On a moon at my navel & heart are the mantras of the Mother; on a sun at my throat & the top of my head are the mantras of the Father.

On a sun at the Mother's navel & heart are the mantras of the Father; on a moon at her throat & the top of her head are the mantras of the Mother.

And the mantras become thick with red-colored light, & they descend through the secret place of the Father up into the Mother's place of space, and they circle around between face & face.

And I make offering with the lust that arises; I take hold of spontaneous knowledge, & enter into contemplative union, and it becomes my offering of reality.

And all the goddesses praise the Lord with his mantras.

The Speech of the God

And the deity himself is upon a lotus in my heart, and in his heart is a moon, & upon the moon in his heart is the syllable *HŪṂ*.

And the dot of the *HŪM* is the essence of the five Buddhas, & its light is like a rainbow halo; and in the midst thereof I clearly see the whole mandala & its retinue.

And every time my breath goes out, the divine hosts of the Blessed Cakrasamvara radiate forth on the tips of beams of light, to purify the world of inanimate objects into a divine palace, & the beings of the world of animate objects into a divine mandala like themselves. And then my breath gathers them all back in to me; & this happens over & over again as I breathe.

Then the syllable *HŪM* appears where the secret places of the Father & Mother join together; and then it appears on the tip of my penis, within the vagina of the Mother; & thereby my mind & my breath are firmly fixed within my central channel; and this alone is the very highest of recitations of the mantra.

Then the mantra issues forth with light from the *HŪM* in my heart; it descends the diamond path; it passes through the central channel; it circles through my vajra into the lotus of the goddess & upward from mouth to mouth.

And this is the forward recitation of the mantra; if the direction is reversed, upward through the diamond path & into the mouth of the goddess, this is the fierce recitation; & I practice each of these in turn.

And I recite the mantras in a whisper.

The Mind of the God

The final emptiness. The vowels & consonants issue forth from my right nostril, with five-colored beams of light; and on the tips of these beams of light there radiate forth the deities of the mandala; they purify the entire triple world & render it into the essence of their divine body & speech & mind.

And the whole world is made equal to these gods & goddesses, whose deity is forever innate; and the world is gathered back into me with the vowels & consonants; they enter through my left nostril & reach the level of my navel.

And the vowels & consonants transform into a moon of red & white radiance: the gods & goddesses transform into a white & red syllable *HŪM*.

And the syllable *HŪM* transforms into a two-armed Blessed One, Father & Mother, doing the sport of lust; and by the sound of their inner experience of spontaneous joy, the whole mandala is aroused & satiated with Great Bliss.

And the cemeteries are gathered into the gates; & the gates into the central lotus, & the lotus into me, the Lord at the center of the mandala: and I am gathered into the Father & Mother at my navel.

And the Father & Mother melt into light and transform once more into the moon & its syllable *HŪM*.

And the moon dissolves into the $H\bar{U}M$, and the U-vowel into the HA, and the HA into the head-stroke, and the head-stroke into the crescent, and the crescent into the dot; and the dot dissolves into Pure Sound.

And my mind is bound to that Pure Sound, and as it grows fainter & fainter I enter into the inconceivability which imposes no constructs upon reality.

The return to the world. And then there arises the Pure Sound, and from that there arises the syllable $H\bar{U}M$, and from the syllable $H\bar{U}M$ the mandala instantaneously appears again: & I am the god himself in the world . . .

7
the spontaneous way

1. SESSIONS ON THE GREAT SYMBOL

Freedom and spontaneity are the goals of meditation: in Mila's words, to be happy as all manner of things appear before one. To know the true nature of events is to be able to respond to them genuinely: realization does not reduce people to a drab sameness, but rather frees them to be themselves. From the earliest disciples to the modern masters, Buddhism has set itself the goal of producing holy people—and holy people are wonderful and strange. They are free to act from the very roots of their own personalities, spontaneously and without any thought at all; there is a childlike authenticity in everything they do.

This freedom is won at the cost of great discipline. It is easy for us to confuse the result with the process and to think that by acting bizarrely we can counterfeit realization. The Buddhists had too much experience to make the same mistake; even where they themselves rebelled against the arduous tedium of long and frustrating contemplative training, even where they sought to find a more rapid path to the goal, they understood the effort that freedom demands; it is never easy to break through the chains that have bound us for eons. Among our own philosophers, Martin Buber has faced this problem of authentic action and has written: "All living with the whole being and with unconstrained force means danger; for there is no thing, no relation, no happening in the world that thus known does not reveal its bottomless abyss, and all thinking threatens to shatter the stability of the knower . . ."*

The Great Symbol is a general name for a number of related meditative techniques, all of which seek to shatter our conceptions and break through to the genuine: the cotton-clad Mila and White Lotus were both followers of this tradition, and their poems are filled with its teachings. There are remarkable parallels between these meditations and the techniques of Zen. Both aim directly at freedom, and seek the swiftest means of creating an authentic and spontaneous mode of being in the world; both use the intellectual categories of insight only where they lead directly to the goal, and as readily use paradox and poetry to cleanse away the constructs we impose upon reality. Both see freedom from "thought" to be freedom in the world; both speak of the "original mind"—our innate and childlike response to the magic show we call the world, the Buddhahood inherent in all living creatures.

Many scholars have thus postulated that early Chinese Zen exerted considerable influence in Tibet. I feel, on the other hand, that we must seek the

*Martin Buber, *Daniel: Dialogues on Realization* (N.Y.: McGraw Hill, 1965), 89.

common roots of both Zen and the Great Symbol in India, as part of an underground movement away from the rapidly ossifying intellectual traditions of the great monastic academies, in the gospel of the Crazy Wanderers, who mocked at stiff-necked righteousness and carried on a guerilla theater of freedom on the streets of India.

The following text by White Lotus is a series of meditative sessions placing the Great Symbol largely within the framework of the standard contemplative structure; but there is still a directness about the technique, a seeking for Buddhahood within this very life, which aims for the immediate experience of freedom and will let nothing stand in its way.

Pad-ma dkar-po, Chos-rje 'brug-pa'i lugs-kyi phyag-rgya chen-po lhan-cig skyes-sbyor-gyi khrid-yig [*Manual of the spontaneous great symbol*], *in* Gdams-ngag mdzod, *ed.* 'Jam-mgon Kong-sprul Blo-gros mtha'-yas (1813–99 A.D.) (Delhi: N. Lungtok and N. Gyaltsen, 1972), 7, folios 19–32.

The Practice of Calm

In these sessions you will try to achieve the state of calm which is the root of all meditation, and you will learn to contemplate one-pointedly. You will first use external objects to meditate upon and only then begin to meditate without using any external objects at all; and in these first sessions you will focus upon an inert object, such as an ordinary pebble or twig, or a holy image of the Buddha.

Session One

Focusing upon an ordinary pebble or twig. For this session, set out a small pebble in front of you as your meditative object; and just stare at it one-pointedly, letting your awareness neither stray from it nor identify with it.

Now visualize your master upon the top of your head and think of him as being truly the Buddha himself; and pray to him, that he may empower you to gain the highest attainment.

Then think that he dissolves into you, and that his mind is mixed with yours: remain in this state of communion as long as you are able; and, throughout these sessions, meditate as though you were telling your master everything that happens in your mind.

If you should ever become drowsy, just lift your gaze and look out over the broad landscape, to refresh yourself; and do the same whenever you become sluggish or apathetic, and discipline yourself with mindfulness. If you should become distracted, then go sit within the hermitage and concentrate upon trying to relax.

Session Two

Focusing upon a holy image of the Buddha. Here you may concentrate upon an image to symbolize the body of the Buddha, a syllable to symbolize his speech, or a glowing dot to symbolize his mind.

Thus, in this session, you will focus upon a statue or a painting; or you may visualize the Buddha in front of you, dressed in his monastic robes, yellow as the purest gold, shining with light and with all his signs upon him, and concentrate upon this.

Session Three

In this session you will focus upon a syllable; so visualize in front of you the disc of a moon, the size of a fingernail, and upon it the syllable *HŪM*, as fine as if it were written with a single hair, and concentrate upon this.

Session Four

Now you should focus upon a glowing dot visualized in front of you, in the shape of an egg and about the size of a pea, shining and wondrous, and concentrate upon this as before.

Session Five

In the next sessions you will meditate not upon an inert object but upon your own breath, first as it moves in and out, and then as you hold it within.

Focusing upon the moving breath. Let your body and your mind be tranquil, and focus upon the inhalation and exhalation of your breath; and, with no other thoughts, simply count your breaths, from one and two and so on all the way through the entire session. In this way you will become experienced in counting your breaths as they move in and out.

Session Six

In this session you will mentally follow your breath as it is inhaled and exhaled; and note for how long the breath is exhaled, and for how long it is inhaled, and through how much of your body it moves. In this way you will become experienced in defining your breath.

Session Seven

Now let your awareness move with your breath, from the tip of your nose all the way down to your navel, and watch how it goes and comes and is held within. In this way you will accurately see the different colors of the air, and its periods of rest and motion as it moves in and out.

Session Eight

Now spend the session examining individually the five elements which make up your body, and you will become aware of how the breath increases and decreases as it moves in and out.

Session Nine

And finally visualize the air to be a white syllable *OM* as it is exhaled, a blue syllable *HŪM* as it is inhaled, and a red syllable *ĀḤ* as it is held within, and the motion of the breath in and out will become visible to you.

Session Ten

Holding the breath. Breathe out forcibly three times, then gently draw in the upper air through your nose and draw up the lower air from your intestines, and try to hold it as long as you can.

For the mind is hard to control, yet it depends upon the breath to relate to the external world; and when the motion of the breath is stopped, then your thoughts are also stopped, and your mind can no longer stray toward external objects.

Session Eleven

Thus in these next sessions you will begin to meditate without using any external objects at all; you will first learn to cut off every thought that occurs, then to leave each thought unformed, and finally to leave your mind entirely alone.

Cutting off every thought that occurs. Continue to contemplate as in the previous session; and you will find your mind following after external objects, imposing its constructs upon them, and thinking that things are real.

Do not let this continue, but discipline yourself with mindfulness, and try to prevent every single one of these thoughts. And thus contemplate, cutting off at its very root any thought that occurs.

Session Twelve

During this session, you should be able to contemplate like this for an ever increasing period of time; indeed, it will seem that these thoughts are becoming more numerous than before, and following one after the other as if in a continuous stream.

This is what we call recognizing your thoughts, as you might become aware of an enemy; it is what we call the first state of calm, like the rushing of a mountain cataract.

It seems as if your thoughts are becoming more numerous because you are now aware of them arising and ceasing with each passing instant. Your thoughts always appear in sequence, occurring in one instant and ceasing in the next, so there can be neither more nor less of them; but you are now seeing them as they really are.

Session Thirteen

Leaving each thought unformed. In this session you will let these thoughts now do whatever they want, not cutting them off at all, yet not falling under their spell. And thus contemplate, setting out the mind itself as its own sentinel.

Session Fourteen

Thus your thoughts can no longer move you one way or the other, and you can begin to abide one-pointedly in a state of calm. When your thoughts flash by, contemplate as before, and you will be able to remain in this state for an ever increasing period of time.

This is what we call the middle state of calm, like the gentle flowing of a river.

To remain in this state continuously settles all the sediment in your mind. As Gampopa says: If you do not stir the water, it is clear; and if you leave your mind alone, it is blissful.

And the cotton-clad Mila sang: Leave your mind in the genuine and the fresh, and realization dawns: nurture the flowing river, and it grows complete. Cast aside all your attention and your labels, and ever abide in meditation.

And Saraha spoke of the two ways of meditating when he said: Bind it, and it tries to go in all directions; let it loose, and it stands firm and unwavering. O I realize it is as stubborn as a camel.

Session Fifteen

Leaving your mind alone. In this session you will keep your mind as if you were spinning a thread, keeping an even tension upon it.

For if your contemplation is too tight, then it snaps; and if it is too loose, then you slip into indolence.

So begin by cutting off every thought that occurs until you find your mind becoming tense and tired, then relax by leaving each thought unformed. And thus keep an even tension upon your mind by alternately tensing and relaxing it in this way: this is what we call keeping your mind as if you were spinning a thread.

Session Sixteen

Now in this session you will keep your mind as if it were a snapped rope.

For all our prior antidotes to thought have been thoughts themselves: it is a thought to think that you must impose no constructs upon reality. You have simply substituted one thought for another: this is what we call mindfulness chasing after its object, and it is a fault in contemplation.

So cast aside your mindfulness itself: keep your mind free of all effort and let it flow naturally and spontaneously in the stream of calm; this is what we call keeping your mind as if it were a snapped rope.

Session Seventeen

Now you will try to keep your mind as if it were a child looking at the murals painted on a temple wall.

For you are now without thought, and without feeling in your body and mind: and thus you will see visions of smoke, and other forms of emptiness: you may feel you are fainting, or as if floating in empty space.

When these ecstatic visions occur, you must neither enjoy them nor fear them, and thus neither think they are important nor try to stop their appearance. Do not cut them off, and do not cling to them: this is what we call keeping your mind as if it were a child looking at the paintings in a temple.

Session Eighteen

And finally you will keep your mind as if it were an elephant being pricked by a pin.

For while your mind is fixed, your mindfulness is automatically recognizing every thought that occurs. What is to be cast aside and that which casts it aside meet each other, and your thoughts can no longer jump about from one to the next. The antidote to thought now occurs spontaneously and naturally, without needing any effort at all on your part: this is what we call mindfulness holding its object.

Thus you feel your thoughts occur, but you yourself neither cut them off nor react to them in any way: this is what we call trying to prick an elephant with a pin.

And this is what we call the final state of calm, like an ocean without waves. You recognize the flickering within the fixed, and you simply leave it alone, for you see the fixed within the flickering. This is the gap between the flickering and the fixed: this is to realize one-pointedness of mind . . .

Session Nineteen

In these sessions you will now analyze this fixed and flickering, to gain the realization of insight, and you may finally reach the state of meditation-less meditation.

The Practice of Insight

Analyzing the fixed and the flickering. In this session, enter the state of calm wherein you are no longer imposing any constructs upon reality, but simply letting it appear before you. Look upon your fixedness: see its true nature, see how it is fixed, and see how it flickers from its state of fixedness.

Is the flickering in your mind something other than the fixedness, or is it a flickering within the fixedness itself? What is the true nature of this flickering? And how does the flickering stop?

Session Twenty

And now you are beginning to realize that you cannot see the fixed apart from the flickering, or the flickering apart from the fixed; you cannot find the true nature of the fixed and the flickering.

And what about this awareness with which you are watching both of them: is it something different from them? Or could it be that they are watching themselves?

You are beginning to see that your introspection is finding nothing there at all, that the watched and the watcher are both the same. You cannot set out its true nature: it is what we call the vision beyond all thought . . .

As it says in scripture: Fire comes from rubbing two sticks together, and then the fire burns both sticks. Wisdom is born of the senses, and both are consumed . . .

Session Twenty-one

The realization of insight. Now you know how to leave every thought and passion entirely alone, not cutting it off at all, yet not falling under its spell.

During this session, try simply to recognize every thought for what it is: let it spontaneously become emptiness, pure in and of itself, without your casting it aside. In this way you learn how to make use of all hindrances: this is what we call making a hindrance into the path itself.

By just recognizing the thought, the imposition of a construct, you are freed from it spontaneously; you realize that there is no difference at all between what you cast aside and that which casts it aside: this is what we call the reverse contemplation, the essence of the practice of the diamond vehicle.

And now too there is born in you exceeding compassion for all those living creatures who do not realize the essence of their own minds.

You will spend your lives working for the sake of these others, but all our meditations have now cleansed away any idea that these others really exist. And nothing can harm you; everything in this world is like poison which has been consumed by a magic spell.

And it is with regard to practice such as this that we say: I neither keep nor cast aside anything that happens on the path . . .

This is the path whereon is cleansed away belief that anything is real, for everything is reality. Even after you arise from meditation, all events appear to you as an illusion.

As it is said: Before and behind and all about me, whatever I see is reality. For today my error is cut off: now I shall not ask anyone at all . . .

Conclusion

Meditationless meditation. And now you have realized that every event is innate and spontaneous, and is the body of reality itself, as the world appears before you in your meditationless meditation.

For the passions are finished; the antidote which cast them aside is finished; and the circle is broken.

There is no place else to go; the journey is over; there is no place higher than this. This is the attainment of the highest attainment; this is the great symbol, the unfixed nirvana.

As it is said: Ha! This is the knowledge of my own experience. It is beyond the ways of speech: it is not an object of the mind. I have nothing to teach at all: know it yourself, for you yourself are its symbol. Do not think, do not ponder, do not ask, do not meditate: but keep in your natural and spontaneous flow . . .

2. THE SIXTH PATRIARCH SPEAKS OF MEDITATION

The sixth Chinese Zen master in direct descent from the founder Bodhidharma was Hui-neng, who lived from 638 to 713 A.D., if indeed he existed at all. We have considerable circumstantial detail about his life, and it is somehow appropriate that the man himself disappears as soon as we look for him with the tools of modern scholarship: it is a very Zen thing to do.

Zen masters have written very little on contemplative technique, for they consider meditation an art learned only in actual practice. The preceding text on the Great Symbol, however, shares many of its methods with Zen, and not a few of its sessions could as well have been held in a Sōtō monastery. I once translated portions of the text for a Zen meditator, and he was surprised at how closely it reported his own contemplative experience.

But the masters have been quite willing to discuss the theoretical foundations of their art. Hui-neng teaches directness above all things: that is, the immediate and spontaneous perception of reality, without imposing "thoughts" or labels upon it. He is quick to point out that no-thought does not mean no thinking, but rather genuine freedom and authenticity. Events appear: thoughts appear—and it is all quite marvelous.

Hui-neng, Nan-tsung tun-chiao tsui-shang ta-ch'eng mo-ho pan-jo po-lo-mi ching liu-tsu hui-neng ta-shih yü shao-chou ta-fan ssu shih-fa *t'an-ching* [*The platform scripture of the sixth patriarch (from the Tun-huang manuscript)*], in Taishō Shinshu Daizōkyo, gen. eds. Takakusu Junjirō and Watanabe Kaigyoku (Tokyo: Taishō Issaikyō Kankokai, 1924–29), 48, no. 2007.

My good & learned friends: all people already possess enlightenment & wisdom; it is only because their minds are deluded that they cannot attain to realization themselves, but must seek out a spiritual guide to show them how to see their own nature.

My good & learned friends: to gain this realization is to gain true knowledge.

My good & learned friends: meditation & wisdom are the foundation of my teaching. But never make the mistake of saying that meditation & wisdom are different; they are one substance, not two; meditation is the substance of wisdom, & wisdom is the activity of meditation. Where there is wisdom, meditation is there; & where there is meditation, there is wisdom.

My good & learned friends: this means that meditation & wisdom are the same. Students of the Way: be careful: do not say that wisdom comes after meditation, or that meditation comes after wisdom, or that meditation & wisdom are different; to hold such a view implies that there is duality in the world.

If your words are good, but your heart is not, then your meditation & your wisdom will not be the same; but if your heart & words are both good, then the inner & outer are of one piece, and your meditation & your wisdom are the same.

The practice of your own realization does not lie in argument: if you argue about what comes after what, you are deluded, you never settle the argument: you think that things really exist, and you never escape from birth & being & decay & death.

We are told to practice the meditation wherein we see all things as one; and this means simply to make your mind direct, whether walking or standing or sitting or lying down. The scriptures say: A direct mind is the object of the Way; a direct mind is the Pure Land.

Do not let your mind be crooked & your mouth speak of directness: if you say that all is one, yet do not see things deep & sharp, then you are no disciple of the Buddha; but to make your mind direct & to be attached to no event, is called the meditation wherein all is one.

Deluded people who like to label things say that this meditation, this direct mind, is to sit unmoving, to cast aside error & let no thoughts occur. If this were so, their teaching would simply turn us into inanimate objects, & set up a barricade upon the Way. But the Way should flow freely: why should we clog it like that? When the mind is not attached to events, then the Way flows freely; it is when the mind is attached that it gets all tangled up . . .

My good & learned friends: I see, too, that there are those who teach people to sit & examine their minds, to see the mind's purity, that it does not move & nothing occurs there. They then work very hard at this, and the poor fools gain no realization; yet they so cling to it that they become quite disordered. There have already been several hundred such cases; thus I know that to teach this way is a great mistake.

My good & learned friends: how then are meditation & wisdom the same? They are like a lamp & its light: when there is a lamp, there is light, & there is no light without a lamp. The lamp is the substance of the light, & the light is the activity of the lamp. They have two names, but their substance is not two: my teaching of meditation & wisdom is like that.

My good & learned friends: in the Law there is no "sudden enlightenment" or "gradual enlightenment," but people may be intelligent or dull. The deluded understand gradually, & the realized practice suddenly. This realization is to know for yourself your original mind, to see for yourself your original nature, and then there is no difference. But without this realization you wander in the world for long eons.

My good & learned friends: my teaching from the very beginning has established no thought as its doctrine, no label as its substance, & no attachment as its foundation.

No label means to make no labels in the midst of labels; no thought means not to think in the midst of thought; no attachment is the original nature of man.

Thought after thought, & they do not stop; past thought & present thought & future thought, thought after thought continues on, & they never cease. But if you can detach just one of these thoughts from events, you can separate the Body of Reality from the Body of Form, & in the midst of thought you will yet be without attachment. If a single thought is attached to an event, then all your thoughts will be attached, & this is called bondage; but if none of your thoughts are attached to anything, then this is freedom from bondage. Thus we take no attachment as our foundation.

My good & learned friends: no label means to be free of all labels; when you just stop sticking labels on it, the substance of your very nature is pure. Thus we take no label as our substance.

To be undefiled by the thought that things are real is called no thought. When your mind frees itself from thinking that things really exist, then your thoughts do not move toward events. But never cease being aware of things as they happen, or sit there trying to cast aside all your thoughts; to cut off thought completely is simply to die & then be reborn somewhere else. Students of the Way, take heed: if your mind is not aware of events, then you mislead yourself: & how much worse when you encourage others! Deluded, you do not see your own delusion, & you slander the teachings of the scriptures. Thus we take no thought as our doctrine.

When deluded people think about things, they think of them as being real, & hence are born all their error & defilement. Our school has established no thought as its doctrine; but when worldly people cease thinking things are real, then they just stop their thoughts from occurring; they just stop thinking; & this is not what we mean by no thought. *No* means no what? *Thought* means thinking what? *No* means freedom from the duality which causes defilement; *thought* means thinking the original nature of reality. Reality is the substance of thought, & thought is the activity of reality.

When thoughts occur spontaneously & naturally, from their own nature, whether seeing or hearing or perceiving or knowing, then you are undefiled by the thought that things are real, & you are forever free. The scriptures say: Externally he well discriminates all the labels of events; internally he abides in the first principle, & he does not move.

My good & learned friends: to sit in meditation in this teaching does not mean to examine your mind, nor to see its purity; we do not speak of unmoving. Suppose you say we should examine the mind: the mind is false, the false is the illusory, & there is nothing to examine. Suppose you say we should see its purity: but man's original nature is pure; it is false thoughts that obscure reality, & free of false thoughts his original nature is pure. If you do not see that your own nature is pure already, & make up your mind to see its purity, you are simply creating a purity which is false, which is not there. We know that what you are looking at is false, for purity has neither form nor label; but you set up the label "purity" & say that it is what we should learn. To hold such a view is to block your original nature, to be entangled in purity.

If people who practiced this "unmoving" meditation would just stop looking around for everyone else's mistakes, then perhaps their nature would indeed be unmoving. A deluded man may be unmoving in his body, but whenever he opens his mouth he says yes & no; he is in violation of the Way. Examining the mind, & seeing its purity, just cause the Way to get clogged.

Now if this is the case, what does our teaching mean by sitting in meditation? *Sitting* means to be unhindered by anything, to have no thoughts occur which move outward toward objects; *meditation* means to see your original nature without confusion . . .

If externally you label nothing, then internally your mind is not confused; your original nature is itself pure & is itself meditation: it is contact with things you think are real that causes confusion . . .

My good & learned friends: see that your own nature is pure in itself; practice for yourself & achieve for yourself your own nature, which is the Body of Reality. Your own practice is the Buddha's practice; your own achievement is the Way to Buddhahood.

8
the search

1. THE BUDDHA'S QUEST

The quest for wisdom is long and difficult: it is hard to give up home and family, and hard to cast aside the passions of the mind. Here, as always, the model is found in the life of the Buddha, who was raised in luxury and surrounded by sensual delight, so that the prophecy of his wandering forth from home might be forestalled by pleasure; and the vision of death and decay granted him by the gods might symbolize our own chilling and sudden confrontation with the realities of human existence.

His final look upon his wife and infant son is one of the most poignant moments in Buddhist literature, and artists have never tired of depicting it, but it too is a symbol. Movingly contrasted with the cloying delights of the harem, the tender love of his family is a more effective trap than pleasure or power. This too, as Kazantzakis saw it, was the last temptation of Christ.

For it is, finally, simple peace that is the way to enlightenment: the Buddha moves through the most fearsome austerities to discover the Middle Way, that neither indulgence nor self-flagellation is the path to tranquility of spirit, and that it is only tranquility that can perceive the truth of the world. And the anonymous author of our texts was not unacquainted with hardship: his descriptions of starvation and suffocation have the ring of truth, and the direct simplicity of the account is more convincing than the most polished rhetoric.

Nidānakathā [*Introduction to the former lives of the Buddha*], *in* The Jātaka together with its Commentary, *ed. V. Fausböll (London: Pali Text Society, 1877), 1: 58–62.*

The Four Signs

Now one day the bodhisattva wished to go to the park; so he called his charioteer, and bade him harness the chariot. Very good, said the charioteer; and he adorned the splendid chariot with all its ornaments, and harnessed the four horses of state, as white as the petals of a lotus; and he told the bodhisattva.

So the bodhisattva mounted his chariot, which was like a palace of the gods, and he went toward the park.

And the gods said to each other: The time draws near for the enlightenment of the prince, and we must show him a sign.

So they transformed a son of the gods into a decrepit old man, his teeth broken, his hair gray, crooked and bent and trembling, and leaning on a stick; and they revealed him to the bodhisattva, that only he and the charioteer could see him.

And the bodhisattva said to the charioteer: My friend, who is this man? Even his hair is not like that of other men.

And when he heard the answer, he said: Shame on life, truly; for those born therein grow old.

And his heart was disturbed; and he returned, and went up into the palace.

Then the king said: Why has my son returned so quickly? And they told him that his son had seen an old man; and that he would now leave home, and wander forth.

And the king said: Why do you kill me? Quickly prepare plays for my son, that he may feel pleasure, and not think of wandering forth from home. And the king increased the guard, and placed them for half a league in all directions.

And again one day the bodhisattva was going toward the park; and he saw a diseased man whom the gods had created. So he asked as before; and he returned with his heart disturbed, and went up into the palace.

Then the king asked again, and again they told him as before. And the king increased the guard, and placed them for three quarters of a league in all directions.

And again one day the bodhisattva was going toward the park; and he saw a dead man whom the gods had created. So he asked as before; and he returned with his heart disturbed, and went up into the palace.

Then the king asked again, and again they told him as before. And the king increased the guard, and placed them for a full league in all directions.

And again one day the bodhisattva was going toward the park; and he saw a monk, carefully and duly clad, whom the gods had created.

And the bodhisattva said to the charioteer: My friend, who is this man?

Now there was no Buddha in the world, and the charioteer knew neither monks, nor the virtues of wandering forth from home; but by the power of the gods he said: My lord, this is called a monk. And he praised the virtues of leaving home, and of wandering forth.

And the bodhisattva conceived a wish to wander forth from home, and that day he continued on to the park . . .

The Wandering Forth

And at that time the great king heard that the bodhisattva's wife had given birth; and he sent a messenger, saying: Announce these glad tidings to my son.

But when the bodhisattva heard of this, he said: An impediment has been born; a fetter has been born.

And the king said: What did my son say? And he heard the answer and said: From this day onward my grandson's name shall be called Prince Impediment.

Then the bodhisattva mounted his splendid chariot, and entered the city with great glory and with great magnificence. And a maiden of the warrior caste went up to the palace roof, to behold the beauty of the bodhisattva as he circled the city; and joy awoke within her, and she sang this joyful song:

> Serene indeed is the mother
> and serene is the father
> serene indeed is the woman
> to whom is such a lord.

And the bodhisattva heard her song and thought: This she said, that serene is the heart of a mother, and serene the heart of a father, and serene the heart of a wife to behold such a man. But what is this serenity of heart?

And his mind was turned away from passion, and he thought: When the fires of lust are extinguished, this is serenity; when the fires of hatred and delusion are extinguished, this is serenity. And it is serenity when the pains of corruption are calmed.

This is the lesson she has taught me: I shall wander in search of nirvana; I shall cast aside the household life, and wander forth from home, and seek for peace.

Now his pearl necklace was worth a hundred thousand pieces of gold; and he took it off from about his neck and sent it to the maiden, saying: Let this be for her a teacher's fee.

And great was her happiness, for she thought that the prince was in love with her and had sent her a gift.

But the bodhisattva went up into the palace with great magnificence, and he lay upon his royal bed.

And his women gathered about him, and they were beautiful and adorned with all their ornaments; they were skilled in song and dance and like the daughters of the gods. And they took up their musical instruments, that he might take pleasure in song and dance and music.

But his mind was turned away from passion; he took no pleasure in their dance, and he fell asleep.

Then the women said: He for whom we are dancing has fallen asleep; why should we trouble ourselves? And they scattered their instruments about, and lay down. And the lamps of scented oil burned.

Then the bodhisattva awoke, and sat with crossed legs upon the bed; he saw the women sleeping, with their instruments scattered about them.

And some of the women were drooling in their sleep, and their bodies were wet with saliva; and some were grinding their teeth, or snoring, or muttering, and they lay with their mouths open. And the clothes of some had fallen off, to disclose their disgusting nakedness.

And he saw their disgrace, and more than ever was his mind turned from passion; for his royal hall was adorned to appear as a palace of the gods, yet it seemed a cemetery of unburnt bodies, filled with corpses scattered about; the entire world seemed to him as a house on fire, and he cried: Indeed it is oppressive and stifling.

So he thought once more of wandering forth from home, and he said: This very day let me set forth upon my wandering.

And he arose from his bed, and he went to the door and called: Who is there?

And Channa his charioteer was sleeping with his head upon the threshold, and he said: It is I, my lord; it is Channa.

And the prince said: Saddle my horse, for today I shall set forth upon my wandering.

Very good, said the charioteer; and he took the saddle and bridle and went into the stable. And there among the shining lamps of scented oil was Kanthaka, the king of horses, standing beneath a canopy of jasmine cloth. And he saddled Kanthaka, thinking: This is the horse to saddle on this day.

And the horse felt the saddle put upon him, and he thought: The girth is tight: it is not as on other days when we galloped in the park for sport; today must be the day my master sets forth upon his wandering. And he neighed a loud neigh in his delight; and the sound would have spread throughout the town, had not the gods silenced it, and let no one hear it.

And after the bodhisattva had sent Channa to the stable, he thought: I will take a last look upon my son. And he arose from the bed, and went to the quarters of the mother of his son, and opened the door of the inner chamber.

And the lamps of scented oil burned within her room; and the mother of his son slept upon a bed strewn with jasmine flowers, her hand resting upon the head of her son.

And the bodhisattva paused with his foot upon the threshold, and gazed upon them, and thought: If I move the hand of my queen to take my son, then she will awaken and will hinder my wandering forth. I will become a Buddha, and then I will return and see my son.

And he turned away, and went down from the palace . . .

Mahāsīhanādasutta [*The great lion's roar*], in Majjhima-nikaya [*Collection of Medium Discourses*], gen. ed. Bhikkhu J. Kashyap (Bihar: Pali Publication Board, 1958), Sutta XII, 1: 109–13.

The Quest

Now I know the fourfold religious practice: for I was an ascetic, and the foremost in asceticism; and I was loathsome, and the foremost in loathsomeness; and I was abstinent, and the foremost in abstinence; and I was secluded, and the foremost in seclusion.

And this was for me in my asceticism: I went naked, and gave up politeness, and licked my hands after I ate; I did not come when I was called, and I did not stay when I was asked; I did not take food which was offered me, or prepared for me, or to which I was invited.

I did not take food from a pot, nor from a vessel, nor upon the threshold, nor by the woodpile, nor in the threshing yard; I did not take food from two people eating together, nor from a pregnant woman, nor from a woman nursing a child, nor from a woman fresh from love; I did not take food from gleaners in the fields, nor where a dog stood, nor where flies swarmed. I did not eat fish or meat, and I drank neither liquor nor gruel.

I visited but one house a day and asked for but one bit of food; and then I visited but one house a week and asked for but one bit of food. I lived on one small offering a day, and then I lived on one small offering a week. I ate food but once a day, and then I ate food but once a week. And in this way I dwelt, intent upon the discipline of taking food but once in every fourteen days.

And I ate herbs and millet and raw rice, I ate wild rice and water plants and the husks of rice, I ate rice scum and crushed seeds, and I ate straw and cowdung. I lived on forest roots and berries, and I ate fallen fruit.

And I wore coarse hemp, and coarse cloth, and shrouds from the cemetery; I wore rags from the garbage heap, and bark from the trees, and the skins of antelopes; I wore strips of antelope skin, and grass, and bark; I wore blankets of human hair and the feathers of wild birds.

I pulled out my hair and beard, intent upon the discipline of pulling out my hair and beard; I stood upright and refused a seat; and I squatted down, intent upon the effort of squatting. I lay upon a bed of thorns, and I made my bed upon a pile of thorns, and I dwelt intent upon the discipline of bathing three times in a night.

And thus I dwelt, intent upon the discipline of tormenting and mortifying my body in many different ways.

And this was for me in my loathsomeness: the dust and dirt of many years gathered upon my body, that it fell off in pieces; and the dust and dirt gathered upon me, as the dirt and dust of many years gathers upon a tree stump, that it falls off in pieces.

But I did not think: Indeed, I could wipe away this dust and dirt with my hand, or someone else could wipe away this dust and dirt for me. This did not occur to me: and this was for me in my loathsomeness.

And this was for me in my abstinence: when I was going out, or coming in, kindness was ever present in me, even toward a drop of water, and I thought: Let me not kill even one of these tiny creatures. And this was for me in my abstinence.

And this was for me in my seclusion: I plunged into the depths of the forest, and there I dwelt. And when I saw a cowherd or a shepherd, or when I saw a gatherer of grass or a gatherer of sticks or a worker in the forest, then I fled from wood to wood, from thicket to thicket, from low ground to low ground, and from high ground to high ground.

And why did I flee? I thought: Let them not see me, let me not see them. And I fled as a deer flees in the forest when he sees a man. And this was for me in my seclusion.

And I crawled on my hands and knees to a stable, which the cowherds had deserted and the cows had left, and there I lived by eating the dung left by suckling calves. And as long as I still had my own excrement and urine, there I lived by eating my own excrement and urine. And this was for me in my eating of loathsome food.

And I plunged into a dense and terrifying forest, and there I dwelt; and so terrifying was that dense and terrifying forest that it was said: He who is not free of lust and enters into this dense forest, his hair stands on end.

And during the cold winter nights, when the snow was falling, I passed the night in the open air and the day in the dense forest; and during the last month of the hot summer, I passed the day in the open air and the night in the dense forest.

And then all at once this song occurred to me, never before heard:

> Scorched and chilled
> alone in the terrifying forest
> naked he sits, and fireless
> the sage intent upon his quest

And I lay down in a cemetery, with a skeleton as my pillow. And cowherd boys came up to me, and spat upon me, and urinated upon me, and poured dirt upon me, and stuck twigs in my ears. But I was aware and thought no evil thoughts against them. And this was for me in my equanimity . . .

Mahasaccakasutta [*The scripture of Saccaka*], in Majjhima-nikāya [Collection of Medium Discourses], gen. ed. Bhikkhu J. Kashyap (Bihar: Pali Publication Board, 1958), Sutta XXXVI 1:301–306.

And I thought: Let me now clench my teeth and press my tongue against my palate; and let my mind restrain my mind, and subdue it, and burn it out.

So I clenched my teeth and pressed my tongue against my palate; and my mind restrained my mind, and subdued it, and tried to burn it out. And sweat poured from my armpits.

As a strong man might seize a weaker man by his head, or by his shoulders, and restrain him, and subdue him, and torment him, so I restrained my mind; and sweat poured from my armpits.

And I began to strive actively, and I set up mindfulness without confusion; yet my body was turbulent, for I was overcome by effort in striving against the pain. And painful feelings arose and stayed within me, but they did not overpower my mind.

And I thought: Let me now enter the trance of holding my breath.

So I stopped my breathing in and breathing out, through my mouth and through my nose; and I heard the roaring sound of winds escaping through my ears, as if a roaring sound were coming from a blowing bellows.

And I began to strive actively, and I set up mindfulness without confusion; yet my body was turbulent, for I was overcome by effort in striving against the pain. And painful feelings arose and stayed within me, but they did not overpower my mind.

And I thought: Let me still enter the trance of holding my breath.

So I stopped my breathing in and breathing out, through my mouth and through my nose and through my ears; and great winds shook my head, as if a strong man were slicing my head with the sharp edge of a sword . . . And I had pains in my head, as if a strong man had strapped my head with a tight leather strap . . . And great winds cut through my belly, as if a skillful butcher were cutting through the stomach of a cow with a sharp butcher knife . . . And there was a blazing heat in my body, as if two strong men had seized a weaker man by his limbs, and were tormenting him over a pit of blazing coals, and making him burn . . .

And I began to strive actively, and I set up mindfulness without confusion; yet my body was turbulent, for I was overcome by effort in striving against the pain. And painful feelings arose and stayed within me, but they did not overpower my mind.

And the gods saw me and said: The recluse Gautama is dead. And other gods said: The recluse Gautama is not dead, but he is dying. And other gods said: The recluse Gautama is not dead, nor is he dying; but he is a Worthy One, and this is the way a Worthy One abides.

And I thought: Let me now set myself to eat no food.

But the gods approached me, and they said: Sir, do not do this thing. If you set yourself to eat no food, then we will feed you with divine essences through your pores, to keep you alive.

And I thought that if I should eat no food at all, yet the gods kept me alive and fed me with divine essences through my pores, then this would be hypocrisy in me.

So I rejected those gods, and I said: Enough.

And I thought: Let me then take food a little at a time, a drop at a time: bean soup, or pea soup, or chickpea soup.

So I took food a little at a time, a drop at a time: bean soup, or pea soup, or chickpea soup. And my body became exceedingly thin.

And all my joints became like the knots of a black and withered creeper, because I ate so little. My buttocks became like a camel's hoof, and my backbone like a chain of balls; my gaunt ribs stuck out like the crazy rafters of an old shed, and the pupils of my eyes in their sockets lay deep and far, as the sparkling of water lies deep and far in a deep well. My scalp shrivelled like a bitter gourd shrunk by hot winds, and all because I ate so little.

And if I thought to touch the skin of my belly, then I seized my backbone; and if I thought to touch my backbone, then I seized the skin of my belly. For the skin of my belly was stuck to my backbone, and all because I ate so little.

And if I thought to defecate or urinate, then I fell face down upon the earth, because I ate so little. And if to soothe my body I stroked my limbs with my hand, then the hairs fell from my body. For they were rotten at the root, and all because I ate so little.

And men saw me, and said: The recluse Gautama has turned black. And other men said: The recluse Gautama has not turned black, but he has turned deep brown. And other men said: The recluse Gautama has turned neither black nor brown, but he has turned yellow. And thus was my clear pure complexion spoiled, and all because I ate so little.

And the thought occurred to me: Recluses and brahmans in the past have felt pain that was sharp and severe and bitter; but this is supreme, there is nothing worse than this. And recluses and brahmans in the future may feel pain that is sharp and bitter and severe; but this is supreme, there is nothing worse than this. And recluses and brahmans in the present are feeling pain that is sharp and bitter and severe; but this is supreme, there is nothing worse than this.

But with all this bitter hardship I could not attain to being more than human, nor could I gain the knowledge and vision of the Noble Ones. And I thought: Is there some other way to enlightenment?

Then I remembered one time when my father was plowing in the fields, and I was sitting in the cool shade of a tree; and I was detached from desire and detached from impure states: and I entered and dwelt in the first trance, with discursive thought and reasoning, and with the enthusiasm and pleasure born of detachment.

And I thought: Could this be the way to enlightenment? And I saw that this indeed was the way to enlightenment.

And I thought: Am I afraid of happiness? For this pleasure is different from desire and different from impure states. And I realized that I was not afraid of happiness, when it is different from desire and different from impure states.

And I thought: It is not easy to attain to happiness with a body exceedingly thin. Let me then eat sufficient food, some gruel with sour milk.

So I ate sufficient food, some gruel with sour milk. And five monks were with me, and they thought: When the recluse Gautama finds the truth, he will tell us. But when they saw me take sufficient food, they turned from me in disgust, and said: The recluse Gautama lives a life of luxury; he has strayed from effort and returned to abundance. And they left me . . .

Ariyapariyesanasutta [*The great quest*], *in* Majjhima-nikāya [Collection of Medium Discourses], *gen. ed. Bhikkhu J. Kashyap (Bihar: Pali Publication Board, 1958), Sutta XXVI, 1:216–217.*

So I set out to seek the highest path to peace. And I saw a lovely stretch of land: a pleasant wooded grove, and a clear flowing river with beautiful banks, and a village nearby to supply me with my food.

And I thought: Indeed this stretch of land is lovely, and the clear flowing river with beautiful banks, and the village nearby. This suits well the striving of one who seeks to strive.

And there I sat down, thinking: Indeed this suits well my striving.

And I saw that I was subject to birth, and I knew the danger of being subject to birth; so I sought nirvana, the supreme refuge, the unborn; and I attained to the unborn, to nirvana, the supreme refuge.

And I saw that I was subject to old age, and decay, and death, and sorrow, and defilement, and I knew the danger of being subject to these things; so I sought nirvana, the supreme refuge, the unaging, the undecaying, the undying, the unsorrowing; and I attained to nirvana, the supreme refuge.

And knowledge and vision arose in me, and unshaken was my freedom; and I knew it was my last birth, and never more would I exist again . . .

2. MILA AND THE TOWER

The Buddha found the Way by himself, but when the Buddha is no longer in the world, we must seek out a master to guide us. Thus the quest for wisdom traditionally becomes the quest for a spiritual guide to lead us on the path.

But the model remains, and the search leads through hardship and self-sacrifice, for the demands made by such a perfect master may be high indeed. The model becomes the ideal, and the ideal is enshrined in the traditional tales of disciples who sacrifice their limbs and even their lives in the service of their masters. And in the harsh mountain land of Tibet, where political strength and spiritual power reinforce each other, we find the brooding and explosive figure of the master Marpa, whose demands seem to symbolize the most chaotic moods of nature itself.

The autobiography of his disciple Mila is a classic text of its kind, yet its theme could be matched in almost any Buddhist tradition. In Zen, too, we find the harsh unyielding master, the slow transformation of the disciple from pride to realization, and the compassion of the teachings hidden beneath a cloak of sudden and unexplained rage; for Marpa is once again the type of the hidden saint, transformed by the author of our text into a human being who struggles to conceal his love for his chosen disciple while sternly cleansing him of sin.

Our text is not an autobiography at all: it was written by a wandering saint named Sangs-rgyas rgyal-mtshan (1452–1507 A.D.), known more popularly as the Crazy Man of Gtsang. He was a unique literary genius, for he single-handedly invented the novel in Tibet, and made the established genre of simple biography into an almost mythic exploration of character. His achievement has never been matched in Tibet, for after him biography became once more a recitation of careful fact, and derived its drama from fact and not from personality.

Our text is an exploration of people and of the reality of relationship. It is written in a vigorous and colloquial style, and draws happily upon the Tibetan tradition of broad and almost slapstick humor. The image of Mila jumping out of a window while his master chases him with a stick is burlesque comedy, and the comedy derives from a very human relationship between the brusque and fearsome master and the young proud disciple whom he loves so much. It is a comedy of transformation, for the occasionally weak disciple will become the cotton-clad Mila, the greatest saint and most beloved poet of Tibet.

Sangs-rgyas rgyal-mtshan, Mi-la ras-pa'i rnam-thar [*The life of Mi-la ras-pa*], ed. J. W. de Jong ('S-Gravenhage: Mouton and Company, 1959), pp. 57–81, 102–103.

... Now by this time I was beginning to get worried, and to suffer from my longing for the Law. Again and again I begged my master to teach it to me and to tell me how to practice it. Finally he said: "I have many faithful disciples who come to me from central Tibet, but the nomads of Talung and Ling rob them on their way, steal their provisions, and prevent them from bringing me any offerings. Go cast down a hailstorm upon these people; that is the religious thing to do. Then I will give you my teachings."

So I sent a great hailstorm upon them, and I asked him again to teach me.

"Ridiculous," he said. "You send down a few lumps of hail, and you think that it earns you this Law that I struggled so hard to bring from India. You say you are a mighty magician; then if you really want the Law, go do some magic on the mountain men of Lhodra. They, too, have often robbed my disciples and have shown contempt for my authority. When I see that your magic has worked, I will give you my teachings and show you how to become a Buddha in this very life."

So I cast my magic spells and made feuds break out among the mountain men; I saw many of them die upon the sword, and I was sick at heart.

"Well, you told the truth when you said you were a magician," my master said, and he started calling me his Great Magician.

I asked him to teach me how to become a Buddha.

"I went to India for these teachings at the risk of my life; I sacrificed my wealth, gave away my gold, and saved nothing. My teachings still breathe the breath of the goddesses who taught them, and you say you want them as a reward for your wickedness! Now that is a joke, and if it were only funny I could laugh at it. If I were anyone else I would have killed you by now. Go restore the harvest that you ruined and bring all the mountain men back to life. If you can do that I will give you the teachings, and if you cannot, then never return to my presence again."

His rebuke was as sharp as if he had struck me; and I cried bitterly in despair, as my master's wife tried to console me in my sorrow.

The next morning, my master himself came to me and said:

"We quarreled too much yesterday. Do not be so unhappy and do not be so impatient: I will give you the teachings eventually. You are a clever person, so just help me build a house for my son. When you finish it, not only will I give you the teachings, but I will provide you with food and clothing while you meditate upon them."

"But what will happen to me," I cried, "if I die in the meantime without the Law?"

"I guarantee that you will not die. Mine is not a Law which promises nothing: you are quite diligent, and if you can meditate upon my teachings it is up to you whether you become a Buddha or not. My tradition is different from all the rest; it is a lineage of great power."

I was quite happy at his good counsel, and I asked him to lay out the plan of the house for me.

Now this was not only a means to cleanse me of my sins; it was also a clever plot to build a tower overlooking a narrow pass, which my master and his relatives had all agreed not to fortify, so that no one would have a strategic advantage over the others. So my master took me to an eastern ridge of the mountain and said, "Build me a house like this."

So I started to build a circular house, as he had indicated; and I was only half finished when my master came and said, "I did not think enough about this. Tear this house down to its very foundation and take the earth and stones back where you found them."

I did as he ordered, and he took me to a western ridge of the mountain and said, "Now build me a house like this."

He seemed to be a bit drunk as he spoke to me, but I started to build the semi-circular house he had indicated, and I was only half finished when again he came and said: "Now this will not do at all. Take the earth and stones back where you found them."

Again I did as he ordered, and he took me to a northern peak and said: "My Great Magician, I drank a little too much beer last time. You really should not have listened to me. But now you can build me a really nice house right here."

"It is very difficult for me to keep building houses like this and then tearing them down again," I said, "and it is a waste of your money, too. Please think about it carefully this time."

"I am not drunk now, and I have thought about it quite carefully. A house for a mystic should be triangular, so build one for me: you will not have to tear this one down."

So I started to build a triangular house, and I had only finished a third of it when my master came and said: "Magician, whose house is this you are building? Who told you to do this?"

"You yourself told me to build such a house for your son," I replied.

"I do not remember telling you to do any such thing. You may well be right, but I was probably crazy at the time, or not in full possession of my faculties."

"I was afraid something like this might happen, and I begged you to think about it carefully, and you said that you had. You said that this time I would not have to tear it down, and you really seemed quite lucid about it."

And my master became furious and shouted at me: "Then who is your witness? Did you think to work magic upon us and cast us into a triangular house shaped like a pit of sacrifice? And if you sought not to enchant us, and you really want the Law—well, a house like this will anger all the local spirits. So take the earth and stones back where you found them. If you want the Law I can give it to you, and if you do not want it, then you can just go away."

I was miserable, but I wanted the Law: so I did as my master ordered, tore down the triangular house, and took the earth and stones back where I found them.

By this time there was quite a sore on my back, but my master would only have yelled at me had I shown it to him; nor did I show it to his wife, lest she think that I was bragging about how hard I was working. So I wept and did not show it to her, but I begged her help in asking for the Law.

So she went in to see my master and said to him: "Really, my lord, the child is miserable with all this useless building. Show a little compassion and give him the Law."

"Well, make me some nice food," he said, "and bring him to me."

So she brought me in with her when she took him his dinner, and he said to me: "Magician, you really should not tell such lies about things I never did. But if you want the Law I will give it to you."

And he taught me how to go for refuge, and he gave me the precepts and vows of a disciple. "This is the ordinary Law," he said. "If you want the special Law of my Tantric teachings, then you must act like this." And he told me briefly about the hardships suffered by his master in seeking the Law, and he added that it would be hard indeed for me to do such things. But I wept as the deepest faith awoke within me, and I vowed that I would do whatever my master said.

A few days went by, and my master invited me to go for a walk with him. We came to the narrow pass kept by his relatives, and he said: "Now you can build an ordinary square tower for me, nine storeys high, and with a turret as a tenth story. You will not have to tear this one down. When it is completed, I will give you the teachings, and I will give you the provisions you need while you are meditating upon them."

"May I ask your wife to be a witness to this?" I asked, and he agreed.

So my master laid out the ground plan while I went to ask his wife to come; and before them both I said: "I have built three houses now and torn them all down again. The first time, my master said he had not thought about it carefully; the second time, he said he was drunk; and the third time, he said he must have been crazy, for he could not remember telling me anything of the sort. And when I told him that he himself had given me the orders, he yelled at me and asked me who my witness was. So this time I am asking his wife to be my witness."

"Certainly I will be your witness," she said. "But my lord is such a tyrant that you cannot count on him for anything. He just keeps on building houses for no reason, and then for no reason tears them down again. And this place is not ours anyway, for we have all taken a vow not to build here. I have said as much to him, but he pays no attention to me."

"Just be a witness like you are supposed to!" he shouted. "I will do whatever I have said I will do. Stop concerning yourself with things that are none of your business, and leave me alone."

Now while I was laying the foundation for the square tower, three of my master's disciples rolled up a great boulder for sport, and I used it as the foundation stone just under the doorway. I had reached the second storey when my master came and looked at everything very carefully. Then he pointed to the rock that his three disciples had rolled up, and he said, "Magician, where did you get this rock?"

"Some of your disciples brought it here for sport."

"You cannot use their rock to build your tower! Take it out and put it back where it belongs."

"But you said I would not have to tear this building down."

"I did not say you could use my most advanced disciples as your servants! And you need not tear down the whole thing; just take out the foundation stone and put it back."

So I had to tear down the whole building to get to the stone, and I put it back where it came from. And my master said, "All right, now you can fetch it yourself, and put it in the foundation again."

So I took the rock, and with the strength of three men I dragged it back into place by myself, nor did I use my magic powers to help me. And I built the tower as before, and the rock became famous thereabouts as my Giant Stone.

Now as I was building the foundation, the relatives of my master were counseling together, and they felt that they should stop him from fortifying the pass where they had all vowed not to build. But some of them said: "Marpa has gone crazy. He has got himself a strong little disciple from the hills and has him building unorthodox houses on every ridge; then he has him tear them down again when they are only half finished and put the earth and stones back where he found them. He will tear this one down too. Just wait and see; there is still plenty of time to stop him."

But I was working on the tower without interruption and without tearing it down. I had reached the seventh storey—and another sore had appeared on my waist—when his relatives said: "This time he is not tearing it down. Tearing down the others was just a wicked plot to build this one! We must destroy it."

And so they prepared for war, but my master magically created an armed host which filled the tower inside and out. His relatives were terrified, and they could not discover where he had gotten such an army; and since they could not fight with him, they came to him secretly one by one, and gave him presents, and submitted to him.

Now about this time Meton Tshonpo came to receive the initiation of Cakrasamvara, and my master's wife said to me, "This time we will somehow get you your initiation." For I had built a great tower without anyone giving me a piece of rock, or a basket of earth, or a jug of water, or a shovelful of clay, and I thought that this time at least I would be given an initiation. So I bowed down before my master, and took my place in the rows of his disciples.

"Magician," he said, "what fee have you brought for your initiation?"

"I have nearly finished the tower for your son. You promised you would give me the initiation and the teachings, and I am here hoping you will keep your word."

"Ridiculous," he said. "You build a turret a few feet high, and you think that it earns you this Law that I struggled so hard to bring from India. If you have a fee for your initiation, then bring it here, and if you do not, then you cannot stand in line for my profound Tantric initiation." And he hit me in the face and dragged me from the room by my hair.

I would have been happy to die right then, and I cried all through the night.

But my master's wife came to console me, and she said: "My lord is always saying that he brought the Law from India with the hope of benefiting all beings; he will teach it even to a dog that wanders in front of him, and finish by giving the animal all his merit. Do not worry. I do not know what he is doing, but think no evil of him."

The next morning, my master himself came to me and said: "Magician, leave off building the rest of the tower for a while and build me a courtyard with twelve pillars and a shrine room. When you finish that, I will give you the initiation and the teachings."

So I laid the foundation of the courtyard, as my master's wife brought me food to eat and a little beer to drink, and gave me what consolation she could.

And when the courtyard was almost finished, Tshurton Wange came to receive the initiation of Guhyasamāja; and my master's wife said to me, "This time we will somehow get you your initiation." So she gave me some butter, a roll of woolen cloth, and a small copper pot; and I set them out as offerings before my master and took my place in the rows of his disciples.

"Magician," he said, "what fee have you brought me, that you stand in line for my initiation?"

"This butter and cloth and copper pot," I said.

"Those are mine!" he shouted. "Those are things which my followers have given me! You cannot pay for your initiation with things that are mine already. If you have something of your own, then bring it here, and if you do not, then you cannot stand in line for my initiation." And he jumped up, yelling at me, and drove me out of the room with a volley of kicks.

I would have been happy to sink into the earth. I have killed many men with my magic spells, I thought, and this is my recompense for destroying the harvest with hailstorms. Or perhaps my master knows that I am unfit for the Law, or perhaps he just does not like me. But whatever the reason, what use is my sinful life without the Law? I might as well kill myself.

And my master's wife brought me some of the food from the ritual and sought to console me. But when she left, I had lost all taste for the food, and I cried all through the night.

The next morning my master came to see me again and said, "Just finish the courtyard and the turret, and I will give you the initiation and the teachings."

So I went back to work and had almost finished the courtyard when yet another sore broke out on my back. All three of my sores oozed pus and blood, and my whole back became an open wound. I showed it to my master's wife, reminded her of what my master had promised when I first started the tower, and begged her help in asking for the Law. She looked at my wounds, and began to cry, and said, "I will speak to my lord."

So she went in to my master and said: "The magician has worked so hard on your tower that all his limbs are cracked; he has three sores on his back which ooze pus and blood. Now I have heard of such sores on horses and donkeys, and seen them too, but I have never heard of a man with such sores, nor ever seen such a thing. We should be ashamed for other people to hear of it, and you are supposed to be such a great master! You should be ashamed of yourself. Have a little pity on him and give the child the Law, as you said you would when he finished the tower."

"I said I would give him the Law when he finished a tower ten storeys tall. Where are my ten storeys?"

"But he has built a courtyard larger than a ten-storey tower."

"I will give him the Law when he can finish the ten storeys without talking so much! But is his sore back really all that bad?"

"You get pleasure from being so cruel," she said sharply. "He has more than a sore back; his whole back is one big sore." And she hurried away.

"Well then," he called after her, "let him come see me."

So I came running in, thinking he might give me the Law, but he only said, "Magician, show me your sores."

I showed them to him, and he looked carefully at them and said: "My master's hardships were much greater than yours, and I myself served him without considering my life or sparing my wealth. So if you really want the Law, stop bragging so much, and finish the rest of the tower." And I knew that he was right.

And my master made his robe into a bandage for me, and he told me that such pads are put on horses and donkeys when they carry rocks.

"But what use is a pad when my whole back is an open wound?" I asked.

"Well, at least it will keep the dirt out."

So I thought that this was what my master wanted, and I carried the baskets of earth in front of me as I laid the plaster, to save my back.

And my master watched me while I worked, and he thought, "Wondrous indeed is such a man, who does whatever his master says." And he turned aside and wept.

But my wounds became inflamed, and I grew sick. So I begged my master's wife to ask for the Law once again, or at least to ask that I might rest until my wounds had healed. So she spoke to my master, but he only said, "He gets no Law until the tower is finished. Let him do as much work as he can, and if he cannot work, then I suppose we shall have to let him rest."

So his wife told me I could rest and not work until my sores were healed. And while I rested she brought me tasty food, but I was still unhappy and could think of nothing save that I had not gained the Law.

And when my wounds had gotten better, my master said to me, but still without mentioning the Law, "Magician, it is time to get back to work on the tower." And I was about to do so, when his wife said to me, "Now we shall contrive a plan to get you the Law."

So we counseled together and decided that I would pile my books and small possessions on top of some sacks of flour in a place where my master could see us, and I would pretend to leave, crying out to her, "Please, let me out of here!" And she would cling to me and say, "I will ask the master for you, and you will get the Law. Please stay."

And so my master saw us, and he said, "Now what are you two doing?"

"The magician came to his master from a distant land," she said, "with his heart set upon the Law. But you have not given him the Law; he has gotten nothing from you but abuse and blows. He is afraid to die without the Law, and he is leaving, saying that he will go and seek another master. I have said that I will be responsible for getting him the Law and will intercede for him; I am trying to stop him from going."

"I see," said my master, and he came over to us, and hit me in the head many times, and yelled at me: "When you first came to me, you said you would give me your body and your speech and your mind. So now where are you going? If you do not please me, I could chop you into a hundred pieces, for I own you. And if you want to leave anyway, what right have you to carry off my flour?" And he knocked me down and beat me, and he grabbed the sacks of flour and took them back inside.

And my heart was crushed, as a mother who has lost her only son. I counseled with my master's wife, but we were awed by the majesty of my master, so we went back into the house, and I stayed crying . . .

So I went on carrying earth and stones and finishing the plastering of the courtyard and shrine room. Then one day Ngogdon Chodor came with his retinue, bearing many gifts, to receive the initiation of Hevajra. And my master's wife said to me: "If my lord is not satisfied with all your work on his tower, and is pleased only by material things, then this time we will give him something to get an initiation for you. Give him this and ask him ahead of time, and if he does not grant it to you, then I will ask him also." And from among her own private possessions she gave me a beautiful deep blue turquoise.

I offered the turquoise to my master and said, "This time, I beg you, grant me the initiation."

He turned the turquoise around and looked at it.

"Magician, where did you get this?"

"Your wife gave it to me," I said.

He smiled. "Ask my wife to come in here."

And when she arrived he said to her, "Where did we get this turquoise?"

"It does not belong to my lord," she said, bowing before him. "My parents gave it to me when they brought me here to marry you. They said you were a hot-tempered man, and I might need it if we separated. They gave it to me as my own private property and told me to put it away without showing it to anyone. And now I have given it to this child, for I feel the greatest pity for him. My lord, please accept this turquoise; have compassion on him and grant him the initiation. He has suffered enough already by being cast out from among your disciples. Help me, master Ngogdon, and all your retinue, in pleading with my lord." And she bowed down many times before my master.

But Ngogdon and his retinue knew my master's temper, and they could not bring themselves to do anything save bow down with her, nodding, "That is so, that is so."

And my master said to his wife, "Do you realize that your actions nearly lost us this lovely turquoise?" He hung it around his neck. "Do not be so silly; you yourself are mine altogether, so I own this turquoise as well. If the magician has something of his own, let him bring it to me, and I will give him the initiation. But this turquoise is mine."

But I stayed, thinking that he might have been softened by his wife's offer of the turquoise. And he got up in a terrible rage and shouted in anger: "I told you to get out! What impertinence is this, that you do not leave?" And he hit me so hard that he knocked me face down on the ground, and he hit me again when I rolled over. He was just picking up his stick when Ngogdon grabbed him, and in the confusion I managed to jump out the window in terror . . .

The fall did not hurt me, but I was so miserable that I thought to kill myself. But my master's wife came to me weeping, and she consoled me, saying: "Magician, do not be so sad. There will never be a disciple as dear and devoted as you are. If you really want to ask another master for the Law, then I will arrange a meeting for you and give you provisions and offerings." And though she was supposed to take part in the ritual, that evening she stayed by my side, lamenting with me as I wept.

The next morning my master told me to come and see him, and I went thinking that perhaps he might give me the Law. "Yesterday I did not give you the initiation," he said. "Did that not displease you? Did you not think evil of me?"

"It did not shake my devotion to my master," I replied, "for I thought that it was recompense for my sinful deeds. But I am so unhappy." And I burst out crying.

"What arrogance to cry before me," he shouted, "and say I am unjust! Get out!"

And as I left, I was so miserable that it seemed a whirlwind pierced my heart. When I was sinful I was rich, I thought, but now that I am practicing the Law I have no wealth at all. If I had now but half the gold I had when I was sinful, I might obtain the initiation and the teachings, for this master will not give them to me unless I make him an offering. I could go somewhere else, but anyone else would want an offering too; without wealth you cannot gain the Law. I would be happy to kill myself; certainly it would be better than this sinful life without the Law. How awful, how awful! Perhaps I should be a servant to some rich man and save my wages to pay my fee for the Law. Or I could go back home again, where I did such evil deeds with my magic powers. I would be glad to see my mother again, and I might earn some money. But I must either seek for the Law or seek for wealth, and in either case I must leave. And now I would even be ashamed to take my master's flour.

So I took only my own books and set out without saying anything to my master's wife. But on the way I thought of her kindness to me, and love for her welled up within me.

I was half a day's journey from my master's house when it was time to eat, so I begged a little flour and borrowed a pot, gathered some water and firewood, and cooked my meal. It was past noon when I had eaten, and I thought that half of the work I had done for my master was in return for my food. I thought of the trouble I had getting just this one meal, and how his wife had always given me food already prepared, nourishing and spicy, and how wicked I was not even to say goodbye. Perhaps I should return, I thought, but I did not dare go back.

As I was returning the pot I had borrowed, an old man said to me: "You seem to be young and able-bodied. If you know how to read, you can earn your living reciting the Law; it is better than begging. If you cannot read, then be a servant for someone, and you will get both food and clothes. Do you know how to read?"

"I do not beg all the time," I said. "And I know how to read."

"That's fine. Read the scriptures to me for a few days, and I will pay you well."

I gladly accepted and stayed with him as I read the Perfection of Wisdom to him; and there I saw the story of Ever-Weeping, and how he had no money, yet paid no heed to his life for the sake of the Law. To tear out one's heart is to ask for death; yet he had resolved to sell even his own heart. And as I considered this, I realized that I had really suffered no hardships at all for the Law, and that my master might yet give the Law to me. And even if he did not, his wife had promised to arrange a meeting with another master. So I gathered my courage to return, and I started back.

Now when I had left, my master's wife had said to him: "Well, the enemy you could not conquer has gone. He is not here. Are you quite happy now?"

"What are you talking about?"

"Did you not make the magician suffer as if he were your deadliest enemy?"

And his face darkened, and he began to weep. "My masters!" he cried. "Goddesses and protectors of my lineage! Send me back my son." And he wrapped his head in his robe, and he sat there without moving.

When I arrived, I went to my master's wife, and bowed before her. She was delighted to see me again. "Wonderful," she said. "I think the master will give you the Law now, for when I told him you had gone, he wept, and cried out to the gods to send him back his son. I think you have been summoned back by the compassion of my lord."

But I thought that she was only comforting me. If it were true, I was quite happy that he had cried for me and called me his son, but it seemed that I was not his son at all, since he would not give me any initiations or teachings. But I had nowhere else to go, and I wondered how much I would suffer here by not attaining the Law.

And the master's wife said to him: "The magician could not forget us, and he has returned. May he come in and bow down to you?"

"It is not that he could not forget us: he just could not forget himself. But he can come in and bow if he wants to."

So I went in and bowed down before him, and he said: "Magician, if you really want the Law, you cannot flit about and keep changing your mind, but you must cast aside even your life for it. Finish the top three storeys of the tower, and then I will give you the teachings. If not, you are nothing but a waste of food, and if you have someplace else to go, you can go there." . . .

*
* *

. . . "My anger is not like the anger of the world," said my master. "However it may appear, it is all for the sake of the Law, to banish pride, and to lead upon the path to enlightenment. You who are seated here may not understand, but you must not be shaken from devotion to your master . . .

"And now I shall bless my faithful disciple, and give him the teachings so dear to the heart of an old man; I shall give him the provisions he needs while he meditates, and lead him to contemplation. So rejoice."

. . . And my master said to his wife: "Set out the food and the excellent offerings upon the altar. Mila is about to go now, and I have given him my permission."

So she laid out the offerings to the masters and the high patron deities, food for the goddesses and protectors, and the excellent feast for my diamond brothers. And before the assembly my master appeared as all the high patron deities, and as their emblems; he appeared as a drop of brilliant light, and finally vanished.

These many things Marpa showed, and he said: "These things I have formed are called magical transformations of the body. They must never be shown in a spirit of falsehood, but I have shown them now as a parting gift for Mila."

And I saw that my master was truly the Buddha himself: I felt immeasurable joy, and I thought that I too must obtain through contemplation magic power such as his. My master said: "My son, did you see? Did you believe?"

"I saw, and I could not help but believe," I replied. "And I thought that I too must do likewise through my contemplation."

"My son, that is good. And now you may go. I have shown you that all things are like an illusion, so do you experience likewise, adhering to the rocky wastes, the snowy ranges and the solitary forests . . . In these places make meditation your foremost aim."

. . . And with tears flowing down he said: "My son, we two shall not meet again in this life. I shall not forget you; do not forget me. If you do as I have said, surely we will meet again in the celestial realms . . . "

9
the experience

1. THE ENLIGHTENMENT

The enlightenment of the Buddha provides the basic model for the experience of wisdom. It is the central act in the history of Buddhism, and the Buddhists were fortunate to find it a drama full of ambiguity, for from the ambiguities of the experience came all the potential for growth and change within the tradition.

The enlightenment was as ineffable as any human event, yet has always been held to be in some sense communicable. The earliest tradition couched it in a mythic mode, where the encounter of the darkness with the light took place at the navel of the world. It was an ecstatic and visionary experience, with roots reaching back to the earliest shamanic sources of Indian religion: the Buddha was given the epithet of *muni,* "silent one," a type described centuries before in a Vedic poem as flying with the gods in his trance, with wild hair and soiled yellow garments, while mortals could see only his body here below.

We should emphasize the visual aspects of the experience: it is described over and over again as "seeing," a vision that permeates the world with meaning. The Buddha encounters the forces of the Evil One and conquers first lust and then terror, penetrating through the most primordial layers of the human condition that binds him to the world. The mythic mode expresses acute psychological insight into the experience of realization in meditation: but what then is the content of the realization? Here the tradition took the mythic materials in hand and made a metaphysics.

The poet Aśvaghoṣa (first century A.D.) is not concerned with doctrine so much as he is with the visionary experience: his poetic care is lavished upon the assaults of Evil, and his treatment of the doctrinal realization is so much less inspired that scholars have doubted his authorship. But he was aware of the dramatic necessity for content in the revelation, and used the traditional materials available to him. Tradition held that the Buddha first saw all his own past lives, then the moral ordering of the universe and the retribution for deeds, and finally saw through to the final principles that govern the world, sometimes given as the four noble truths, and sometimes as the chain of causation. It is the vision and the sequence of penetration into reality that are important here, and constitute a mythic search for the meaning of the world. Aśvaghoṣa managed to manipulate the mythos into an epos, without sacrificing the directness of the visionary experience.

Aśvaghoṣa, Buddhacarita [*The deeds of Buddha*], ed. *Mahanta Śrī Rām-candra Dās Śāstrī, (Vārānasī: Caukhambā Vidyābhavan, 1966), Cantos XIII-XIV, 1: 178–211.*

Then sat the great seer, resolved on freedom
        son of a house of royal seers
while the earth rejoiced : but the Evil One trembled
        the enemy of the true Law
        whom the world calls god of love
            (with divers weapons : with flowery arrows)
        whom they call Evil One, hater of freedom

And his sons were Confusion, and Thrill, and Arrogance
and his daughters were Lust, and Joy, and Desire
        & they asked of his despair, and he said to them:

This sage has donned the armor of resolution
        he has drawn the arrow of wisdom on the bow of reality
and I despair: for he would conquer my realm

and should he overcome me
        proclaiming to the world the path of happiness
my realm will be made desolate: but as long as
        he stands within my power : his vision unattained
I will move against him, to break his vow
        as a swollen flood against a dam

And he took his flowery bow
        his five arrows which delude the world
he approached the tree with his sons & daughters
        the troubler of minds
his left hand was on his weapons : he played with his arrows
and he said to the seer seated tranquilly there
        eager to cross over the sea of existence:

Arise, coward warrior, afraid of death
        follow your duty : give up this law of freedom
and conquer the world with arrows & with sacrifices
        let the world gain you lordship of the gods

for it is glory to tread the path
        traveled by former lords of men
(and shame it is for a son of royal seers
        to live by begging)

if you remain resolute, & do not arise
if you stay firm, & do not quit your resolve
   I have this arrow ready
     which I shot at the sun (& pricked
     the grandson of the moon, to drive him mad) and
     which made the best of kings my slave
in this degenerate age: shall one weaker than they prevail?

then quickly arise : come to your senses
    my arrow waits, darting its tongue
    more powerful than that I shoot at the ruddy geese
     who are slaves of love, & servants to desire

But when he spoke, the lion sage
    did not move : nor pay him heed
(and he loosed the arrow, parading his sons & daughters before him)
    yet even as it flew he paid no heed
    nor wavered in his constancy
the Evil One despaired : fell into thought, & slowly said:

He heeds not this arrow
    (which has pierced the Lord himself
    & made him lust for the daughter of the mountains)
is he then unfeeling? is this not that arrow?
    he is unworthy of my flowery arrows : deserves not thrill nor lust
     but rather the abuse and blows (the terror
      of cruel hosts of demons)

and he called to mind his legions
    eager to break the calm of the sage:
   his retinue surrounded him in divers forms
    and picked up rocks & trees
    held their swords & clubs in their hands

      pig-faces & fish-faces
      faces of horses and bulls
      tiger-faces & bear-faces
      faces of lions and elephants

     one-eyed : many-faced : three-headed
     hanging bellies and speckled bellies
     blended with goats : knees of pots
     armed with fangs & armed with claws
     skull-faced : many-bodied
     with half the face broken & smashed
     great-mouthed : red with ashes
     and speckled with drops of blood
     clubs in hand : yellow smoky hair

chains dangling : elephant ears hanging
leather-clad or naked
half their faces white or yellow
red as copper : grey as smoke
arms long as snakes
and belts hung with sounding bells
large as a palm tree : grasping spears
small as a child : fangs gaping
ram-faces and bird-bodies
cat-faces and man-bodies
hair wild or half-shaven
red-clothed with mad headdresses
faces rejoicing : faces frowning
strength-destroying : mind-destroying

some attacked : galloping crazily
    & others leaped upon each other
they danced in the sky & wandered in the treetops

one danced and whirled his trident
another roared and dragged his club
one bellowed like a bull in triumph
another blazed from every hair

and thus the hosts of demons stood all about the tree
eager to seize : eager to destroy
    & awaited the command of their lord

the heavens darkened : the earth trembled
the regions of space blazed & roared
the wind blew all about in a hurling rush
the moon did not shine : nor did the stars glow

there spread a darkness deeper than the night
and the oceans shook
as they saw the battle of Evil with the bull of men

the virtuous (longing for the freedom of the world)
wailed in space : for they saw the tree
covered with the hosts of cruel Evil

and the great seer saw the legions of Evil standing there
to assail the Knower of the Law
yet he did not tremble : nor did he become afraid
as a lion lies in the midst of cattle

And the Evil One gave the command
hurling his demon legions to terrify him
his army resolved to crush his fortitude
each with his own power

& they advanced upon him (terrifying
with many hanging tongues) with
sharp fangs with sunbright eyes
(with gaping mouths) with spike-stiff ears

some flew into the sky
to fling rocks & trees & axes upon him
(but they hung in space and did not fall
: like multicolored twilight clouds) & some
cast blazing straw upon him
large as mountain peaks loosed upon him (which
hung in the sky) by his power : burst
into a hundred pieces
& some rose like a blazing sun to pour forth from the sky
a great rain of blazing coals upon him
(as blazing Mount Meru at the end of the world
pours forth the lava of its golden ravines) but
the sparkling
rain of coals scattered
upon the tree : became
(by the power of the best of seers)
: a rain of red lotuses

(& such scorching assaults upon body & mind
were brought down upon him
yet the sage did not stir from his seat
embracing his resolution like a kinsman)

then others vomited snakes from their mouths
(as from a rotting tree) but they did not move
near him : nor hiss : nor strike
(as though bound by a magic spell) & others became
vast clouds with lightnings
& the fierce sound of thunder : to pour forth upon him
a rain of rocks : became
: a shining rain of flowers (or set
blazing arrows in their bows)
which did not fly forth : fell slack
(like the smoldering resentment
of an impotent man) & some took on the form
of hyenas & lions : and roared great roars

(that beings cowered all about
& thought a thunderblasted sky had burst
the deer and elephants cried out in distress
fled & hid themselves
and screaming birds fluttered in that night
and flew about as if in day)

but when all these beings trembled
        the sage did not fear : nor cower from their cries
            as an eagle at the screech of crows (for the more
     terrifying were the assembled hosts the less
        did the sage fear : the more did Evil despair) in grief & rage
         the enemy of those who bear the Law

And then some great invisible thing in the sky
        (seeing Evil in his rage yet seek to harm the seer)
        spoke to the Evil One in a great voice:

Evil One! you are not worthy for this useless labor
        cast aside your malevolence : become safe once more
(for you cannot cause this one to tremble)
        Mount Meru is not shaken by the wind

                        (for fire might lose its heat
                   water its wetness : earth its firmness)
                     but he will not lose his resolve
                       whose merit was gathered over eons

for such is his determination
        his valor : his power : his love for beings
            that he will not arise until he has attained the truth
        (as a thousand-rayed sun until it has dispelled the darkness)

he pities this tortured world
            which lives amidst the plague of lust
        a great physician ought not be hindered
                when he labors for the medicine of knowledge

for when the world is led astray on many wrong paths
        the guide who seeks the one true path
            ought not be hindered
        as a guide when a caravan has lost its way

& when beings are lost in the great darkness
            it is not good to put out the light of knowledge
        the lamp which is kindled in the night

& when he desires to free all creatures
        (their hearts firm bound by the noose of delusion)
            you ought not desire to seize him
        who wearies himself to free the world from bondage

and now the time has come
        he has gathered the merit for enlightenment
        and he sits upon this place
            as did the sages of the past

(for this is the navel of the earth
        endowed with all the highest splendor
    there is no other place upon the earth
        could bear the flood of his contemplation)

do not grieve: but attain to peace
      Evil One
          let not your greatness be arrogance
             for glory is fickle and transient
             set not your pride upon unsteadiness

And when the Evil One heard these words
      & saw the sage untrembling
he despaired : he abandoned his purpose, & went away
          with his arrows which torment the mind
    & his army fled in all directions
          (gone their triumph : useless their efforts)
       their stones & straw & trees used up
          as an army with its camp destroyed by the foe

And the lord of the flowery banners was overcome
      fleeing with his hosts
the great sage was victorious

            (who had overcome the darkness
            who was free of passion)

       & the sky shone with the moon
          like a smiling maiden
       a rain of flowers fell
          fragrant and wet with dew

and the Evil One was overcome, and fled away
      the regions of the sky grew bright : the moon appeared
        a rain of flowers fell upon the earth
      and the night shone like a stainless maiden

                 *

             *   *

He had conquered the hosts of Evil
      with his firmness : with his peace
    he wished to know the highest reality : & he meditated
        (the master of meditation)
    he mastered all the ways of meditation
        and in the first watch of the night
          he remembered all his former lives

    (in such a place I had such a name
    I passed away from there & I came here)

: he remembered a thousand lives
as if experiencing each one
he remembered his birth : his death in each destiny
& the compassionate one felt compassion
for all living creatures

& the conviction arose in him as ne remembered
(the controlled one):

this world is insubstantial as a hollow reed

And in the second watch of the night he attained
(he of unequaled might)
the divine eye : the supreme eye
(he who is the best of those with eyes to see)
& with that pure divine eye he saw the entire world
as in a clear mirror

saw beings appear & pass away according to their deeds

& grew in compassion : for surely those of evil deeds
go to evil destiny (& those of virtuous deeds
set forth for heaven)

& some are born in hell
in terror : in fierce pain
tormented with wretched sufferings
are made to drink molten iron : fiery & boiling
made to mount screaming
on blazing iron pillars
pitiably burned in heaps of blazing coals : and eaten
by fierce dogs with sharp iron fangs
by gloating crows with iron beaks

(& wearied by burning they long for cool shade
are driven into the black sword-leaf forest)

they bitterly suffer who have done evil for pleasure
does their enjoyment grant them a moment of happiness?
(for the deeds the wicked do with laughter
they experience with screaming
when the time has come)

if only those of sinful deeds could see these fruits
they would vomit forth hot blood
as if smitten in their very bowels

& some are born in the wombs of wretched animals
                because their deeds were born of violence
        and they are slaughtered in the sight of their kinsmen
                (for their flesh or fur : their skin or teeth)
                slaughtered for hatred
                        slaughtered for fun

        are driven as horses & oxen (their bodies pierced
                by goads) tortured by hunger
        by thirst and weariness
                        unable : unwilling

                                are driven as elephants
                their heads tormented by hooks
        beaten by foot and heel : the strong
                        driven by the weak

& some are born as hungry ghosts
        whose thoughts were filled with envy
                        eating their doleful fruit in darkness
                (mouths small as needles : bellies big as mountains)
                        their lot is suffering (tormented
with hunger & thirst) inflicted by their own deeds
                who do not find even filth to eat

                        & some are born among men
        in the filthy hellish pool they call a womb
                                (vermin fit for suffering)
                weak : they scream
        seized by rough hands
                        as if chopped by sharp swords

        and they play : enjoy themselves with kinsmen
                gather possessions with love
        are tortured by divers sorrows
                        and all by their own deeds

                & some go to heaven
                        who have done good deeds
        and burn in the flames of lust as in a blazing fire
                unsatisfied

                        & by their lust fall downward
        their garlands faded
                stricken with regret
                        their glory gone . . .

And in the third watch of the night
          he sought to know the truth of the world : & be meditated
              (the best of meditators)
            abiding in courage : unseized by ignorance

           nowhere do creatures find peace or stability
             they are born : they grow old : they die
                again & again
surely the vision of the world is covered over with lust & delusion
       for they cannot see how to set out on the true path
            because of their suffering

        and what is it that through its mere existence
          is the cause of the suffering of old age & death?

and he thought : & he understood why this state exists
                  (the best of those who know)
          for old age & death exist
             only when there is birth
      (where there is a body there is illness : where there is a tree
          it is cut down) & he saw
              (the most excellent of sages)
         everything with his inner eye

    and the sage thought further: what could be
          the cause of birth? & he saw that birth was caused
          by the coming to be of deeds

                he saw that birth
      was set in motion by deeds
          (not by matter : not by a god)
        not without a cause
          not by a self

once a man has broken the first joint of a bamboo
     the rest are easy
                and thus his knowledge grew
       for the sage meditated
       carefully
     on the cause for this coming to be : & he saw
               that it lay in clinging

        all the deeds of beings (practices : observances)
      come from clinging
         as fire from fuel

& he considered: this clinging
      is born through a cause
          and it is because of craving

a spark can consume a forest
when joined with the wind
desire joined with craving
roars through the forest of deeds

& he meditated: what is the cause
of this craving?
and he knew the cause was feelings
(he who was absorbed in meditation)

the world is dragged along by feelings
it rushes after satisfaction
for the world yearns for water
only when it is thirsty

& he meditated, to know the root of feelings : and he saw
(he whose senses were conquered)
the riverbed of feelings was contact
(he who had made an end of feelings)
& he said

contact is the joining of the mind
to a sense & its object
from this contact come feelings
as fire from sticks rubbed together

& again he meditated upon the cause of contact
(the best of those who know the world) & knew
it was the senses & their objects

for a blind man does not see a pot
because it is not in contact with his vision
when there are the senses & their objects
contact is born

& he knew the truth of the senses
he understood their cause was name-and-form
ever thinking with his insight

where there is a sprout
leaves & branches grow
where there is name-and-form
there grow the senses & their objects

& again he meditated upon the cause of name-and-form
(he whose knowledge had gone beyond)
and saw their root was awareness

for when there is awareness
name-and-form appear
as the shoot grows
from the germinated seed

& he considered : whence is awareness born?
and saw that it appears
dependent upon name-and-form

he knew the order of the causes
& traversed the order of effects

(his mind fixed steady upon them
not wandering elsewhere)

for awareness is the condition
whence name-and-form appear
and name-and-form are the foundation
on which awareness depends

a ship carries a man upon the water
the man carries the ship upon dry land
& he thought
awareness & name-and-form cause each other

hot iron sets a blade of glass aflame
and the blazing grass will heat the iron

cause & effect are bound together . . .

but old age & death will cease
when birth is done
and birth will be destroyed
with the destruction of becoming

and the coming to be of deeds will cease
when clinging is cast aside

(& thus he meditated
his inner enlightenment increased)

clinging ends when thirst is over
and there is no thirst when feelings are destroyed
feelings cease when contact is no more
and contact vanishes
when the senses & their objects are destroyed
the senses end when name-and-form are finished
and name-and-form will cease
when there is no more awareness

and surely awareness ceases when one yearns no more for existence
　　(& the sage knew the causes one by one)
　for there is no more yearning for existence
　　　when ignorance vanishes

And he knew what was to be known : he became a Buddha
awoke from his meditation and saw a self nowhere in the world
　　gained the highest peace by the eightfold noble path

I have attained this path : I have fulfilled this path
　　which the great seers followed
　　　(who knew the true & the false)
　　for the benefit of others

And in the fourth watch, when dawn appeared
　　and the whole world was tranquil
he gained omniscience : the imperishable state

& the earth trembled like a drunken maiden when he was enlightened
the heavens shone with his success
　　and kettledrums sounded in the sky

2. WISDOM IS A WAY OF SEEING

What was the content of the enlightenment experience? Its mythic ambiguities provide a range of choices, and the Buddhist tradition was strong
enough to take full advantage of the interpretive options. The ecstatic vision
certainly had an intellectual component: it was (as in the contemporary
movements that produced the *Upaniṣads*) a seeing-through to the real nature of
the world, and it revealed to the Buddha that the world was impermanent,
suffering, and devoid of any fixed substance anywhere.

Thus wisdom becomes a way of looking at the world, of penetrating its
true meaning, and seeing the causal connections that bind us to it. Wisdom is a
mode of being in the world, of looking upon all events with insight, and casting
aside the chains of ignorance. But here the meaning of events is their ultimate
inutility and inadequacy, and the ecstatic projection of meaning upon the
events of the world becomes an enstatic search for separation and disentanglement. We shall see how far this leads.

*Buddhaghosa, Visuddhimagga [The path of purity], ed. Henry Clark
Warren (Cambridge: Harvard University Press, 1950), Chapter XIV, sections 3–7, pp. 369–70.*

In what sense is this called wisdom? In the sense of insight. And what is
this insight? It is a special sort of apprehension, different in kind from
either perception or knowledge.

Now perception and knowledge and wisdom are all equally states of apprehension. But perception is the naked cognition of an object as being simply blue or yellow: it cannot penetrate into its true nature of impermanence, suffering, and not-self.

Knowledge knows the object as being blue or yellow, and penetrates into its true nature: yet it cannot bring about the manifestation of the path, even with the greatest striving.

And wisdom knows the object as above, and penetrates into its true nature, and it brings about the manifestation of the path when one strives therein.

Suppose there were a heap of coins piled on a moneychanger's table, and three people looked at them: an ignorant child, a country villager, and a professional moneychanger.

The ignorant child would know only that the coins were bright and ornamented, long or square or round; he would not know that they were considered treasures for the use and enjoyment of the people.

The country villager would know the coins were bright and ornamented, and also that they were considered treasures for the use and enjoyment of the people; but he would not know which were genuine, which were false, and which were only half-value.

But the professional moneychanger would know all of these things, and he would know them by simply looking at a coin, listening to its sound when struck, smelling it, tasting it, or weighing it in his hand; and he would know that it was made in a certain village or town or city, or on a certain mountain or river bank, or by a certain master.

This is to be understood as an analogy.

For perception is like the ignorant child looking at the coins; it grasps only the outward appearance of the object as blue and so on.

Knowledge is like the country villager looking at the coins; it grasps the outward appearance of the object as blue and so on, and further penetrates into its true nature.

And wisdom is like the professional moneychanger looking at the coins; it grasps the outward appearance of the object as blue and so on, penetrates into its true nature, and further attains to a manifestation of the path.

Thus wisdom should be understood as a special sort of apprehension, different in kind from either perception or knowledge. This is why we said that it was wisdom in the sense of insight.

Now this wisdom does not necessarily accompany all perception and knowledge; but when it does accompany them, then it is not something separate from them, that they can be distinguished one from the other: the difference is very subtle and hard to see. This is why it was said:

"Great King, it is a difficult thing which the Blessed One has done."

"Venerable one, what is the difficult thing which the Blessed One has done?"

"The difficult thing done by the Blessed One was to explain all the mental events which take place upon a single object, that this is contact, this is feeling, this is an idea, this is a volition, this is a thought."

What is the definition, the function, the manifestation, and the cause of wisdom? Wisdom is defined by its penetration to the essence of events. Its function is to destroy the darkness of delusion that conceals the essence of events. Its manifestation is the absence of delusion. And its cause is meditation, for it is said: He who is in meditation knows and sees things as they really are.

3. NIRVANA

The world is ultimately unsatisfactory: it is made, become, changing, suffering, useless. The search is then for what is not made, what is not suffering. The very existence of the unsatisfactory has for its corollary the existence of the ultimately satisfying. Let us give it a name; let us call it the end of suffering; let us call it nirvana.

The extension of the experience of penetration to include the corollary of nirvana took place very early: it is extremely probable that the Buddha saw the world and nirvana as two sides of the same coin of reality. The twelve-fold chain of dependent origination (or any of its earlier and shorter versions) can be read backward as well as forward; it can be seen as a chain of causation leading to bondage, or as a disentanglement from the world, a gradual process of elimination leading to an enstatic withdrawal rather than an ecstatic penetration. The following passages are the source for all future descriptions of disentanglement from occurring events, and for the postulation of a transcendent permanence beyond the world. In twenty-five centuries, they have not been exhausted, as philosophers have sought to explain, somehow, the nature of this ultimate transcendence.

Udāna [*Utterances*], *in* Khuddaka-nikāya [*Collection of little texts*], gen. ed. Bhikkhu J. Kashyap, (Bihar: Pali Publication Board, 1959), Chapter VIII, sect. 1–4, pp. 162–63.

Monks, there is that sphere wherein is neither earth nor water, fire nor air: it is not the infinity of space, nor the infinity of perception; it is not nothingness, nor is it neither idea nor nonidea; it is neither this world nor the next, nor is it both; it is neither the sun nor the moon.

Monks, I say it neither comes nor goes, it neither abides nor passes away; it is not caused, established, begun, supported: it is the end of suffering.

What I call the selfless is hard to see, for it is not easy to see the truth. But he who knows it penetrates his craving; and for him who sees it, there is nothing there.

Monks, there is an unborn, unbecome, unmade, unconditioned. Monks, if there were not an unborn, unbecome, unmade, unconditioned, then we could not here know any escape from the born, become, made, conditioned.

But since there is an unborn, unbecome, unmade, unconditioned, then we know there is an escape from the born, become, made, conditioned.

For the attached there is wandering, but for the unattached there is no wandering: without wandering there is serenity; when there is serenity there is no lust; without lust there is neither coming nor going; without coming or going there is neither passing away nor being reborn; without passing away or being reborn there is neither this life nor the next, nor anything between them. It is the end of suffering.

4. THE WAY OUT OF THE WORLD

Given the transcendent and thus ineffable nature of nirvana, Buddhist tradition has been accused of both pessimism and obscurantism. Neither charge is true: our own religious traditions have struggled with the problems of finding value in a world where ultimate value lies ultimately beyond the world, where transcendence becomes alienation and loss. The struggle is between robbing the world of all meaning and building it into a graven image: as transcendence merges into loss, so does immanence become idolatry—of images of stone, of pleasure, of money, of the state. This world is where false gods live.

The tension is a creative one, but still it must be resolved, and the early Buddhist philosophical traditions made a choice for transcendence and a devaluation of the world. Nirvana was the goal, and nirvana was freedom from the filthy pit of occurring events, the open air after a blazing fire, security and peace. The world is suffering; nirvana must then be bliss.

Milinda-pañha [*The questions of King Milinda*], ed. V. Trenckner, (London: William and Norgate, 1880), pp. 313–26.

"Venerable one, is nirvana all bliss, or is it mixed with suffering?"

"Nirvana is entirely bliss, Great King, and there is no suffering in it."

"We cannot believe that nirvana is all bliss; we maintain that it is mixed with suffering. For we can see that those who seek nirvana torment their bodies and their minds: they restrain their standing and walking and sitting and eating; they interrupt their sleep; they oppress their senses; and they cast aside their wealth and friends and kinsmen.

"But those who are happy and full of bliss in the world delight their senses with pleasure. They delight their eyes with all manner of beautiful sights, and their ears with all manner of music and song; they delight their nose with the scent of fruits and flowers and fragrant plants, and their tongue with the sweet taste of food and drink. They delight their body with the touch of the soft and fine, the tender and the delicate; and they delight their mind with thoughts and ideas both virtuous and sinful, both good and bad. And they do these things whenever they like.

"But you do not develop your senses; you slay and destroy and hinder and prevent them, and thus torment your body and your mind. When you torment your body, then you feel suffering in your body; when you torment your mind, then you feel suffering in your mind. And that is why I say that nirvana is mixed with suffering."

"What you call suffering, Great King, is not what we call nirvana; it is the preliminary to nirvana, the search for nirvana. Nirvana is all bliss and is not mixed with suffering. And I will tell you why. Is there what we might call a bliss of sovereignty which kings enjoy?"

"Indeed, venerable one, there is a bliss of sovereignty."

"But the borders become disturbed, and a king must put down the revolt; and he surrounds himself with advisors and soldiers and goes sojourning abroad. He runs about over the rough ground and is oppressed by flies and mosquitoes and wind and heat; he fights great battles and is in doubt of his very life."

"But, venerable one, that is not what we call the bliss of sovereignty; it is but a preliminary in search thereof. The king seeks for power with suffering, and then he can enjoy the bliss he has sought. The bliss of sovereignty is not mixed with suffering: the bliss is one thing and the suffering another."

"Even so, Great King, nirvana is all bliss and is not mixed with suffering. Those who seek nirvana torment their bodies and their minds: they restrain their standing and walking and sitting and eating; they interrupt their sleep; they oppress their senses; they sacrifice their bodies and their lives.

"They seek for nirvana with suffering, and then they can enjoy the bliss they have sought, even as a king enjoys the bliss of sovereignty when he has destroyed his enemies. Nirvana is all bliss and is not mixed with suffering: the bliss is one thing and the suffering another.

"And I will tell you another reason. Is there what we might call a bliss of learning which is enjoyed by learned masters?"

"Indeed, venerable one, there is a bliss of learning."

"Is that bliss of learning mixed with suffering?"

"No, it is not."

"But a student torments himself with bowing down and standing up before his teacher: he fetches the water and sweeps the house; he massages and bathes his teacher's feet; and all he gets are scraps of food. He casts aside his own mind and follows the mind of another; he sleeps in discomfort and eats bad food."

"But, venerable one, that is not what we call the bliss of learning; it is but a preliminary in search thereof. The student seeks for learning with suffering, and then he can enjoy the bliss he has sought. The bliss of learning is not mixed with suffering: the bliss is one thing and the suffering another."

"Even so, Great King, nirvana is all bliss and is not mixed with suffering. Those who seek nirvana torment their bodies and their minds: they restrain their standing and walking and sitting and eating; they interrupt their sleep; they oppress their senses; they sacrifice their bodies and their lives.

"They seek for nirvana with suffering, and then they can enjoy the bliss they have sought, even as a learned master enjoys the bliss of learning. Nirvana is all bliss and is not mixed with suffering: the bliss is one thing and the suffering another."

"Excellent, venerable one. Thus it is, and thus I accept it."

*

*   *

"Venerable one, you are always speaking of nirvana: can you give me a metaphor, or a reason, or an argument, or an inference to show me its form, or its nature, or its duration, or its size?"

"Great King, nirvana is unique and incomparable: there is neither metaphor nor reason, neither argument nor inference, which can show its form, or its nature, or its duration, or its size."

"But venerable one, nirvana is a real thing: I simply cannot accept that there is no way to make intelligible its form, or its nature, or its duration, or its size. Explain this reasonably to me."

"Very well, Great King, I shall explain it to you. Is there such a thing as the ocean?"

"Of course there is such a thing as the ocean."

"Suppose someone were to ask you how much water there was in the ocean, and how many creatures lived therein. How would you answer such a question?"

"Foolish person, I would say, you are asking me an unaskable thing. No one should ask such a question; such a question should be put aside. Scientists have never analyzed the ocean: no one can measure the water there, nor count the creatures who live therein. That is the way I would answer the question."

"But, Great King, the ocean is a real thing: why should you give such an answer? Should you not rather count and then say: There is so much water in the ocean, and so many creatures living therein?"

"But I could not do so, venerable one. The question is impossible."

"So the ocean is a real thing, yet you cannot measure its water nor count its creatures; and in the same way nirvana is a real thing, yet there is neither metaphor nor reason, neither argument nor inference, which can show its form, or its nature, or its duration, or its size. And even if there were a man with magic powers, who could measure the waters of the ocean and count its creatures: even he could not find the form, or the nature, or the duration, or the size of nirvana."

"Venerable one, let us accept that. Is there not at least some quality of nirvana which is also found elsewhere, that it may serve as a metaphor?"

"Nothing has the same form as nirvana, but we can indeed find some things to serve as metaphors for its qualities."

"Excellent, venerable one. Quickly tell me, that I may gain some insight into even one of the qualities of nirvana. Allay the fever of my heart with the cool sweet breezes of your speech."

"One quality of the lotus is found in nirvana, Great King, and two qualities of water; three qualities of medicine, and four of the ocean; five of food, and ten of space; three of the wish-granting gem, and three of red sandalwood; three of the finest butter, and five qualities of a mountain peak are found in nirvana."

"What is the one quality of the lotus which is found in nirvana?"

"The lotus is unstained by water, Great King, and nirvana is unstained by any passion."

"And the two qualities of water?"

"Water is cool, and calms fever; and nirvana is cool, and calms the fever of all the passions. Water allays the thirst of men and beasts who are weary and thirsty, parched and overcome by heat; and nirvana allays the thirst of craving for pleasure, craving for existence, and craving for wealth."

"And the three qualities of medicine?"

"Medicine is a refuge for creatures tormented by poison; and nirvana is a refuge for creatures tormented by the poison of passion. Medicine puts an end to disease, and nirvana puts an end to all suffering. Medicine is the nectar of immortality, and nirvana is the nectar of immortality."

"What are the four qualities of the ocean which are found in nirvana?"

"The ocean is empty of all corpses, and nirvana is empty of the corpses of passion. The ocean is great and limitless, and it is not filled by all the rivers that flow into it; and nirvana is great and limitless, and it is not filled by all the beings who enter it. The ocean is the abode of great creatures; and nirvana is the abode of the great Worthy Ones, the stainless, the strong, the powerful. The ocean seems to flower with the vast and various blossoms of the waves; and nirvana seems to flower with the vast and various blossoms of purity and knowledge and freedom."

"And the ten qualities of space?"

"Space does not arise, nor decay, nor die, nor pass away, nor reappear; it cannot be overcome, nor stolen by thieves; it is not supported by anything; it is the path of the birds, without obstruction, infinite. And nirvana does not arise, nor decay, nor die, nor pass away, nor reappear; it cannot be overcome, nor stolen by thieves; it is not supported by anything; it is the path of the Noble Ones, without obstruction, infinite."

"And the three qualities of the wish-granting gem?"

"The wish-granting gem grants every wish, and nirvana grants every wish. The wish-granting gem causes joy, and nirvana causes joy. The wish-granting gem shines with light, and nirvana shines with light."

"And the three qualities of red sandalwood?"

"Red sandalwood is hard to find, and nirvana is hard to find. Red sandalwood has an unequaled fragrance, and nirvana has an unequaled fragrance. Red sandalwood is praised by the discriminating, and nirvana is praised by the Noble Ones."

"And the three qualities of the finest butter?"

"The finest butter is beautiful in color, and nirvana is beautiful in virtue. The finest butter is beautiful in fragrance, and nirvana is beautiful in righteousness. The finest butter is beautiful in taste, and nirvana is beautiful in experience."

"What are the five qualities of a mountain peak which are found in nirvana?"

"Nirvana is as lofty as a mountain peak and as unmoving. A mountain peak is hard to climb, and nirvana cannot be reached by the passions. No seeds can grow upon a mountain peak, and no passion can grow in nirvana. A mountain peak is free of fear or favor, and nirvana is free of fear or favor."

"Excellent, venerable one. Thus it is, and thus I accept it."

*

* *

"Venerable one, it is said that nirvana is neither in the past, nor in the future, nor in the present; that it is not produced, nor is it unproduced, nor is it producible. Then say a man rightly practices, and realizes nirvana: does he realize something already produced, or does he produce it first and then realize it?"

"He neither realizes something already produced, Great King, nor does he produce it first and then realize it. And yet the realm of nirvana exists, that he may rightly practice, and realize it."

"Venerable one, do not explain the question by making it dark; explain it by making it open and unconcealed. Willingly heap upon me all that you have been taught, for people are bewildered and perplexed, and full of doubt. Destroy this dagger in my heart."

"The realm of nirvana exists, Great King, calm and blissful and exalted. And a man may rightly practice, and know conditioned things according to the teachings of the Buddha, and realize nirvana with his wisdom.

"Even as a student might learn an art according to the teachings of his master, a man may rightly practice, and know conditioned things according to the teachings of the Buddha, and realize nirvana with his wisdom.

"And how may nirvana be known? It may be known by its safety, its security, its peace, its calm, its joy, its bliss, its purity, its coolness.

"Suppose a man were being burned in a blazing scorching fire heaped high with wood. And with great effort he freed himself and escaped into the open air where there was no fire; then he would feel the greatest happiness.

"Even so, Great King, a man may rightly practice and by careful attention realize nirvana, the highest happiness, wherein the three-fold fires blaze no more. For these fires of passion are the fire heaped high with wood; and the man who rightly practices is the man cast into the fire; and nirvana is the open air.

"Or suppose a man had fallen into a pit filled with excrement and the corpses of snakes and dogs and men, that he was entangled in the hair of the corpses. And with great effort he freed himself and escaped into the open air where there were no corpses; then he would feel the greatest happiness.

"Even so, Great King, a man may rightly practice and by careful attention realize nirvana, the highest happiness, wherein there are no corpses of passion. For the pleasures of your senses are the corpses; and the man who rightly practices is the man fallen into the pit; and nirvana is the open air.

"Or suppose a man had been taken by his enemies, and he shivered and trembled in his fear, and his heart was confused and distressed. And with great effort he freed himself and escaped into a place of safety, firm and secure; then he would feel the greatest happiness.

"Even so, Great King, a man may rightly practice and by careful attention realize nirvana, the highest happiness, wherein there is neither fear nor terror. For the terror you feel at birth and decay and disease and death is the fear of the man among his enemies; and the man who rightly practices is the terrified man; and nirvana is the place of safety.

"Or suppose a man had fallen into a muddy swamp, all filthy and dirty and slimy. And with great effort he removed the slimy mud and went into a place which was pure and clean; then he would feel the greatest happiness.

"Even so, Great King, a man may rightly practice and by careful attention realize nirvana, the highest happiness, wherein there is no mud of passion. For your possessions and honor and fame are mud; and the man who rightly practices is the man fallen into the swamp; and nirvana is the place which is pure and clean.

"And how does this man rightly practice, and realize nirvana? He knows conditioned things as they really are; he sees in them birth, and decay, and disease, and death; he sees in them neither happiness nor joy, nor anything worth grasping, in the beginning or the middle or the end.

"Suppose a lump of iron were heated all day, and became scorching and glowing and hot: a man could find no place to grasp it, in the beginning or middle or end.

"Even so, Great King, he knows conditioned things as they really are; he sees in them birth, and decay, and disease, and death; he sees in them neither happiness nor joy, nor anything worth grasping, in the beginning or the middle or the end.

"And his heart grows discontented when he sees nothing worth grasping, and his body begins to sweat; for he is without refuge or protection, and he is weary of all his existences.

"Suppose a man had fallen into a great blazing mass of fire: he would be without refuge or protection, and he would weary of the flames.

"Even so, Great King, his heart grows discontented, and his body begins to sweat; for he is without refuge or protection, and he is weary of all his existences.

"And when he has seen the terror of this world, he thinks: Blazing it is, burning and blazing and full of sorrow. If I could only find something else, something calm and exalted, something passionless and peaceful; if only I could find nirvana, wherein all these conditioned things come to rest, where clinging to rebirth is given up, where craving is destroyed.

"And his heart leaps forward from the world, and he finds peace. For he is happy, and rejoices: I have gained my freedom from the world.

"Suppose a man had chanced into a strange land and lost his way. And when he found the way out his heart would leap forward; he would be happy, and rejoice: I have found the way out at last.

"Even so, Great King, his heart leaps forward from the world, and he finds peace. For he is happy, and rejoices: I have found the way out at last.

"And he pursues that path, and strives upon it, and practices it: his mindfulness is fixed upon the goal, and his striving is fixed upon the goal, and his joy is fixed upon the goal.

"He is forever aware of the goal; and he passes beyond the world and gains his freedom. And when he has gained his freedom from the world, Great King, then this man has rightly practiced, and has realized nirvana."

"Excellent, venerable one. Thus it is, and thus I accept it."

5. THE TRANCE OF CESSATION

Buddhism was not the only Indian tradition to choose transcendence. The Vedas reveal to us an ecstatic mode of being in the world, a visionary experience of present deity that culminated in the profound immanence of the *Upaniṣads*; but this vision was early challenged by the enstatic mode of Yoga and Jainism, which preached the most radical withdrawal from the world and the erection of impenetrable boundaries around the untouched self, insisting upon the absolute transcendence of salvation, a monadology of freedom.

The Buddhist trance of cessation is in many ways a logical extension of the gradual sensory withdrawal of the four trances: all the so-called formless trances were worked into the standard structure of the contemplative process as part of the practice of calm and considered preliminary exercises to the application of insight. But just as there is reason to believe that insight was originally an independent process of ecstatic penetration into reality (as evidenced by the anomalous status of Mindfulness within the structure), the following text suggests that trance itself was once an independent approach to a goal defined as utterly apart from this world of pain and sorrow.

There are many parallels between this Buddhist trance and the procedures of classical Yoga. Despite deep clashes in metaphysical superstructure, there is considerable similarity in the ultimate experience of enstatic disentanglement from the world. The trance of cessation is structurally equivalent to the final *samādhi* of the yogic texts: both are states wherein all thoughts and feelings cease; neither relies upon the external support of a meditative object; both culminate a sequence of withdrawals from sensory experience, and both are the highest happiness that can be achieved in this life. The yogic word for salvation is "isolation," and though the Buddhist texts do not use the term, it is an apt description of ultimate transcendence.

Buddhaghosa, Visuddhimagga [The path of purity], ed. Henry Clarke Warren (Cambridge: Harvard University Press, 1950), Chapter X, sections 1–63, pp. 271–83, and Chapter XXIII, sections 17–52, pp. 604–11.

The Realm of Infinite Space

And the monk wearies of the material thing which is the object of his fourth trance, and he wishes to go beyond it; he emerges from the now familiar trance, and he sees the danger in it, thinking: This trance has for its object a material thing, and I am weary of material things . . .

And he sees the danger in the fourth trance, and his longing for it disappears; and he concentrates upon the realm of infinite space, for he sees that it is peaceful.

So he takes his meditative object and extends it to the very ends of the universe, and then he eliminates the object itself and concentrates upon the space which was touched by it, saying: This is space; this is infinite space.

And in eliminating the object he does not roll it up like a mat, nor pull it out like a cake from a pan, but he simply concentrates upon it no longer, nor does he notice it, or contemplate it. He eliminates the object by ceasing to concentrate upon it, and he concentrates exclusively upon the space which was touched by it, saying: This is space.

Thus the meditative object does not change its position, but it is eliminated; for he no longer concentrates upon it, but concentrates instead upon space; he perceives only the space left by the elimination of the object. We may call it the space left by the elimination of the object, or the space which was touched by the object, or the space from which the object was removed: it is all the same.

He concentrates again and again upon the mental image of the space left by the elimination of the object; he strikes at it with discursive thought and reasoning. And as he does so, the hindrances are cast aside, his mindfulness is established, and his mind is concentrated.

Again and again he pursues the image of infinite space, cultivates it and practices it. And in concentrating upon it again and again, his mind becomes fixed in the realm of infinite space . . .

And when this formless trance occurs, the monk is like a man who has plugged a hole in a pot with a blue rag, or a yellow or red or white rag, and is looking upon it; and the wind comes and tears the rag away, and he finds himself looking at space.

For the monk had been looking with the eye of his trance upon a meditative object; and the object has been torn away by his attention upon the space from which it was removed, and he finds himself looking at space . . .

The Realm of Infinite Perception

. . . And the monk sees the danger in the realm of infinite space, thinking: This trance may easily slip back into the realm of material things; it is not as peaceful as the realm of infinite perception.

And he sees the danger in the trance of infinite space, and his longing for it disappears; and he concentrates upon the realm of infinite perception, for he sees that it is peaceful.

So he concentrates upon his own perception pervading infinite space, saying: This is perception; this is infinite perception.

He concentrates again and again upon the mental image of his perception pervading infinite space; he strikes at it with discursive thought and reasoning. And as he does so, the hindrances are cast aside, his mindfulness is established, and his mind is concentrated.

Again and again he pursues the image of infinite perception, cultivates it and practices it. And in concentrating upon it again and again, his mind becomes fixed in the realm of infinite perception . . .

The Realm of Nothing-at-all

. . . . And the monk sees the danger in the realm of infinite perception, thinking: This trance may easily slip back into the realm of infinite space; it is not as peaceful as the realm of nothing-at-all.

And he sees the danger in the trance of infinite perception, and his longing for it disappears; and he concentrates upon the realm of nothing-at-all, for he sees that it is peaceful.

So he concentrates upon the absence and emptiness and removal of his perception of infinite space. And how does he do this? He eliminates his perception and concentrates upon its absence, saying: It is not there; it is empty; it is removed.

He concentrates again and again upon the absence of his perception pervading infinite space; he strikes at it with discursive thought and reasoning. And as he does so, the hindrances are cast aside, his mindfulness is established, and his mind is concentrated.

Again and again he pursues the image of nothing-at-all, cultivates it and practices it. And in concentrating upon it again and again, his mind becomes fixed in the realm of nothing-at-all . . .

And when this formless trance occurs, the monk is like a man who sees an assembly of monks in the assembly hall, and then goes away. And the monks finish the business for which they had assembled, and they depart; and the man returns and stands in the doorway, looking at the place. He sees that it is empty and deserted, but he does not think: These monks have died; these monks have left the district. But rather he sees only that the place is empty and deserted, and that the monks are absent.

For the monk had been looking with the eye of his trance upon his own perception; and his perception has been eliminated by his attention upon its absence, and he finds himself looking at absence . . .

The Realm of Neither Idea nor Non-idea

. . . And the monk sees the danger in the realm of nothing-at-all, thinking: This trance may easily slip back into the realm of infinite perception; it is not as peaceful as the realm of neither idea nor non-idea. For ideas are a disease; ideas are an abscess; ideas are a dagger in the heart. It is peaceful and exalted to abide in neither idea nor non-idea.

And he sees the danger in the trance of nothing-at-all, and his longing for it disappears; and he concentrates upon the realm of neither idea nor non-idea, for he sees that it is peaceful.

So he concentrates upon the realm of nothing-at-all, with absence as its object, saying: This is peace; this is peace.

He concentrates again and again upon this peace; he strikes at it with discursive thought and reasoning. And as he does so, the hindrances are cast aside, his mindfulness is established, and his mind is concentrated.

Again and again he pursues the image of neither idea nor non-idea, cultivates it and practices it. And in concentrating upon it again and again, his mind becomes fixed in the realm of neither idea nor non-idea . . .

. . . Now the monk achieves the first of these formless trances by transcending material things, the second by transcending space, the third by transcending his perception of space, and the fourth by transcending the elimination of his perception of space . . .

Suppose there were a tent pitched in a filthy place, and a man came and climbed up on to the tent to avoid the filth, and hung there by his hands. And another man came and clung to the man who was hanging on to the tent.

And yet another man came, but he thought: The man who is hanging on to the tent, and the man who is clinging to him, are both in danger, for surely they will fall if the tent collapses. I will stand outside.

So he did not cling to the man who was clinging to the first man but stayed outside. And yet another man came and considered how insecure was the man hanging on to the tent, and the man clinging to him, and he thought that the man standing outside was well placed, so he clung to him instead.

Now the tent pitched in the filthy place is like the space left by the elimination of the material object. The man who hangs on to the tent to avoid the filth is like the trance of infinite space: for the trance takes space as its object to avoid the filth of material things.

The man who clings to the man hanging on to the tent is like the trance of infinite perception: for that trance depends upon the trance of infinite space, which has space as its object.

The man who sees their insecurity and stands outside without clinging to the man hanging on to the tent is like the trance of nothing-at-all: for that trance does not take the realm of infinite space as its object, but rather takes as its object the absence of the perception of space.

And the man who considers that the man outside is well placed and clings to him instead is like the trance of neither idea nor non-idea: for that trance depends upon the trance of nothing-at-all, which in turn stands outside, in the absence of perception . . .

The Trance of Cessation

What is the trance of cessation? It is the total stopping of the mind and all its thoughts through a gradual process of elimination.

Why does one enter the trance? One grows weary of the arising and ceasing of conditioned things, and thinks: Let me be without thought and dwell in bliss; here and now let me gain the cessation that is nirvana.

How does one enter the trance? The monk who wishes to enter the trance of cessation first finishes his meal, washes his hands and feet, and sits upon the appointed seat in a secluded place.

He sits down with his legs crossed, holds his body straight, and sets up mindfulness before him.

Then he enters the first trance, and he emerges therefrom and sees with insight that the conditioned things therein are impermanent, and suffering, and not-self.

Now this insight is of three sorts: the insight which comprehends conditioned things, the insight which leads to the trance of fruition, and the insight which leads to the trance of cessation.

The insight which comprehends conditioned things may be either quick or slow, yet still leads to the path; the insight which leads to the trance of fruition works only when it is quick, as when one cultivates the path; and the insight which leads to the trance of cessation works only when it is neither too quick nor too slow. And so the monk sees conditioned things with insight that is neither too quick nor too slow.

Then he enters the second trance, and he emerges therefrom and sees with insight that the conditioned things therein are impermanent, and suffering, and not-self.

And similarly with the third trance, and the fourth trance, and the trance of infinite space, and the trance of infinite perception, and the trance of nothing-at-all: he emerges therefrom and sees with insight that the conditioned things therein are impermanent, and suffering, and not-self.

And when he emerges from the trance of nothing-at-all, he must do the four-fold preparation. He resolves that anything he has about him which belongs to someone else shall not be damaged while he is in his trance; he resolves to emerge from his trance should the community need his presence; he resolves to emerge from his trance should his master call him; and he determines how long he shall live, lest his trance be interrupted by death . . .

And then he enters the trance of neither idea nor non-idea, and when one or two moments of thought have passed, he becomes without thought, and he attains to cessation.

Why do his thoughts not continue after only two thoughts? Because he practices cessation; he joins his calm and his insight together, and he ascends through the eight trances; he practices a gradual process of elimination . . .

How long does the trance last? It lasts as long as the monk has decided, unless it is interrupted by death, or the needs of the Community, or the summons of his master.

How does he emerge from it? He emerges from the trance having attained the fruit of being a Worthy One . . .

And where does his mind tend? When he emerges from the trance, his mind tends toward nirvana. As it is said: When a monk emerges from the trance of cessation, wherein are neither ideas nor feelings, then his mind tends toward solitude, inclines to solitude, goes to solitude.

But what is the difference between one who is in this trance and one who is dead? This too is explained in scripture: When one is dead, the elements of his body are ceased and still, the elements of his speech are ceased and still, and the elements of his mind are ceased and still: his life has ended, his warmth has subsided, his senses are cut off.

When a monk has attained the trance of cessation, the elements of his body are ceased and still, the elements of his speech are ceased and still, and the elements of his mind are ceased and still: but his life has not ended, his warmth has not subsided, and his senses are not cut off . . .

This peaceful trance is practiced by the Noble Ones, and it is considered nirvana in this very life. The wise man cultivates his noble wisdom, and enters into it, to attain this trance: it is called a blessing of wisdom upon the noble path.

6. ALL THINGS ARE ENLIGHTENMENT

The creative tension between transcendence and immanence has been one of the most fruitful sources of renewal in the Buddhist tradition. The religious movement known as the Great Vehicle drew upon ancient visionary modes to support the value of action in the world and create a metaphysical structure wherein the vows of compassion could be effective. The movement was revivalistic in the sense that it saw itself as returning to the roots of its tradition, and in exactly the same sense it was radical as well; for wisdom was now seen as immanent within all events, if they could but be penetrated to their true nature. Enlightenment was reaffirmed over nirvana, and enlightenment became once more a mode of being rather than an ontological state: once more the world became an arena of salvation rather than a pit of corpses, and events in the world were permeated with ecstatic meaning. Disentanglement did not mean escape from the world, but freedom within the world itself.

Śāntideva, Śikṣāsamuccaya, [An anthology of teachings] ed. P. L. Vaidya, (Darbhanga: The Mithila Institute, 1961), Chapter XIV, p. 137.

This much is to be known: ·the conventional & the absolute: and the Blessed One has well seen & well known & well experienced it, and it is emptiness. Therefore he is called the omniscient one.

The Buddha sees the conventional: it is ordinary experience. But the absolute is inexpressible, unknowable, unperceivable, untaught, unrevealed, inactive; neither gain nor loss, praise nor blame, happiness nor sorrow, form nor formlessness . . .

What was it that the Blessed One revealed in his supreme & perfect enlightenment? Was it form or feeling or idea or motive or perception that the Blessed One revealed in his supreme & perfect enlightenment? It was none of these, for form does not occur, & enlightenment does not occur: how can the unoccurring be enlightened about the unoccurring?

When no event at all can be apprehended, what is the Buddha? what is enlightenment? what is a bodhisattva? what is a revelation? For form & feeling & idea & motive & perception are all empty.

All this is nothing but usage, nothing but names, nothing but agreed signs, nothing but convention, nothing but designation, & wise men do not believe in it . . .

For all events are the limit of reality, the final limit, the limit of vision, the limit of the unfixed. All events are enlightenment . . .

We laugh at those who seek nirvana: for if they had ever indeed fallen into the world, then they might seek for nirvana.

The limit of reality! We do not apprehend any limit; we do not apprehend any reality. Whoever apprehends reality apprehends its limit: & he courses in duality . . .

7. NIRVANA IS HERE AND NOW

The philosopher Nāgārjuna (second century A.D.) was the major intellectual spokesman for the immanence of holiness within the world. The limit of nirvana is the limit of the world, he declared; nirvana is not a thing to be gained or lost. Nirvana is enlightenment, and enlightenment is a mode of apprehension: it is not a thing in itself; it is as unreal as any "thing." But it is a way of relating to the world by ecstatic penetration into the true reality of events; it is to be free and spontaneous in the midst of events, and to know them in their emptiness.

The meditator breaks through to freedom by destroying the reality of the world. When he destroys the objective referent of his own subjectivity, he eliminates the subject as well: he systematically empties every description of its reference to a real thing. In his philosophical works, Nāgārjuna applies this process of metaphysical emptying-out to every concept of real existence—and hence to every concept of real nonexistence—wherever it is found. Space and time, persons and events, nirvana and the world can have existence neither predicated of them nor denied them. All of our reality—the arising and abiding and perishing of events—neither exists nor nonexists; it is an illusion and a dream; it is a reality wherein the Buddhas walk in perfect freedom, and are masters of the magic show. The chains that bind us are a bubble we can burst by waking to the dream.

Nāgārjuna, Madhyamaka-śāstra [*The middle stanzas*], ed. P. L. Vaidya, (Darbhanga: The Mithila Institute, 1960), Chapter XXV, verses 4–24, pp. 229–37.

nirvanas not any some : thing
(lost or gained) eternal
or ending   arisen or
destroyed

if nirvana were some any : thing
absurdly it
would decay & die
(all any some : things decay & die)

if nirvana were any some : thing
it would be caused
no every)any : thing(where
is unconditioned

if nirvana were some any : thing
it would be
clinging to existence
(every any some : thing clings)

& if

nirvanas not any some : thing
nirvanas not some no : thing

(where there is not some : thing
no : thing not is there where)

if nirvana were any no : thing
it would be
clinging to existence
(every any no : thing clings)

but coming & going
clinging dependent
made free unclinging
is called nirvana

abandon   the Teacher said
being & unbeing
so nirvana is
not some : thing not no : thing

if nirvana were both
any some : thing some no : thing
absurdly freedom
would be
some no : thing any some : thing

if nirvana were both
any some : thing some no : thing
it would be
clinging to existence
some)both(no : things cling

how can nirvana be both
some no : thing any some : thing
nirvana is not caused
no some (any no) : thing
is unconditioned

how can both (any some) some no : thing
pertain to nirvana
not both where)any(when together
(like light & darkness)

we could know nirvana is
not any some (some no) : thing
if we only knew what
some no (any some) : thing was

if nirvana were
not some no (any some) : thing
who could establish
not (any some) some no : thing

after his final cessation
the Blessed One isnt is
(isnt isnt) isnt is & isnt
isnt isnt is & isnt

during his lifetime
the Blessed One isnt is
(isnt isnt) isnt is & isnt
isnt isnt is & isnt

there is no difference at all
between this world & nirvana
between nirvana & this world
there is no difference at all

the limit of nirvana is
the limit of this world
between the two
any even not most subtle is

to say   the final end
is eternal
means there is
before) nirvana (after &

when all events are empty
what is endless
what is ending (what is endless
& ending) what is neither
endless nor ending

which is this
which is the other

which is eternal (which
noneternal) which both
which neither

happiness is
calming all realmaking
calming all busywork
Buddha didnt teach
where)any(when
events

Nāgārjuna, Mahāyāna-vimśikā [*Twenty verses on the great vehicle*], *in
Minor Buddhist Texts, ed. Giuseppi Tucci (Rome: Instituto Italiano per il
Medio ed Estremo Oriente, 1956), 1: 201–203.*

homage to the Buddha (inconceivable
glory) mind unattached : whose compassion
taught the Law (expressed
the inexpressible)

Buddhas & beings are of one essence
(like space) do not arise
through an essence : do not cease
in reality

(& we are impelled to this world :
to nirvana) by what does not occur
by what is born in dependence
by what the omniscient know

for all things
are pure (& calm :
beyond duality) like a reflection
: reality

& we think there is a self
where there is no self
happiness & sorrow
are real for us : & realization

the six destinies & this
world : highest happiness of heaven
great suffering in hell
old age : disease : & death

are real for us

we see what isnt there (& burn
in hell) burn
by our own fault (as reeds
are burned by fire)

& experience things
at the magic show
(go to a destiny :
born in dependence)

at the magic show

fools fear the world (a painter
paints a demon
& screams) a child digs
a mudhole : falls in

sunk in the mud of imposing upon reality
& cant get out (& see no:thing
as real) feel sorrow : false things
tormenting with the poison of fear

but the Buddhas : constant
in compassion (seek
to help) see us helpless
& lead us to enlightenment

that we may be Buddhas : knowledge
attained : & freed from the net
of things (friends of the world)

they see reality (unborn
unmade) they see the world :
empty (and without beginning
without middle : without end)

they see there is no world
(no nirvana) stainless it is
unchanging (and radiant in the beginning
in the middle : in the end)

he who has awakened does not see
what he saw in his dream (he who has awakened
from delusion does not see)
the world

a magician puts on a magic show
when he stops : nothing
nothing : the nature of reality
nothing (but thought)

a magic trick (& then we do
good & evil) and go
to good & evil
destiny

we construct a world
(& we do not occur) occurrence
is a construct : & things
do not exist

fools conceive of permanence
(& self & happiness) in things
essenceless : & are wrapped
in darkness (wander
in the ocean of existence)

8. THE SILENCE OF STAINLESS FAME

I have always pictured Stainless Fame as being like Socrates: old, and rather ugly, and most bothersome to nice well-intentioned people. You can be going about your ordinary righteous daily business, and suddenly realize: Oh no, here he comes again.

For Stainless Fame is the answer to the question posed by the surrealist André Breton: "What if everything in the Beyond is actually here, now, in the present, with us?" When the sacred is immanent in the world, then all things are holy, and nothing is impure. The only authentic response to the magic show is something very much like laughter and what Martin Buber called "the magic power of unconstrained acting."

A bodhisattva wanders in the world with his skillful means; his vows of compassion lead him to the world, even as his wisdom penetrates its emptiness. The world is unreal, because it is a dream; the world is real, because it is a dream; the world is a magic land that lies upon the Middle Way between yes and no. Stainless Fame is once again the hidden bodhisattva, the stranger, the disturber of the smugly conventional; he is the prototype embraced by the followers of the Spontaneous Way, and the following text (translated into Chinese by Kumārajīva in 406 A.D.) has long been a cornerstone of the Zen tradition. Stainless Fame is the ultimate iconoclast, for he knows that all our idols are figures in a dream, but he also knows—to quote one more surrealist maxim—that the dream alone entrusts to man all his rights to freedom.

Wei-mo-chieh so-shuo ching [Vimalakīrti-nirdeśa], *in* Taishō Shinshū Daizōkoyō, *gen. eds. Takakusu Junjirō and Watanabe Kaigyoku (Tokyo: Taishō Issaikyō Kanakōkai, 1924–29), 14, no. 475.*

The Skillful Means of Stainless Fame

And in the city there lived an elder named Stainless Fame, who dwelt there as a skillful means for the salvation of men.

For he used his measureless wealth to convert the poor, and his own pure virtue to convert those who broke the precepts; he controlled himself with patience to convert the scornful, and strove with diligence to convert the lazy; he used his calm meditation to convert the confused, and his firm wisdom to convert the ignorant.

He wore the white robes of a layman but observed the pure conduct of a recluse: he lived the household life but was not attached to the world. He had a wife and children but ever practiced the religious life: he kept a household but ever delighted in solitude.

He wore jewels and ornaments but adorned his body with the signs of greatness: he ate and drank but delighted in the taste of meditation. He went to the gambling hall but worked for the salvation of men; he took on the ways of the heretics but never strayed from the true faith; he knew all the worldly texts but ever delighted in the teachings of the Buddha.

And truly he was honored by all as the best among the worthy, for he upheld justice; he converted the old and the young.

He knew all businesses, but he took no pleasure in the worldly profits he gained. Rather he went out upon the streets to benefit all living creatures: he entered the courts to defend the oppressed; he attended the debates to lead the people to righteousness; he went to the schools to educate the untaught; he entered the brothels to show the follies of lust; he went to the wine houses to make firm the wills of men.

When he was with the elders, he was the most honored among them and taught them the highest teachings; when he was with the householders, he was the most honored among them and taught them to cast aside attachment; when he was with the warriors, he was the most honored among them and taught them forebearance.

When he was with the priests, he was the most honored among them and taught them humility; when he was with the judges, he was the most honored among them and taught them justice; when he was with the princes, he was the most honored among them and taught them loyalty.

When he was in the inner palace, he was the most honored person there, and he converted all the harem girls to virtue; when he was with the common people, he was the most honored among them and taught them the power of merit . . .

The Illness of Stainless Fame

And thus with innumerable skillful means the elder Stainless Fame brought benefit to living creatures, and using his skillful means he made his body appear to be sick.

And the kings and ministers, the elders and householders, the priests and princes heard of his illness, and thousands upon thousands of people came to inquire after his health. And Stainless Fame made use of his illness to receive them and to preach to them the Law . . .

True Meditation

And the elder Stainless Fame thought to himself: Here I am sick and upon my bed, yet the Blessed One has no compassion upon me, nor does he think of me.

But the Blessed One knew his thoughts.

So the Buddha said to Śāriputra: Go and call on Stainless Fame, and inquire about his illness.

And Śāriputra said to the Buddha: Blessed One, I am not worthy to call on him and inquire about his illness. For I remember that once I was sitting quietly in meditation at the foot of a tree, and Stainless Fame came up to me and said:

"Śāriputra, to sit quietly is not necessarily to sit in meditation. But rather to sit in meditation is to let neither your body nor your mind appear in the universe; it is to let all your activities appear without arising from your trance of cessation.

"To sit in meditation is to act like everyone else while casting aside no quality of enlightenment; it is to let your mind neither abide within or wander without.

"To sit in meditation is to be unmoved by error while you practice all that conduces to enlightenment; it is to enter nirvana without cutting off the passions of the world.

"It is when you can sit like this that you win the seal of the Buddhas."

And when I heard this, Blessed One, I remained silent and could make no reply. That is why I am not worthy to call on him and inquire about his illness . . .

True Nirvana

Then the Buddha said to the great Kātyāyana: Go and call on Stainless Fame, and inquire about his illness.

And the great Kātyāyana said to the Buddha: Blessed One, I am not worthy to call on him and inquire about his illness. For I remember that once the Buddha had preached an outline of the Law to a group of monks, and I was expanding upon it, teaching them the meaning of impermanence, and suffering, and emptiness, and not-self, and nirvana; and Stainless Fame came up to me and said:

"Kātyāyana, do not use arising and ceasing thoughts to teach about reality. For all events ultimately neither arise nor cease: that is the meaning of impermanence. And the five aggregates are empty and occur nowhere: that is the meaning of suffering.

"No event ever really happens: that is the meaning of emptiness. Self and not-self are the same: that is the meaning of not-self. And events have never been as they are, and so will never cease: that is the meaning of nirvana."

And when he taught this teaching, the minds of all the monks gained freedom. That is why I am not worthy to call on him and inquire about his illness . . . .

True Purity

Then the Buddha said to Upāli: Go and call on Stainless Fame, and inquire about his illness.

And Upāli said to the Buddha: Blessed One, I am not worthy to call on him and inquire about his illness. For I remember that once two monks had committed an offense, and they were so ashamed that they dared not tell the Buddha.

And they confessed to me, and said: "Resolve our doubt and our remorse, that we may cleanse our guilt." So I was teaching them in accordance with the Law, and Stainless Fame came up to me and said:

"Upāli, do not aggravate the sin of these two monks, but rather wipe it out at once, without tormenting their minds. For the true nature of their sin abides neither within nor without, nor does it abide in between.

"The Buddha has said that living creatures are impure when their minds are impure, and pure when their minds are pure. And the mind abides neither within nor without, nor does it abide in between: as their minds are, so are their sins. Every event is the same, and does not depart from reality. Upāli, tell me, is your mind impure when it gains its freedom?"

I said that it was not.

"And even so the minds of all living creatures are without impurity. Misconceptions are impurity: purity is to be without misconceptions. Error is impurity: purity is to be without error. Clinging to a self is impurity: purity is to be without clinging.

"All events arise and cease, and do not abide: like an illusion, like lightning, events do not wait for each other, and do not stay for an instant. All events are false vision: like a dream, like fire, like the moon in water, like an image in a mirror, they are born of false vision.

"He who knows this is said to be a keeper of the rule; he who knows this is said to be truly free."

And the two monks said: "This is the highest wisdom, and it is beyond the ability of Upāli: he is the highest in keeping the rule, yet he cannot explain it . . . "

And the two monks had their doubt and remorse resolved, and awakened the thought of supreme and perfect enlightenment. That is why I am not worthy to call on him and inquire about his illness . . .

True Enlightenment

Then the Buddha said to the bodhisattva Maitreya: Go and call on Stainless Fame, and inquire about his illness.

And Maitreya said to the Buddha: Blessed One, I am not worthy to call on him and inquire about his illness. For I remember that once I was preaching to the King of the Gods and his retinue, explaining the conduct of one who can no longer be turned back from enlightenment, and Stainless Fame came up to me and said:

"Maitreya, the Blessed One has prophesied that in one more life you will attain to supreme and perfect enlightenment. Tell me, for which life did you receive this prophecy? Is it the past, or the future, or the present?

"For if it is the past, then your past life is already finished; if it is the future, then your future life has not yet come; if it is the present, then your present life does not abide. For the Buddha has said that at this very moment you are born, and decaying, and passing away.

"And if you received the prophecy for no lifetime at all, then no lifetime at all is the fixed abode of nirvana; and in nirvana there is no receiving of prophecy, and no attaining to supreme and perfect enlightenment.

"Maitreya, tell me, how did you receive the prophecy that in one more life you would attain to enlightenment? Did you receive the prophecy from the birth of reality? Did you receive the prophecy from the cessation of reality?

"If you received the prophecy from the birth of reality, then reality has no birth; if you received the prophecy from the cessation of reality, then reality has no cessation.

"All living creatures are reality; all events are reality; all the saints and sages are reality; even Maitreya is reality.

"If Maitreya receives a prophecy, then all living creatures should receive a prophecy, for reality is always the same, and never different.

"If Maitreya attains to supreme and perfect enlightenment, then all living creatures should attain to it, for all living creatures are the manifestation of enlightenment.

"If Maitreya gains nirvana, then all living creatures should gain nirvana; for the Buddhas know that all living creatures are already calm and ceased, and this is nirvana; and they shall not cease hereafter.

"Therefore do not mislead these sons of heaven with your teachings; for there is no such thing as awakening the thought of enlightenment, and there is no such thing as turning back from it.

"But rather you should urge these sons of heaven to give up thinking that enlightenment is something real, or something different; for enlightenment cannot be attained by the body, and it cannot be attained by the mind.

"Enlightenment is calm cessation, for there all manifestation ceases. Enlightenment is nonseeing, for it is beyond all connection. Enlightenment is nonaction, for it is without thought. Enlightenment is cutting off, for it sees nothing as real. Enlightenment is separation, for it imposes nothing upon reality.

"Enlightenment is blocking, for it blocks all desire. Enlightenment is nonentering, for it clings to nothing. Enlightenment is adapting, for it adapts to reality. Enlightenment is abiding, for it abides in the true nature of events. Enlightenment is reaching, for it reaches the limit of reality.

"Enlightenment is oneness, for it is free of thought and its objects. Enlightenment is sameness, for it is the same as empty space. Enlightenment is the unconditioned, for it neither arises nor abides nor ceases. Enlightenment is knowledge, for it knows the workings of the minds of living creatures. Enlightenment is nonmeeting, for it confronts nothing at all.

"Enlightenment is disentanglement, for it is free of passion. Enlightenment is nowhere, for it has neither shape nor form. Enlightenment is an unreal name, for it is empty of names and terms. Enlightenment is illusion, for it accepts and rejects nothing.

"Enlightenment is nondisturbance, for it is tranquil of itself. Enlightenment is true calm, for it is inherently pure. Enlightenment is nontaking, for it is free of all connection. Enlightenment is nondifference, for it sees all events as the same.

"Incomparable is enlightenment, for it is beyond description; profound is enlightenment, for events are hard to know."

Blessed One, when Stainless Fame taught this teaching, two hundred sons of heaven realized that no event in this world is truly real. That is why I am not worthy to call on him and inquire about his illness . . .

The Visit of Sweet Glory

Then the Buddha said to the bodhisattva Sweet Glory: Go and call on Stainless Fame, and inquire about his illness.

And Sweet Glory said to the Buddha:

Blessed One, this excellent man is hard to answer. Deeply he has reached reality; skillfully he teaches the essentials of the Law. His eloquence is unhindered and his insight boundless: he knows all that a bodhisattva must do, and has penetrated into all the secret treasures of the Buddha. He has overcome the Evil One, and exercises magic powers: he has gained both wisdom and skillful means. But I will accept the command of the Buddha, and go and inquire about his illness.

And all the bodhisattvas who were present—the great disciples and the kings of the four heavens—all thought to themselves: Now these two great men shall meet together; surely they will discuss the wonderful Law.

So eight thousand bodhisattvas, and five hundred disciples, and hundreds of thousands of men and gods followed after Sweet Glory to the house of Stainless Fame . . .

The Buddha Way

And Sweet Glory asked Stainless Fame: How does a bodhisattva set forth on the Way of the Buddha?

And Stainless Fame replied: If a bodhisattva treads what is not the Way, then he has set forth on the Way of the Buddha.

And Sweet Glory asked: How does a bodhisattva tread what is not the Way?

And Stainless Fame replied: A bodhisattva walks among those who have committed the most grievous sins, yet feels no anger; he goes to the deepest hell, yet has neither sin nor stain . . .

He may seem to be aged and sick, but he has cut off all disease, and has no fear of death; he may seem to be born with property, but he ever looks upon impermanence, and desires nothing. He may seem to have wives and concubines, but he is far from the swamp of desire; he may seem to be dull and stammering, but he is perfect in eloquence and unfailing in memory; he may seem to have entered the wrong crossing, but he saves all living creatures. He may seem to be in the world, but he has cut off the causes of becoming; and he may seem to be in nirvana, but he has not cut off arising and ceasing.

And if a bodhisattva thus can tread what is not the Way, then he has set forth on the Way of the Buddha.

And then Stainless Fame asked Sweet Glory: What is the seed of Buddhahood?

And Sweet Glory replied: The body is the seed of Buddhahood; ignorance and craving are the seeds of Buddhahood; lust and hatred and delusion are the seeds of Buddhahood . . . The senses are the seeds of Buddhahood; evil and passion are the seeds of Buddhahood.

And Stainless Fame asked: What do you mean by that?

And Sweet Glory replied: Whoever sees the unconditioned, and enters into the fixed abode of nirvana, cannot awaken the thought of supreme and perfect enlightenment. For the lotus flower does not grow on the high dry plain, but in the muddy swamp; and only in the swamp of passion are there living creatures to produce the qualities of Buddhahood.

And a seed planted in the sky cannot grow, but flourishes in manured fields; and even so, whoever sees the unconditioned, and enters into the fixed abode of nirvana, cannot gain the qualities of Buddhahood.

You can raise up views of self as great as Mount Meru, and still you can awaken the thought of supreme and perfect enlightenment, and gain the qualities of Buddhahood.

And thus you should know that all the passions are the seed of Buddhahood: for you cannot gain a priceless pearl unless you enter into the vast ocean, and you cannot win the pearl of omniscience if you do not enter the great ocean of the passions . . .

Entering the Gate of Oneness

And Stainless Fame said to all the bodhisattvas: Gentlemen, tell me, how does a bodhisattva enter the gate of oneness? Each of you tell me in your own way.

So the bodhisattva Lord-of-the-Law said: Gentlemen, arising and ceasing are two. But events have never arisen, so now they do not cease. To realize that no event in this world is truly real is to enter the gate of oneness . . .

The bodhisattva Never-Blinking said: Perception and nonperception are two. If you do not perceive events, then you do not rest upon them; when you do not rest upon them, then there is neither accepting nor rejecting, neither acting nor doing. This is to enter the gate of oneness.

The bodhisattva Highest-Virtue said: Sin and purity are two. If you see the true nature of sin, then there is no state of purity. To flow in this state of cessation is to enter the gate of oneness.

The bodhisattva Auspicious-Star said: Action and thought are two. If you do not act, then you are without thought; when you are without thought, then you make no discriminations. This is to enter the gate of oneness . . .

The bodhisattva Bright-Moon said: Darkness and light are two. If there is neither darkness nor light, then they are two no longer. For when you enter the trance of cessation there is neither darkness nor light; and so it is with all events. To enter into this state of peace is to enter the gate of oneness . . .

The bodhisattva Precious-Sign-in-Hand said: To delight in nirvana and despise the world are two. If you neither delight in nirvana nor loathe the world, then they are two no longer. For if there were bondage there could be freedom; but if there has never been bondage, then who would seek for freedom? If there is neither bondage nor freedom, then there is neither delight nor loathing. This is to enter the gate of oneness.

The bodhisattva King-of-the-Crown-Jewels said: The right and the wrong are two. If you abide in the right, then you do not discriminate between the right and the wrong. To be free of these two is to enter the gate of oneness.

The bodhisattva Joy-in-Reality said: Reality and unreality are two. But he who truly sees does not see reality; so how could he see unreality? For it is not what the eye can see; only the eye of wisdom can see it; and the eye of wisdom neither sees nor does not see. This is to enter the gate of oneness.

And thus each of the bodhisattvas spoke in turn; and they asked Sweet Glory what it was to enter the gate of oneness.

And Sweet Glory said: I think that when you can neither speak nor talk of any event, when you neither indicate nor know any thing, when you pass beyond both questions and answers, this is to enter the gate of oneness.

And then Sweet Glory said to Stainless Fame: Sir, each of us has spoken. Tell us how a bodhisattva enters the gate of oneness.

And Stainless Fame kept silent, and did not say a word . . .

9. CRAZY JANE AND THE BISHOP

The apparent iconoclasm of true wisdom and the figure of the hidden saint are so intermingled that they become, in effect, a single theme: the mad wanderer who acts upon the shocking truth that the world is holy. It is a revolutionary idea that the crazy mocker of conventional value is nearer sainthood than the established voice of institutional religion, yet the idea is found throughout all of Asia, and becomes within traditional society a means of institutionalizing dissent, of providing an established niche for holy madness within the ecology of the culture.

The crazy saint is a moving and wondrous figure and a constant inspiration to literature. Crazy Jane is Ono-no-Komachi, a beautiful but heartless woman of ancient Japan who slew her princely lover through her constant and exorbitant demands upon his chivalry: his spirit returns to haunt her when she has grown old and ugly. Kwanami (1333–84 A.D.) created from this tale one of the most popular *nō* plays ever written. He was one of the great *nō* actors, and the profoundly Zen atmosphere of the dramatic form—with its emphasis upon allusion, restraint, and sublety—provided a perfect setting for the encounter between Crazy Jane's mad insight into reality and the stubborn moral common sense of the monastic world. Crazy Jane can see the world as holy and sit upon a shrine; the monks protect the sanctity of the shrine and cannot see its holiness.

William Butler Yeats turned to the *nō* drama when he sought a form that was "distinguished, indirect, and symbolic." In naming my characters, I have thought it only fair to return the compliment.

Kwanami, Sotoba Komachi [*Komachi at the shrine*], *in* Yō Kyoshū, *eds. Yokomichi Mario and Omote Akira (Tokyo: Iwanami Shōten, 1963), 1: 82–85.*

The two monks speak:	Shallow mountains for our shelter shallow mountains for our shelter where our deep hearts may hide
The first monk speaks:	I am a monk from the holy hills making my way to the city
The second monk speaks:	The Buddha of the past is gone the future Buddha not yet in the world
The first monk speaks:	And we were born into a dream where nothing matters by chance we gained a precious human form and stumbled on the holy Law that is hard to find
	it is the seed of our salvation and with this single thought our bodies are in inky robes
	we shall not be born again we shall not be born again we have no love for parents who brought us to this world no children to care for us
	a thousand miles is not far to walk we lie in fields and rest on mountains for these are now our home for these are now our home
Crazy Jane speaks:	I am the floating grass the water calls the floating grass the water calls would go if water called me . . .

long ago I was full of pride
with jade pins in my hair
lovely I was and supple
as a willow in spring winds
more lovely than the nightingale
than the dew-soaked rose
when it starts to fall . . .

but now I am foul among the sluts
and all men know my shame
joyless months and days lie upon me
for I am old by a hundred years

in the city I flee their eyes
that they may not know me
under the cover of the dusk
I creep with the moon
I creep with the moon

past the towers of the palace
where no guard challenges
nor questions a poor wanderer
in the shadows of the trees
past the tombs of lovers
and the autumn hills

I see boats on river shallows
but who is rowing them
but who is rowing them?

Ai, it is too hard for me. Here is a withered stump: I shall rest a while.

The first monk speaks: Come along, the sun is setting. We must hasten on our way. But look, surely that is a beggar resting upon a holy shrine. We must tell her to get away.

What do you think you are doing, old woman, that you sit upon the holy shrine? It is a manifestation of the body of the Buddha: get away from it, and rest someplace else.

Crazy Jane speaks: And for all your talk I see no words upon it, nor figures carved: it seemed to be a withered stump.

The first monk speaks: A withered stump in the deep hills
cannot be hid when its flowers blossom . . .

Crazy Jane speaks: And I am a low stump, and well buried:
                               but still there are flowers in my heart
                               that may serve as an offering.
                               But why do you call this the body of the Buddha?

The first monk speaks: This shrine represents the Diamond Buddha, as he
     assumes the transient forms in which he appears to us.

Crazy Jane speaks: And in what forms does he appear?

The first monk speaks: In earth and water and fire and air and space.

Crazy Jane speaks: The five elements of a human body; so what difference is
     there?

The first monk speaks: The form is the same, but the merit is different.

Crazy Jane speaks: And what is the merit of the shrine?

The first monk speaks: One look upon the shrine frees you from all evil
     destinies.

Crazy Jane speaks: And one thought can awaken you to enlightenment: that
     seems just as good.

The second monk speaks: And if you have awakened the thought of enlight-
     enment, then why do you wander in this world of sorrow?

Crazy Jane speaks: My body wanders; my heart has wearied of it long ago.

The first monk speaks: Indeed you have no heart at all, or you would have
     known the body of the Buddha.

Crazy Jane speaks: And perhaps I came because I knew . . .

The second monk speaks: And then you sprawled all over it without a single
     offering.

Crazy Jane speaks: It was on the ground already: what harm did I do to rest
     upon it?

The first monk speaks: It was a sinful act!

Crazy Jane speaks: Sometimes even from sin there is salvation.

The second monk speaks: It was evil . . .

Crazy Jane speaks: . . . as much as love.

The first monk speaks: It was folly . . .

Crazy Jane speaks: . . . as much as wisdom.

The first monk speaks: But what we call evil . . .

Crazy Jane speaks: . . . is good.

The first monk speaks: The passions . . .

Crazy Jane speaks: . . . are enlightenment.

The second monk speaks: Enlightenment . . .

Crazy Jane speaks: . . . is not planted like a tree.

The first monk speaks: . . . is a bright mirror . . .

Crazy Jane speaks: . . . which is not hung on a tower.

The chorus sings:
      Truly nothing is real
no difference between man and Buddha
save the deepest vow of skillful means
to save the ordinary man

sometimes even from sin
there is salvation
carefully she spoke
and the priests said:
surely this beggar has realization
and they bowed their heads to the ground
three times paid homage to her . . .

10. A BODHISATTVA GAINS THE TENTH STAGE

We return once more to the vision. Even as the process of meditation seeks to re-enact the enlightenment of the Buddha, the flash of realization can re-create the mythic mode of his visionary ecstasy. Here too is a "seeing" that opens up the farthest reaches of the universe. The knowledge of the bodhisattva imbues the world with shining brilliance and creates the cosmic glories of his throne and retinue: his compassion and devotion appear as blazing rays of light that penetrate to all the worlds of gods and men. And once more we return to the path, for this vision is the result of eons of striving, a final culmination of the bodhisattva stages. It is the experience of wisdom made manifest, freedom made visible in a new and shining dream, a dream as real and unreal as our own tainted vision of suffering and pain.

Daśabhūmikasūtra [The ten stages], ed. P. L. Vaidya (Darbhanga: The Mithila Institute, 1967), pp. 55–64.

The Song of Praise to Buddhahood

> . . . and heavenly maidens
>> (their senses gladdened) worshipped
>> paid honor to the Well-gone
>>> & a million instruments played
>> to set this song to music
>
> the Buddha abides in a single realm : yet shows
>> himself in all realms (a million bodies
> of divers delights) exhibited
>>> in the broad realm of reality
>>> and from each of his pores stream forth
>>> rays of light : to calm
>>>> the passion of the world
>
> (for you could count the motes of dust in all the world
> yet could not know the number of his rays of light)
>
>> some lights seen : are wise men
>>> with the highest signs of Buddhahood
>>> turning the wheel of the Law (others
> seen : are lords of men
>>> purifying the highest practice
>>> in their realms) and the Lord
> gains the realm of heaven (seen
>> walking : moving) seen in the womb
>>> in millions of realms (seen
>> born in all the realms) wanders forth
>>> for the sake of the world : and once again
>> is enlightened in supreme enlightenment
> and he is seen : turning the wheel of the Law
>>> (entering nirvana)
>>>> in
>>>> millions
>>> of Buddha-realms
>
>> (for a magician skilled in magic
>> shows many bodies
>>> to earn his living
> the Teacher skilled in wisdom
>> produces all his bodies
>> for our sake)

empty : calm : undefined as event
spacelike is
reality (and the Buddha our teacher
shows reality : the highest object
a Buddha knows) the highest object is
essence (and all beings
know reality : sign and no sign
are one sign) for all events themselves are
reality

and he who seeks the knowledge of a Buddha
knows existence & nonexistence are one
does not impose real & unreal
(and quickly will become
the highest lord of men)

sweet-voiced they sang this song
of a thousand sounds (the heavenly maidens
looked at the Conqueror) became
silent : rejoiced in tranquility

The Question

And Moon-of-Freedom saw their readiness. Three times he spoke to Diamond-Womb, and confidently asked the glorious son of the Conqueror: Tell us the qualities (the knowledge, the signs & wonders) of one who enters upon the tenth stage.

The Preliminaries

And the bodhisattva Diamond-Womb said:
Venerable sons of the Conqueror: a bodhisattva (whose mind has discriminated innumerable objects of knowledge up through the ninth bodhisattva stage) is said to have well inquired the inquiry & well fulfilled the good Law: he has gathered up his infinite stocks & well obtained the great stocks of merit & knowledge; he has realized vast great compassion; he is skilled in the distinction & number of worldly realms & proficient in the abyss of entering into the worlds of living creatures; his thoughts & attention seek to enter the realm of Those who Have Come, & he seeks to gain the qualities of Buddhahood, both power & certainty; and he has reached the stage of initiation into omniscient knowledge of all things.

The Meditations

Venerable sons of the Conqueror: to the bodhisattva who seeks such knowledge, who has reached the stage of initiation, there appears the meditative state called PURITY; there appears the meditative state called ENTRY INTO THE DISTINCTION OF THE REALM OF REALITY,

called ARRAY OF ADORNMENT OF THE TERRACE OF ENLIGHT-
ENMENT, called FLOWER OF DIVERS RAYS OF LIGHT, called
WOMB OF THE OCEAN, called WEALTH OF THE OCEAN, called
EXPANSE OF THE REALM OF SPACE, called EXAMINING THE ES-
SENCE OF ALL EVENTS, called KNOWING THE HEARTS & CON-
DUCT OF ALL BEINGS, called STANDING FACE-TO-FACE WITH
ALL THE PRESENT BUDDHAS.

And innumerable millions of meditative states become manifest to
him: he enters into all these meditations & arises from them; he seeks skill
in meditation; he experiences all the effects of these meditations; & after
these innumerable millions of meditations, there appears to him the
meditative state called INITIATION INTO OMNISCIENT KNOWL-
EDGE.

The Initiation

The great lotus throne. And in this meditation there appears to him the
great jeweled king of lotus flowers, a billion immensities studded with all
manner of precious gems: it surpasses every worldly thing; it springs from
his own transcendent merit, a perfect illusion rooted in the realm of reality
itself.

It surpasses every vision of heaven: its stalk is made of precious gems &
its pericarp of sandalwood; emeralds are its filaments, & its leaves shine like
river gold; it blossoms with countless rays of light; it is strewn with jewels &
draped with an endless net of jewels; and it is surrounded by great jeweled
lotus flowers, as many as the atoms of a billion universes.

And as soon as the bodhisattva enters the meditation called INITIA-
TION INTO OMNISCIENT KNOWLEDGE his body grows as great as
the great jeweled king of lotus flowers, and he sits upon it as his lotus
throne. And there appears a host of a billion bodhisattvas to be his retinue,
gathered from all the worldly realms in the ten directions; they sit upon the
great jeweled lotus flowers all about him; they all enter into a million
meditations, & gaze upon the bodhisattva.

And all the worlds tremble as they enter into meditation, for the evil of
the world is cast aside; the realm of reality is made manifest, and all the
worlds made pure: there roars forth the sound of the names of all the
heavens of the Buddhas. All the bodhisattvas of the same deeds & destiny
gather together; all the worlds resound with the song & music of men &
gods; and all living creatures become joyful, and worship all the perfect
Buddhas with infinite worship.

And all the assemblies of Those Who Have Come learn what has
happened.

The rays of light. And how do they learn what has happened? Sons of
the Conqueror: as soon as the bodhisattva sits upon his lotus throne, a
billion rays of light radiate forth from the soles of his feet: they illuminate
the ten directions & shine as far as the deepest hell; and they purge the
beings in hell of all their sufferings.

And a billion rays of light radiate forth from his knees: they illuminate
the ten directions & shine upon all beings born as animals; and they calm

the sufferings of all the animals. And a billion rays of light radiate forth from his navel: they illuminate the ten directions & shine upon the land of the dead; and they calm the sufferings of all the beings among the dead.

And a billion rays of light radiate forth from his sides: they illuminate the ten directions & shine upon all men; and they calm the sufferings of men. And a billion rays of light radiate forth from his hands: they illuminate the ten directions & shine upon the dwellings of the gods & demigods, and they calm the sufferings of the gods & demigods.

And a billion rays of light radiate forth from his shoulders: they illuminate the ten directions & shine upon those who follow the career of disciples; and they set the disciples in the gate of the light of the Law. And a billion rays of light radiate forth from his throat: they illuminate the ten directions & shine upon those who follow the career of solitary Buddhas; and they lead the solitary Buddhas to the gate of tranquil meditation.

And a billion rays of light radiate forth from his mouth: they illuminate the ten directions & shine upon all the bodhisattvas, from those who have just awakened the thought of enlightenment to those who have reached the ninth stage; and they set the bodhisattvas on the way to skill in wisdom & means.

And a billion rays of light radiate forth from the tuft of hair between his brows: they illuminate the ten directions; they eclipse all the dwellings of the Evil One & shine upon all the bodhisattvas who have reached the stage of initiation; and they enter into the bodies of the bodhisattvas.

The worship of the Buddhas. And rays of light radiate forth from all about his head, as many as the atoms of a billion universes: they illuminate the ten directions to the very ends of space, as far as the realm of reality itself, & they shine upon all the assemblies of Those Who Have Come.

And the rays of light three times circle the ten-fold world: they stay in the sky all about, forming circles of great nets of light, and for all Those Who Have Come they set out the great worship & veneration called BLAZING SPLENDOR.

And the worship & veneration the bodhisattva has performed from his first thought of enlightenment up through the ninth stage is not one billionth part of this worship & veneration; for there is no counting or numbering, no metaphor or comparison or resemblance for this worship & veneration.

And from these great nets of light in the ten directions a great rain of flowers pours down on the assemblies of Those Who Have Come: incense & garlands & perfumes & robes & parasols & flags & banners & precious gems rain down upon them, as if it were a great rain of all manner of precious thing, as if it were a great cloud of offerings from the realm of reality.

The offerings surpass every worldly thing, for they spring from the transcendent merit of the bodhisattva & from the gathering of his stocks: they are endowed with all virtues & blessed by the inconceivable power of nirvana. And the living creatures who know this worship shall surely attain to supreme & perfect enlightenment.

And when the rays of light have offered such worship & veneration, they shine once more upon all the assemblies of Those Who Have Come:

three times they circle the ten-fold world, & they enter into the feet of Those Who Have Come, the Worthy Ones, the perfect Buddhas.

And thus the Buddhas know that in this worldly realm a bodhisattva has done such practices & has attained to the stage of initiation.

Sons of the Conqueror: from all the worldly realms in the ten directions there gather the numberless & countless & innumerable bodhisattvas who have reached the ninth stage; they surround the bodhisattva & make him great offerings; they gaze upon the bodhisattva & enter into a million meditations.

And from the bodies of the bodhisattvas who have reached the stage of initiation there radiates forth a ray of light called VICTORY OVER THE EVIL ONE, with a billion rays of light to be its retinue; it illuminates the ten directions & manifests countless wonders, and it enters into the breast of the bodhisattva.

And as soon as it enters into him, the bodhisattva grows great in power & shines with the light of a million virtues.

The consecration. And then, sons of the Conqueror, the rays of light called SUPERKNOWLEDGE OF OMNISCIENCE radiate forth from between the brows of Those Who Have Come, the Worthy Ones, the perfect Buddhas: with their measureless retinue of light they illuminate all the worldly realms in the ten directions; three times they circle the ten-fold world & manifest the countless wonders of Those Who Have Come.

And the rays of light awaken a billion bodhisattvas & shake all the heavens of the Buddhas; they calm all evil destinies & eclipse all the dwellings of the Evil One. They reveal all the seats whereon the Buddhas have been enlightened into perfect enlightenment; they manifest the glory of the array of all the assemblies of Buddhas; they illuminate all the worldly realms to the very ends of space, as far as the realm of reality itself.

And the rays of light return once more & circle again and again the whole assembly of bodhisattvas gathered there; they reveal the great array & come to rest upon the head of the bodhisattva; and their retinue of lights enters into the heads of his retinue of bodhisattvas.

And as soon as the rays of light have gathered together, the bodhisattvas attain to millions of meditations they had not attained before; and when the rays of light fall upon the head of the bodhisattva, then he is said to be initiated in the field of perfect enlightenment; for when he fulfills the ten powers he is numbered among the perfect Buddhas.

Sons of the Conqueror: suppose the eldest son of a universal emperor, the crown prince born of the first wife of the king, were invested with the signs of a universal emperor. The king would place him on the blessed seat of a holy golden elephant; he would bring water from the four oceans, and set out in the imperial palace above him a great array of flowers & incense & garlands & perfumes & robes & parasols & flags & banners & musical instruments.

He would take a golden pitcher and sprinkle the water upon the head of the prince; and as soon as he was thus initiated, he would be numbered among the consecrated warrior kings; for when he fulfilled the ten paths of good conduct he would gain the title of universal emperor.

Even so, sons of the Conqueror, as soon as the bodhisattva is thus initiated, he is said to be consecrated by all the Blessed Buddhas with the initiation of omniscient knowledge; and when he fulfills the ten powers with his initiation into perfect Buddhahood, he is numbered among the perfect Buddhas.

Sons of the Conqueror: this is the initiation of great knowledge of a bodhisattva, for the sake of which he had embarked upon many hundreds of hardships. And it is said that he is consecrated, that he has increased his infinite qualities, that he abides in the bodhisattva stage called THE CLOUD OF THE LAW . . .

10
the celebration

1. WANDERING IN THE WORLD

Enlightened people simply do not behave the way we do; they are tourists in our reality, wanderers in our world. An encounter with a Zen master can be an unnerving experience: it is difficult to confront a spectator to a game you did not know you were playing.

The two texts that follow are a celebration of sainthood. They are separated by perhaps six hundred years in time and by vast differences in philosophy: the first is traditional and anonymous; the second is by Nāgārjuna, a famous metaphysician. Yet, for all their differences in tone and style, they celebrate the same thing—that realization is freedom, and freedom is joy.

Suttanipāta, *in* Khuddaka-nikāya [*Collection of little texts*], *gen. ed. Bhikkhu J. Kashyap (Bihar: Pali Publication Board, 1959), Sutta XII (Munisutta), 1: 298–300.*

> fear is born from intimacy
> passion is born in company
>   so the sage wanders
>   without company
>   without intimacy
> & cuts down what occurs
> nor lets it grow again (and does not feed
>   what happens)
> they call him a sage
>   wandering alone : he has seen
>   the state of peace
> & considers things
> casts aside their seeds (and does not feed
>   desire)
> sees the end of birth and death : casts aside
>   thought
> goes beyond definition
>
> the sage knows all clinging
>   wants none of it (free
> of greed) ungrasping : no effort
> for he has gone across

the wise call him a sage

conquers) all (knows : and wise
            no event touches him
abandoned all (craving
                destroyed)

        :free

the wise call him a sage

strength of wisdom : endowed with virtue
concentrated (delighting in meditation) mindful
free of attachment : open-hearted : un
        drunk

the wise call him a sage

wanders alone : heedful (unshaken
            by praise or blame) a lion
unafraid of noises : or a wind not caught
        in a net (a lotus unsoiled by water)

leader of others : unled by others

the wise call him a sage

(like a pillar at the ford)
            & others speak of his speech
free of lust : his senses concentrated

the wise call him a sage

steadfast as a straight shuttle
            he loathes all evil (examines all
        right & wrong) and the wise

call him a sage

restrained is he : does no evil
in youth in manhood the sage
            is restrained (& is
never angered : nor angers anyone

the wise call him a sage

receives his alms from high and low
            (what there is : what is left)
depends upon what others give
            & does not praise (does not reproach)

the wise call him a sage

wanders : chaste (nor bound
                by youth) un
drunk with pride

        :free

the wise call him a sage

knows the world (vision
                of highest reality) crossed
            over the ocean the waves
chains broken : unbound : un
            drunk

the wise call him a sage

different are they
they dwell far apart
the householder maintains a wife
the sage is disciplined

        unselfish

careless the householder who slays
careful the sage who protects

for the crested blue-necked peacock
cannot fly like the ruddy goose
& the householder cannot equal the monk

        the solitary sage
        meditating in the forest

Nāgārjuna, Niraupamyastava [*Praise of the incomparable*], ed. Giuseppe
Tucci, in Journal of the Royal Asiatic Society *(1932), pages 309–25.*

Homage: incomparable one
                knowing nonessence
                intent to benefit a world
                        afflicted with "reality"

Lord, you see nothing at all with your Buddha-eye
                (seeing reality : ultimate vision)
            you know the nature of things
                which is hard to know
        and there is neither knower nor known
                (from the absolute point of view)

no event occurs or ceases for you
you have attained the highest state
                    (vision of oneness) : for you do not
          seek nirvana by slandering the world
Lord, you have attained peace
                    by nonknowing the world
you know passion & purity as of one taste
you are completely pure
                    (without a box
                    to put reality in)

Lord, without uttering a single syllable
your followers are filled with a rain of the Law

to the senses & their objects : no attachment (& to events
                    no dependence) a mind like space
Lord, you have no concept of a "being"
          yet you are compassionate to beings
                    afflicted with sorrow

Lord, you do not cling to happiness
          or sorrow (self or notself) permanent or
          impermanent : nor think them real
                    events do not come nor go for you
                              nor any aggregate thing
          (for you know reality)

you are everywhere followed (& born nowhere)
seer, you are inconceivable
                    (in birth : in qualities : in body) faultless one
          you know the world as like an echo
                    (free of one & many) beyond
                    change & destruction
          you understand this world as like a magic show
                    as like a dream (free of
                    eternal & noneternal) without predicate
                    or predicable

sinless one, you conquer your passion (whose root
          & end are deeds) you gain immortality
                    through the very nature of passion
resolute one, you see form as nonform : undefined (yet appear
                    in the realm of form) your body blazes
                              with the thirtytwo signs (are seen
                    with form : yet you are not called seen
          you are seen when events are seen

                    (reality is unseeable)

there is no aperture in your body (nor flesh
        nor bone nor blood) you have shown your body
            like a rainbow in space
        no disease nor impurity in your body (no hunger
            nor thirst) yet you act in the world
                conform to the world

sinless one, you are not obscured by deeds
                (yet you leap into deeds
        out of pity for the world) Lord
            there is no distinction of careers : for there is no
                distinction of reality (yet you taught
        the threefold career for the salvation of beings)

your body is permanent (unchanging : auspicious)
        Conqueror
    made of reality : yet you passed into nirvana
                for your followers (& again they behold you
            those who are devoted to you
            throughout the infinite universe)
                longing for your descent & birth
                    your enlightenment
                    your teaching
                    your nirvana
                        again

not for you is there thought : Protector
                (nor birth nor thinking things are real)
        Buddha-deeds happen in the world
                without your tasting them

2. SONGS OF THE NUNS AND ELDERS

The songs in this section are a heritage from the earliest disciples of the Buddha. They are folksongs, simple and unadorned, lyricism reduced to its most basic expression: they celebrate no ecstasies or visions, but rather simple peace, the cessation of passion, the calming of desire.

Above all they reveal the joy that lies in the heart of transcendence, of loss without regret. The singers of these songs did not long for life, they said, and did not long for death; but they awaited their time, as a servant his wages. These songs celebrate serenity amid events, wandering in the world with the heart already beyond the world: the experience that T. S. Eliot described in "Burnt Norton":*

---

*From *Four Quartets*, by T. S. Eliot, reprinted by permission of the publishers, Harcourt Brace Jovanovich, Inc., New York; and Faber and Faber Ltd., London, England.

The inner freedom from the practical desire,
The release from action and suffering, release from the inner
And the outer compulsion, yet surrounded
By a grace of sense, a white light still and moving . . .

Therīgāthā [*Songs of the nuns*], and Theragāthā [*Songs of the elders*], in
Khuddaka-nikāya [Collection of Little Texts], *gen. ed. Bhikkhu J.*
Kashyap (Bihar: Pali Publication Board, 1959), 2: 234–460.

I am thin
I am sick & weak
but leaning on my stick I go
climbing the mountain

I lay aside my robe
turn my bowl upside down
lean against a rock
& smash the mass of darkness

        *
     * *

I was drunk with my beauty
with my form & with my fame
I was stiff with youth
I despised other women

I adorned this body
for the delight of fools
I stood at the whorehouse door
like a hunter laying a snare

O I showed my ornaments
& my nakedness many times
made many sorts of magic
mocked many men

today I went to beg for alms
shaven & dressed in robes
I sat at the foot of a tree
& attained to nonthinking

all bonds are loosed
human & heavenly
I have destroyed all drunkenness
I have become cool : quenched

        *
     * *

a woman in the middle of the highway
a dancing girl dancing to music
dressed and adorned and garlanded
covered with sandalwood perfumes

I entered for alms
going along I saw her
dressed and adorned
like a snare of death laid out

then I considered
I thought carefully
saw the danger before me
became disgusted with the world

then my mind was freed
(see how true is the Law)
for I have attained to wisdom
& done the Buddha's teachings
                    *
              *   *
I shall restrain you, mind
like an elephant at the gate
I shall not urge you to evil
you net of lust : bodyborn

restrained, you shall not go
as an elephant not gaining the open gate
sinful mind, you shall not wander forth again
delighting in evil

as a strong man takes a hook
and turns an unruly elephant
(untamed : newly taken)
so shall I turn you

as a noble charioteer (skilled
in taming swift horses) tames a thoroughbred
I shall stand in the five strengths
and tame you

I shall bind you with mindfulness
harnessed I shall tame you
checked by the bridle of my striving
you shall not go far from here, mind
                    *
              *   *
Kulla went to the cemetery
saw a woman cast away
abandoned in the burning ground
being eaten : filled with worms

see the body, Kulla
diseased impure putrid
trickling and oozing
the delight of fools

I took the Law as a mirror
to attain knowledge & insight
I looked at my body
empty inside & out

as is this so is that
as is that so is this
as below so above
as above so below

as by day so by night
as by night so by day
as before so after
as after so before

fivefold music
does not please so much
as does insight in the Law
for a mind one-pointed

*
*   *

it is twentyfive years
since I wandered forth
not for the snap of a finger
have I experienced calm of mind

not attaining concentration
assailed by lust
I stretched forth my arms and wailed
I went forth from my dwelling

I shall take up a knife
what is the use of my living?
how shall I die
I who have rejected the training?

then I took a razor
sat upon the couch
and placed the razor round
to cut my veins

then I considered
I thought carefully
saw the danger before me
became disgusted with the world

then my mind was freed
(see how true is the Law)
for I have attained to wisdom
& done the Buddha's teachings
                    *
                *   *
if no other is found
before or behind
O it is pleasant
to dwell alone in the forest

well, I shall go alone
to the woods the Buddha praised
pleasant for dwelling alone
for a monk of resolute will

delightful : giving joy to meditators
(where are rutting elephants)
alone : bent on my purpose
swiftly I shall enter the glade

in the cool and flowered woods
in a cool mountain cave
I shall wash my limbs
I shall walk about alone

alone and solitary
in the delightful great forest
when shall I dwell there?
my task done : undrunken

O I wish to do this
may my wish come true
I myself shall do this
no one can act for another

I bind on my armor
I shall enter the glade
shall not come forth from there
until I have destroyed my drunkenness

the cool breeze blows
full of fragrance
sitting on the mountain peak
I shall break my ignorance

in the forest covered with flowers
on the cool slopes
enjoying the pleasures of freedom
I shall delight in the mountain ravines

my purpose is fulfilled
like the moon on the fifteenth day
I have destroyed all drunkenness
there is no more existence for me

*
* *

when I went out to wander
from home to homelessness
I had no thought
ignoble or corrupt

slay them : slaughter them
let these creatures suffer
I had no such thought
for a long time

but I have love
infinite & well-nurtured
slowly grown
as the Buddha taught

friend of all, comrade of all
compassionate to all creatures
I nurture thoughts of love
ever intent on kindness

I gladden my heart
unmoving & unshaken
I nurture the abode of love
unserved by the vile

attained to nonthinking
the disciple of the perfect Buddha
instantly gains
noble silence

as a mountain rock
unmoving & well-founded
a monk does not tremble
when his delusion passes away

to a man unblemished
ever seeking purity
a hair's tip of evil
seems big as a cloud

as a border town is guarded
inside & out
so guard yourselves
let not the moment escape

I do not long for death
I do not long for life
but I await my time
as a servant his wages

I do not long for death
I do not long for life
but I await my time
mindful & attentive

I have worshipped my Master
done the Buddha's teachings
laid down my heavy load
fired my guide to existence

I have attained the aim
for which I went out to wander
from home to homelessness
my bonds are destroyed

strive diligently
this is my advice
well, I shall be quenched
I am everywhere liberated

3. SIXTEEN HAIKU

To wander in the world is not to be unaware of the world, but rather to be aware of events in a special way. The enlightened seem—almost paradoxically—to have a great zest for living: no thing is important, and thus nothing is unimportant; every instant is new, and every event is a surprise.

The Japanese poetic form of *haiku* is an almost perfect setting for the celebration of enlightenment in the world, of the holiness immanent in all things. It is individual and emotional and full of humor; its very concision limits it to the concrete and the momentary, to the meaning hidden within the most transient event. Martin Buber might have been describing *haiku* when he wrote, "Not over the things, not around the things, not between the things—in each thing, in the experience of each thing, the gate of the One opens to you if you bring with you the magic that unlocks it . . . "*

Bashō (1644-94 A.D.) is the outstanding practitioner of this *haiku* of realization, the concrete portrayal of infinite depths in the most minute details of daily life.

*Martin Buber, *Daniel: Dialogues on Realization* (New York: McGraw Hill, 1965), 53.

Matsuo Bashō, Bashō Kushū [The collected works of Basho], eds. Ōtani Tokuzu et al (Tokyo: Iwanami Shōten, 1959).

SUMMER MOON

OCTOPUS IN A POT

. . . transient dreams

OLD POND
+ FROG

SPLASH

*
* *

BLACK AUTUMN DUSK

CROW ON A WITHERED BRANCH

. . . settles

snow
snow
snow
snow
snow
snow

DAFFODILS

bend

light the fire, my friend

and I will show you something lovely

a lump of snow

. . . silence

*
* *

freezing night . . .

OAR

SURF_{SURF}SURF^{SURF}SURF_{SURF}

STRIKES

. . . the sound of tears

A ROSE BY THE ROADSIDE

. . . my horse ate it

NOT SEEING MOUNT FUJI . . .

```
          drizzledrizzledrizzledrizzledrizzledrizzle
mistmistmistmistmistmistmistmistmistmistmistmist
            fogfogfogfogfogfogfogfogfogfogfogfogfogfog
       drizzledrizzledrizzledrizzledrizzledrizzle
mistmistmistmistmistmistmistmistmistmistmistmist
            fogfogfogfogfogfogfogfogfogfogfogfogfogfog
          drizzledrizzledrizzledrizzledrizzledrizzle
mistmistmistmistmistmistmistmistmistmistmistmist
         fogfogfogfogfogfogfogfogfogfogfogfogfogfog
       drizzledrizzledrizzledrizzledrizzledrizzle
mistmistmistmistmistmistmistmistmistmistmistmist
         fogfogfogfogfogfogfogfogfogfogfogfogfogfog
       drizzledrizzledrizzledrizzledrizzledrizzle
mistmistmistmistmistmistmistmistmistmistmistmist
         fogfogfogfogfogfogfogfogfogfogfogfogfogfog
       drizzledrizzledrizzledrizzledrizzledrizzle
mistmistmistmistmistmistmistmistmistmistmistmist
         fogfogfogfogfogfogfogfogfogfogfogfogfogfog
       drizzledrizzledrizzledrizzledrizzledrizzle
mistmistmistmistmistmistmistmistmistmistmistmist
         fogfogfogfogfogfogfogfogfogfogfogfogfogfog
  drizzledrizzledrizzledrizzledrizzledrizzle
```

_____

. . . wonderful day!

MOON

**PLUM
TREE**

_____

. . . and the stage is set for spring

leave all your thoughts to the willow tree

*
* *

HILLS AND FIELDS

MY
SUMMER
ROOM

enter

IT IS TIME FOR THE MARKET FAIR!

maybe I'll go buy a stick of incense

*
* *

sweeping the courtyard . . .

THE

BROOM

FORGETS

the

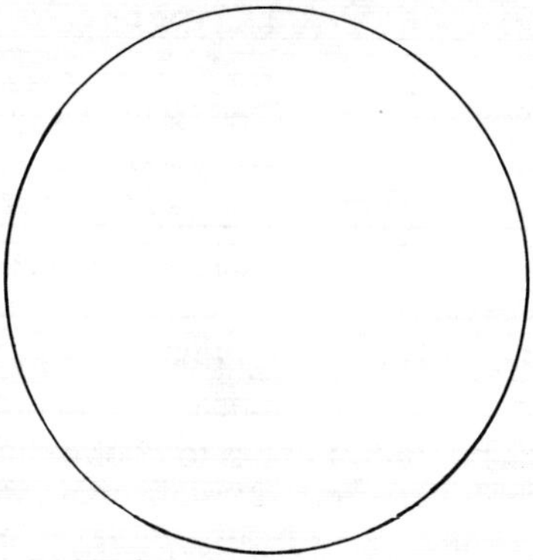

NOBODY

roadroadroadroadroadroadroadroadroadroadroadroadroadroadroad

autumn twilight . . .

*

* *

MORNING MIST ON A NAMELESS MOUNTAIN

SPRING

thank you

4. SONGS OF THE CRAZY WANDERERS

During the sixth to the tenth centuries A.D., as the practices of meditation gradually grew stiff in the Indian academies and the experience of wisdom was bricked up within the monuments of scholasticism, a new type of wandering saint appeared: long-haired, mad, endowed with magic powers, and singing of the bliss that dwelt within the human body.

For within the body lie the magic gates of Buddhahood, the veins and channels wherein the breath and mind and semen pursue their course and are woven into a single symbolic whole. To control one is to control the others: to manipulate the body is to control the mind, and to control the mind is to be master of the source of bliss. Enlightenment and the bliss of wisdom lie dormant and innate within the senses, and will burst forth spontaneously when we but tear aside the veils of accumulated custom that hide us from our authentic and joyful mode of being in the world.

So they sang of wisdom as the great Whore, for she opens herself to every man who seeks her. They sang in puns and riddles, made love to the spontaneous maiden within them, and preached a world turned upside down: they slept in bliss and drowned in emptiness, and were altogether quite outrageous and shocking to all good and sober citizens, and from them sprang all the traditions of the Spontaneous Way.

One of the greatest of these Crazy Wanderers was Kāṇha, the Black One. He sang his crazy songs in a language often called Old Bengali, but which seems to have been a dialect common to all of Northeast India, and from which have descended the modern tongues of Bengal, Assam, and Orissa. It was no learned language, but the language of the streets and markets, for it was in the streets and among the people that he acted out his play of bliss and freedom.

Hājār Bacharer Purāna Bāngālā Bhāsāy Bauddha Gān O Dohā [*Buddhist songs in old Bengali*], ed. *Haraprasad Sastri (Calcutta: Bangiya Sahitya Parisat, 1916), with the emendations of Tarapada Mukherji*, The Old Bengali Language and Text *(Calcutta: University of Calcutta, 1963).*

> The path is blocked by vowels and consonants.
> Kāṇha is disconsolate when he sees it.
> Kāṇha, where will you go to make your abode?
> You are indifferent to all the objects of your mind.
> There are three, there are three, but the three are separate:
> Kāṇha says: it is existence separates them.
> Whatever comes goes away:
> Kāṇha is disconsolate at all this coming and going.
> Hey, Kāṇha! The palace of the Conquerors is found nearby.
> Kāṇha says: I don't understand this.

He tramples the solid posts of reality.
He tears off the bonds which encompass him.
Kāṇha frolics, rutting with wine.
He enters the lotus lake of the spontaneous and finds peace.
The more the elephant lusts for his mate
The more he drips the musk of Suchness.
All the creatures of the six destinies are pure in essence:
Neither being nor nonbeing has a hairtip of impurity.
The ten precious strengths radiate in the ten directions.
Tame the elephant of ignorance with nondefilement.

His staff holds firm the power of his channels,
His drum unstruck gives forth warlike sounds:
Kāṇha, the skullbearer, the yogin, has set out to practice:
He wanders alone in the city of his body.
The vowels and consonants are made his anklets,
The sun and moon are made his earrings.
He smears himself with the ashes of lust, hatred, and delusion,
He takes supreme freedom to be his string of pearls.
He has slain his mother-in-law and sisters-in-law within tne house,
He has slain his mother: Kāṇha has become a skullbearer.

Hey, Whore, your hut is outside the city.
You stroke the brahman boys and go away.
Hey, Whore, I shall join together with you,
I, the shameless Kāṇha, the naked yogin, the skullbearer.
The lotus is one, its petals sixty-four:
I climb upon it and dance with the Whore.
Hey, Whore, honestly I ask you:
In whose boat do you come and go?
The Whore sells string as well as wicker baskets.
For your sake I have given up dancing.
You are a Whore, I a skullbearer.
For your sake I have put on a garland of bones.

I play chess on the board of compassion:
Instructed by my true guru, I capture the chessmen of existence.
Two are removed. Ha! I checkmate the king.
The Conqueror's palace is near, Kāṇha,
In the direction of the castle.
First I take up the pawns and slay them.
I take up the rook and crush the five men.
The bishop sends the king to nirvana.
I keep them from moving, I capture the chessmen of existence.
Kāṇha says: I offer a good stake.
I count out sixty-four squares and take them.

Eight maidens form my boat of the three refuges.
My body is compassion, emptiness my mistress.
I have crossed the sea of existence like an illusion, a dream.
I feel the flow of waves in the middle.
I make the five Who Have Come my oars:
Row your body, Kāṇha, that net of illusion.
Smell, touch, taste: whatever they may be
They are like a waking dream.
My mind is the helmsman in the boat of emptiness:
Kāṇha has gone to live with Bliss.

Easily I ply the triple world.
I sleep in the play of Bliss.
Hey, Whore! How is your flirting?
The patricians are outside, the skullbearers within.
Hey, Whore! You have spoiled everything.
For no reason you have spoiled the moon.
Some people say you are ugly,
But wise men cling to your neck.
Kāṇha sings of his low-caste lover:
There is no better whore than you.

Existence and nirvana are the two drums,
Mind and breath are the two cymbals:
The bass drum resounds *jaa jaa* "Victory victory"
As Kāṇha goes off to marry the Whore.
The Whore is married, birth is eaten up,
The dowry is the highest Law.
Day and night pass in lovemaking.
The night is brightened with my Lady's flame.
The yogin who is devoted to the Whore
Does not leave her for a moment: he is drunk with the spontaneous.

The mind is a tree, the five senses its branches,
Desires its many leaves and fruits.
Cut it down with the axe of the true guru's word.
Kāṇha says: the tree will not appear again.
The tree grows with the water of good and evil.
The wise man cuts it down at the command of his guru.
Whoever doesn't know the secret of cutting it down—
The fool slips and falls, and experiences it as existence.
The tree is emptiness, the axe is the sky:
Cut down the tree! Leave neither root nor branch.

He strikes at existence with the arm of emptiness.
He steals the stores of delusion and eats them.
He is asleep.
He does not know the difference between himself and others.
The naked Kāṇha sleeps in the spontaneous.
Neither aware nor feeling, he has gone full asleep,
And dreams in Bliss that he sets all beings free.
In a dream I saw the empty world
Spinning about, neither coming nor going.
I shall make the great yogin my friend:
The scholars don't see things my way.

The objects of the mind are rubbish.
Texts and traditions are piles of bricks.
Tell me how you can speak of the spontaneous
Where body, speech and mind do not enter.
The guru teaches his disciple in vain.
How can he speak of what is beyond the path of speech?
The more he says, the more he is an old humbug.
The guru is dumb, and the disciple is deaf.
Kāṇha says: what is the jewel of the Conqueror like?
It is like the dumb enlightening the deaf.

The mind spontaneously is full of emptiness.
Do not grieve when you lose your body.
Tell me how Kāṇha doesn't exist any more:
Every day he spreads through the triple world, and measures it.
The fool is sad when he sees the seen destroyed.
Does a breaking wave dry up the ocean?
The fool does not see how the world is:
He does not see the butter in the milk.
Nothing comes or goes in reality.
That's the reality that Kāṇha plays in.

5. RIDDLES OF THE GATELESS WAY

Of all the celebrations of enlightenment, none is more strange and wonderful than the Zen *kōan*. It is a riddle and a joke: it is an active smashing of conventional reality, a verbal breaking-through to the genuine and the spontaneous; it is the most joyous of pranks played upon the world. Literally a *kōan* is an official document, usually implying grave and important legal decisions, but here it is a story of the seemingly mad actions of the earlier masters of Chinese Zen. And to be able to answer their answerless questions, or to understand their peculiar brand of enlightened madness, is to be mad and enlightened oneself. The riddle becomes a device to shatter our fondest prejudices about reality, and reveal the authenticity that lies beneath our thoughts.

Laughter seems an inevitable response to realization. I remember, when I was living in a Tibetan monastery, the yogins in their white cotton robes sitting and laughing together. The overwhelming impression was that they knew a marvelous joke that they really wanted to share with me if they could, but somewhere along the way I had simply missed the point.

The Chinese master Hui-k'ai (1183–1260 A.D.) was a collector of *kōans*. He was also known—most happily—as Wu-men, which means "gateless," and the riddles that he told his disciples are the Gateless Barriers through which one must pass to true wisdom. As we read the text, we must picture the master sitting at the head of the hall, telling each story, commenting upon it, and composing an extemporaneous verse upon its meaning. He condemns the old masters in one breath and praises them in the next, wooing and cajoling his students from established responses to genuine freedom. He challenges them to answer, and he dismisses all possible answers as not to the point. Always he is saying, Tell me something! Tell me something! And always he is smiling.

Selections from Hui-k'ai, Wu-men kuan[*The gateless barrier*], *in* Taishō Shinshū Daizōkyō, *gen. eds.* Takakusu Junjirō *and* Watanabe Kaigyoku *(Tokyo: Taishō Issaikyō Kankōkai, 1924–29), 48, no. 2005.

A monk once asked Chao Chou: Could this dog have the Buddha-nature?

Chao Chou said: NO.

Comment. To practice meditation, you must pass through the barrier of the masters: subtle realizations require that you stop the wandering of your discursive thoughts. If you do not pass the barrier, if you do not stop your thoughts from wandering, then you are a ghost flitting among the weeds. Tell me: what is the barrier of the masters? It is but a single NO, the only barrier to our gate: and thus it is called the gateless barrier to the teachings of meditation.

Whoever passes this barrier is not only kinsman to Chao Chou, but he walks hand in hand with all the generations of our masters: he sees with the same eyes & hears with the same ears. Is this not happiness?

Do you want to pass through this barrier? Then take your whole body, its three hundred and sixty joints & its eighty-four thousand pores, and concentrate upon this NO: day and night hold it in your hand. But do not make it an empty no, as in yes & no; it must be a red-hot iron ball you have swallowed, which you vomit and vomit, but cannot bring forth.

Cast aside all your old misperceptions & mistakes: slowly, naturally, purely, the inner & outer become of a single piece; but (like a dumb man who has a dream) perhaps only you yourself will know it. Then suddenly you arise to startle the heavens & shake the earth; you take in your hand a magic sword; you meet the Buddha: kill him! you meet a master: kill him! In the midst of life & death you have reached the other shore, gaining great freedom; in the midst of the six destinies you wander, playing in your contemplation.

And how do you concentrate on the NO? With every bit of your strength. If you do not falter, you will light a lamp of the Law to benefit the world.

> The dog: the Buddha-nature:
> stern implacable command:
> if you fall into yes & no
> dead man

Whenever Chü Chih was asked a question, all he did was raise one finger. Once a disciple of his was asked by a visitor: What is the main point of the Law your master teaches? So the disciple raised his finger.

When Chü Chih heard about this, he took a knife and cut off the disciple's finger. As he ran screaming from the room, Chü Chih called him back: the disciple turned his head, and Chü Chih raised one finger. The disciple gained a sudden realization.

When Chü Chih was about to die, he said to the assembled monks: It was from T'ien Lung that I received this one-finger meditation; it was more than I could use up in an entire lifetime.

He spoke these words and died.

Comment. The realization of Chü Chih & his disciple does not lie in the raising of the finger. If you can really see this, T'ien Lung & Chü Chih & the disciple & you are all strung on a single skewer.

> Chü Chih made a fool of old T'ien Lung:
> just raised up his sharp knife
> & sliced the little disciple
> The spirit didn't make a fuss:
> just raised up his hand
> & shattered the mountain

Hsiang Yen said: It is like a man up a tree, hanging by his mouth from a branch: his hands can't reach a limb & his feet can't reach the tree. And under the tree someone asks him why Bodhidharma came from the west. If he does not reply, he ignores the question; if he replies, he will die. At that very instant: what should he do?

Comment: You may have a flowing stream of eloquence & it won't help; you may be able to recite the whole Buddhist canon & it won't help. But if you can reply, you can kill the living & raise the dead; if not, we'll have to wait for Maitreya to come, and ask him.

Hsiang Yen has rotten taste:
he never stops his evil poison
he shuts up the mouths of the monks
tears drip from their eyes

In ancient times the Blessed One dwelt upon Vulture Peak, and he held up a flower before the assembly. All were silent; but the venerable Kāśyapa smiled. The Blessed One said: I have the eye of the true Law, the subtle heart of nirvana, the true signless sign, the mysterious gate of the Law: it does not rest in words; it is a separate transmission outside the teachings; and this I commit to the great Kāśyapa.

Comment. Gold-faced Gautama is like no one else: he oppresses the righteous as worthless; he hangs up a sheep's head and then sells dog's meat. And what he says is not all that special. Just suppose that everyone in the assembly had smiled: how could he have transmitted his eye of the true Law? Or suppose that Kāśyapa hadn't smiled: how could he have transmitted it then? If you think the eye of the true Law can be transmitted, then the gold-faced old phoney was shouting it at the village gate; & if you think it can't be transmitted, then how in the world did he give it to Kāśyapa?

Here he comes, holding up a flower
already exposing his ass end
Kāśyapa smiles
men & gods don't know what to do

A monk said to Chao Chou: I have just entered the monastery; I beg the master to teach me.

Chao Chou said: Have you eaten yet?

The monk said: I have eaten.

Chao Chou said: Then go wash your bowl.

And the monk understood.

Comment. Whenever Chao Chou opens his mouth, you can see his gall bladder, he shows his heart & liver. The monk didn't really understand anything: he thought a bell was a pot.

It's all so clear
it takes a while to catch on
the stove was lit in the morning
& the food is cooked already

A monk said to Ts'ao Shan: I am Ch'ing Shui, alone & poor. I beg you, master, give me charity.

Ts'ao Shan said: Master Shui!

The monk said: Here I am!

Ts'ao Shan said: He's already drunk three glasses of good wine, & he swears he hasn't wet his lips.

Comment: Poor old Ch'ing Shui: what's he thinking? Ts'ao Shan saw deep & sharp; he knew what was happening. But even so, tell me: when did this Master Shui drink the wine?

> Poor as a beggar
> spirit of a warrior
> he has no job
> & he fights about money

Chao Chou went to a hermit's cave, and he called: Are you there? Are you there?

The hermit held up his fist.

Chao Chou said: The water is shallow: I cannot anchor my boat here.

He went away. He came to another hermit's cave, and he called: Are you there? Are you there?

The hermit held up his fist.

Chao Chou said: You can give & you can take: you can destroy & you can give life.

And he bowed.

Comment. Both raised their fists in the same way: why did he approve of one & not the other? Tell me: where was the mistake? If you can get the answer, you'll see that Chao Chou's tongue has no bone in it; he raises up & dashes down in perfect freedom. But in any case, the two hermits saw through Chao Chou too. If you tell me that one hermit was better than the other, you are not yet looking with the eyes of the teachings; & if you tell me that one hermit was not better than the other, you are not yet looking with the eyes of the teachings.

> His eyes are meteors
> he flashes like lightning
> a death-dealing knife
> a life-giving sword

Every day Jui-yen Shih-yen would call to himself: Sir!
And he would answer: Yes?
And he would say: Wake up!
OK!
Or sometimes he would say: Don't let people fool you!
OK! OK!

Comment. Old Jui-yen sells to himself & buys from himself; he calls ghosts above him, spirits before him. What's going on here? One calls & one answers; one says wake up & one isn't fooled by people. He recognized that whatever appeared was a payment from his past, that it wasn't so. But if you imitate him: what vain illusion!

A man who seeks the Way
does not see reality
because from of old
he sees a ghost
(the root of birth & death
for measureless eons)
& a fool thinks it is
himself

The monks of the east and west halls were arguing about a cat. Nan Ch'üan picked it up and said: If you can tell me something, I will spare it; & if you cannot tell me something, I will kill it.

No one replied: so Nan Ch'üan killed the cat.

In the evening Chao Chou returned from outside, and Nan Ch'üan told him what had happened. Chao Chou took off his shoe, put it on his head, and went out.

Nan Ch'üan said: If you had been here, I could have spared the cat!

Comment. Tell me: what does it mean, Chao Chou putting his shoe on his head? If you can answer, you see that what Nan Ch'üan did was not without purpose. But if you can't: watch out!

If Chao Chou were there
it would have been different
he snatches away the knife
Nan Ch'üan begs for his life

A monk said to Tung Shan: What is the Buddha?
Tung Shan said: Three pounds of flax.

Comment. Old Tung Shan practices meditation like a clam: open his two halves, and you see his liver & intestines. But even so, tell me: where do you see Tung Shan?

Suddenly: three pounds of flax
word and meaning are kinsmen
whoever comes saying yes & no
is a yes & no man

Chao Chou asked Nan Ch'üan: What is the Way?
Nan Ch'üan said: Your ordinary mind is the Way.
Chao Chou said: Then can I advance upon it?
Nan Ch'üan said: If you try, you won't.
Chao Chou said: But if I don't try, how do I know it is the Way?
Nan Ch'üan said: You cannot know it is the Way, & you cannot not know it is the Way. Knowing is mistaken, & not knowing is stupid. When you really penetrate the spontaneous Way, it is like a great emptiness, a vast openness: how can it be yes or no?

At these words Chao Chou had a sudden realization.

Comment: Chao Chou asked Nan Ch'üan a question: right away the tile broke & the ice melted & the drain got clogged. Chao Chou may have gained a realization, but he'll have to work at it for thirty years before he begins to catch on.

> Spring has a hundred flowers
> & autumn has a moon
> summer has a cool breeze
> & winter has snow
> but if things just hang in your mind
> & don't clog it
> that is the best season

A monk said to Yün Men: What is the Buddha?

Yün Men said: He is a dried turd.

Comment. As for Yün Men, all we can say is this: it is hard to be a gourmet when you are poor & it is hard to write a book when you are busy. And when someone comes holding a turd to prop up the gate & support the door: well, you can see what happens to the Buddha's Law.

> Sudden lightning flash
> sparks from a flint
> in the blink of an eye
> already gone

A monk said to Nan Ch'üan: Is there a teaching no one has taught?

Nan Ch'üan said: There is.

The monk said: What is the teaching no one has taught?

Nan Ch'üan said: It is not the mind & it is not the Buddha & it is not a thing.

Comment. Nan Ch'üan was asked one question, and right away he squandered all his wealth. He's just not as young as he used to be.

> He repeated himself & lost all value
> the truth has power without words
> we let the vast ocean change
> & you can't be right all the time

A temple banner flapped in the wind: two monks were arguing about it. Said one: The banner moves. Said the other: The wind moves. Back & forth, they could not agree.

The Sixth Patriarch said: It is not the wind moving & it is not the banner moving: it is your minds moving.

And the two monks trembled.

Comment. It is not the wind moving & it is not the banner moving & it certainly is not the mind moving: so where is the Patriarch? If you can see this deep & sharp, you'll know that the monks bargained for iron & got gold. The Patriarch just couldn't repress his superiority. Ridiculous.

> Wind & banner & mind moving
> all the same: reprehensible
> he just opened his mouth
> & the words fell out by themselves

Nan Ch'üan said: The mind is not the Buddha, & wisdom is not the Way.

Comment. As for Nan Ch'üan, all we can say is this: he was old, but he was still quite without shame. He just opened his stinking old mouth & told everyone about his family disgrace. And even so, very few people appreciated it.

> The weather clears & the sun comes out
> the rain falls & the earth is wet
> with utmost compassion he explained it all
> & you just don't believe it

Wu Tsu said: When you meet an enlightened man on the road, do not greet him with words & do not greet him with silence. Tell me: how do you greet him?

Comment: If you can greet him deep & sharp, nothing can hinder your happiness. But if you can't, you had better start looking at everything.

> An enlightened man met on the road:
> do not greet him with words or silence
> punch his jaw & split his face
> he'll get the message

Shou Shan held up his bamboo staff before the assembly and said: All you people: if you call this a bamboo staff, you insult it; & if you do not call it a bamboo staff, you deny it. All you people, tell me: what do you call it?

Comment. If you call it a bamboo staff, you insult it; & if you do not call it a bamboo staff, you deny it. You can't get it with words & you can't get it without words. Quick, tell me! Quick, tell me!

> Holding up his bamboo staff
> giving life & death commands
> insult & denial fight each other
> Buddhas & patriarchs beg for their lives

Pa Chiao said to the assembly: If you have a walking stick, I will give you one; & if you do not have a walking stick, I will take it away from you.

Comment. It helps you wade the water when the bridge is broken, it keeps you company on a moonless road: but if you call it a walking stick, you'll fall to hell swift as an arrow.

> In all directions, deep & shallow
> all lie in the palm of my hand
> prop of the heavens, pillar of the earth
> suddenly it stirs the winds of teaching

6. A TOUCH OF SAD FAREWELL

I can think of no better way to end this collection than with the Chinese poems that follow. Many of them have to do with saying farewell, and all of them are touched with a wistful awareness of the transience of our human encounters. And yet the poems always assert the possibility of realization and of beauty in the world. The first possibility is Buddhist, the second is Chinese. To the poets in this selection there is no difference at all.

T'ang-shih san-pai shou [*Three hundred poems of the Tang Dynasty*], ed. Heng-t'ang T'ui-shih (Hong Kong: Lien-yi shu-tien ch'u-pan, 1965).

Passing the Temple of Heaped Fragrance

> I did not know there was a temple there.
> For there was no human path in the ancient woods
> and clouds stretched for miles over the hills:
> where could there be a bell deep in the mountains?
>
> The fountain sang over the voracious rocks,
> the sunlight colored the cool green pines . . .
> And the dusk was thin over winding empty pools
> when my calm meditation conquered the dragon of passion.

Wang Wei

The Hermitage Behind Broken Mountain Temple

> Pure dawn enters the old temple
> and the first light brightens the tall trees.
> The crooked trail winds through the gloom
> to a meditation hut among thick flowers,
> where birds delight in the shimmering mountains
> and the shadows in the pool are my empty mind.
> All the sounds are still:
> I hear only the chiming of the temple bells.

Ch'ang Chien

Looking for an Absent Hermit

Under the pines I spoke to your disciple.
"My master has gone to gather herbs.
But the clouds are deep among the mountains
and I don't know where he is."

Chia Tao

On Hearing the Monk Chün Play the Lute

The monk from Shu carries his green silk lute-case
and goes to the west down O-mei Mountain.
With the smallest gesture of his hand
I hear the pines of a thousand valleys.
His heart is the guest of the clear flowing waters,
his songs are in the icy bells . . .
I cannot see the jade green hills at sunset:
they are hidden by the darkness of the autumn clouds.

Li Po

Looking for Ch'ang in the Southern Stream

On the single road leading to this place
I saw a footprint in the moss.
The white clouds leaned on quiet banks,
the fragrant grasses closed your idle door.
I passed the rain-fed green of pines
and followed the hills to a mountain spring . . .
Streams and flowers spoke to me in meditation,
and I replied: and cannot think of what it was I said.

Liu Chang-ch'ing

Passing the Night at Wang Ch'ang-ling's Retreat

Your hidden hut is a solitary cloud
upon the clear deep waters of your pool.
The pines about it are dewed with the distant moon,
a glow of liquid light to be my friend.
I pass the night in the shadow of flowers,
where garden herbs enrich the patterns of the moss.
I too would leave the world
and fly to the western mountain with the phoenix and the crane.

Ch'ang Chien

Farewell to Ling Ch'e

The temple is in the green bamboo:
its evening bells are small and distant.
Your pilgrim's hat catches the slanting sunbeams
far off and alone in the blue green mountains.

Liu Chang-ch'ing

Farewell to a Monk

Lonely clouds escort the wild cranes:
how can we ask them to stay among men?
And could you retire to Wu-chou Mountain
now that people know the place?

Liu Chang-ch'ing

Visiting the Temple of Master Ch'ao to Recite the Scriptures

I draw water from the well to wash my teeth
and purify my mind as I brush my clothes.
Idly turning the pages of my book
I step out to the eastern library . . .

No one wants the true teachings.
The world follows upon false tracks.
I had hoped the words bequeathed to me would be profound
but how can one write down the true nature of things?

But it is quiet here in the temple courtyard
where the colors of moss join the dense bamboos.
The sun clears away the last of the morning mist
and the green pines seem sleeked with oil.

Weak and wordless I try to speak.
Realization floods my heart with rest.

Liu Tsung-yüan

Mountain Stones

The mountain stones were rough, the path narrow.
Bats flew in the twilight when I reached the temple.
I climbed to the hall and sat on the steps, where the fresh rain
had washed the great palm leaves and sleek gardenias.
The monk said there were fine Buddhas painted on the old walls:
he took a lamp to show me some of them.
He spread the bed, dusted the mats, and set out rice for me:
it was coarse but satisfied my hunger.
Late at night it was quiet, and not an insect murmured
as the clear moon came over the mountains, and entered my door . . .

I left at dawn, alone, and lost my way,
up and down the twisting mountains in the mist
where the red hills glittered in the jade green brooks.
I saw pines and oaks full ten spans around
and my bare feet in swift water stepped on river rocks
where the water boiled and the wind tore my clothes.
A man could make himself happy here.
Why should I bridle myself in crowded towns?
O my own few disciples:
what if I grew old here and never returned?

Han Yü

Farewell to a Monk Returning to Japan

It was predestined that you come to this country.
You came your way as in a dream
and now you float far off on the sky-wide sea,
leaving the world in your fragile boat of the Law.
The water and the moon see your meditation and are still:
the fish and dragons listen to your chanting.
And only the mirrored speck of your lamp of compassion
shines in my eyes for ten thousand miles.

Ch'ien Ch'i

A Letter to the Priest Yüan

Long have I yearned to rest:
but a hermitage is hard when you have no money.
I do not want the north lands
for my master dwells in the eastern woods.
As yellow gold is burned in cinnamon fires
my ambition wanes as the years go by.
A cold wind blows from the setting sun.
The singing cricket makes me think of death.

Meng Hao-jan

Climbing the Pagoda at the Temple of Compassion

The tall pagoda gushes from the earth
alone and lofty as a palace in heaven.
As I climb I seem to leave the world behind
and the coiling steps are poised in empty air.
Its greatness looms above this land of gods
and towers as if built by spirits.

Its four corners block the burning sun,
its seven storeys grope for the blue canopy of space.
Below me I can see the soaring birds,
and bend to hear the startling wind.
The linked mountains seem like rippling waves
which run away together toward the dawning east.
Green trees line the dwindling roads,
and the cities look like lacy jade.
Autumn colors from the west
invade the mountain passes with their green . . .
And in the north are five tombs
lying under the grey and ancient mist
where rest the masters of my former lives
who long ago had realized the truth.
I swear: I shall hang up my official hat and go
to gain the infinite treasure of the Way.

Ts'en Ts'an